TWENTIETH CENTURY VIEWS

The aim of this series is to present the best in contemporary critical opinion on major authors, providing a twentieth century perspective on their changing status in an era of profound revaluation.

Maynard Mack, *Series Editor*
Yale University

MOLIÈRE

A COLLECTION OF CRITICAL ESSAYS

Edited by

Jacques Guicharnaud

A SPECTRUM BOOK

Prentice-Hall, Inc. *Englewood Cliffs, N. J.*

75- 1670

Current printing (last digit):

11 10 9 8 7 6 5

© 1964 BY PRENTICE-HALL, INC.

ENGLEWOOD CLIFFS, N.J.

LIBRARY OF CONGRESS CATALOG CARD NO.: 64-23235

Printed in the United States of America—C

P 59970
C 59971

Table of Contents

Introduction

by Jacques Guicharnaud

Probing the mysteries of a vocation is not our intention here. Besides, in Molière's case such an undertaking would be hopeless: we have no diary, no more or less fictionalized autobiography, no memoirs to provide the elements of a psychobiography or an existential analysis. Grimarest's *La Vie de Monsieur de Molière,* curious as it may be (Molière confiding his personal torments, his turbulent friendship with Chapelle, and so on), was published in 1705, thirty-two years after Molière's death, and is thus considered extremely questionable by most modern scholars. The other rare pieces of evidence from his contemporaries are all of a polemical nature and, consequently, partial.

Actually, what we have to go on is one simple reality: the presence, in France in the second half of the seventeenth century, of a complete man of the theater—actor, leader of a theatrical company, playwright—recognized as such by his contemporaries, transmitted as such by an almost continuous tradition, and obviously shown to be such by his works.

Here, then, are the facts: at a time when actors were more or less outside the law, Jean-Baptiste Poquelin, the son of a good bourgeois family, gave up the security and respectability of the legal profession, at about the age of twenty, renouncing the right to succeed his father as "upholsterer by appointment of the King" (true, he later assumed the title), in order to throw himself body and soul into the mad adventure of the boards. We know nothing about how he came to make that choice. Had he limited himself to writing, like Corneille or Racine, we might fancy that we understood. But he began by taking the extraordinary plunge of becoming an actor, and when later he set about writing, he did so mainly to fulfill his possibilities as an actor.

To be sure, the venture was not so novel as it would at first appear. Valdemar Vedel, in his *Molière,*[1] rightly reminds us that the acting profession, while still hazardous and fraught with danger, was not so discreditable about 1650 as it had been in the past, and that the tragedian Montfleury, among others, had also forsaken a bourgeois career at the

[1] See bibliography at end of volume.

1

bar to give himself to the stage. But if Molière is not the only one on the list, he leads it because of his obstinacy and the scope of his enterprise.

For this was, above all, a case of obstinacy. It is one thing to say no to succeeding one's father; it is another to persist under the worst conditions, never returning to eat the fatted calf. We know that in 1643 he and the Béjart family founded the "Illustre Théâtre." Although that name still calls up wonders, we must not forget that it turned out to be a lamentable undertaking, doomed to failure by its participants' lack of experience and the competition of the large companies, those of the Hôtel de Bourgogne and the Hôtel du Marais. That failure meant debts, prison (Molière did time in Le Châtelet in 1644), and finally, collapse. One might say "cherchez la femme," and no doubt she would be found in the person of Madeleine Béjart. The classic (or rather, romantic) story of the young man of good family seduced by an obscure actress? Perhaps. But it was more the choice of a profession, against all comers. And a definitive choice. Love may have weighed down the scale, but there is still no doubt that Molière needed the theater as much as the Béjarts needed an energetic and learned young companion. More than Molière's loves, what counts is the constancy of the group to which he belonged—a group which, despite the inevitable upheavals and desertions, was to hold together in adversity as well as in success.

When we say that the Illustre Théâtre collapsed, we mean that the undertaking, not the group, fell apart, for Molière and the Béjarts together joined another company, that of Gros-René, in 1645. And it took but four years for Molière to become its leader. Yet it was exile—in other words, the provinces. Thirteen years in the provinces: can one "imagine," along with René Bray,[2] "that those long years, the years of his beautiful youth, were the happiest of his life?" No doubt the troupe grew, the receipts came in, and success smiled on Molière; in addition, an illustrious protector, the Prince de Conti, was found. But the provinces are the provinces; even Lyons, the troupe's home port, although a rich and Italianized center for more than a century, was—in the eyes of a Parisian such as D'Assoucy—merely a "beautiful village." And the Prince de Conti forsook Molière, becoming devout and at the same time his worst enemy. Indeed, it would seem that those years were years of struggle and apprenticeship, with one impatiently awaited goal: the return to Paris.

It was during those thirteen years that Molière discovered a means of survival: writing. He had once studied seriously at the Jesuit Collège de Clermont; he knew how to wield a pen. One can imagine that he and his friends were weary of feeling ill at ease in plays written by others, plays that were common property as soon as they were published, since there was no copyright. On the other hand, the audience reacted favor-

[2] Introduction, *Oeuvres complètes de Molière* (Club du Meilleur Livre); see bibliography at end of volume.

ably to improvisation modeled on the Italians, to spontaneous witticism. Little more was needed to tempt Molière into writing plays "to order." In other words, Molière began to write comedies not because he had some profound message (satirical or philosophical) to communicate to the world, but because he was able to stock up on jokes, gestures, and situations that "worked" with his audience every time, given his troupe's ability and, mainly, his own. *L'Étourdi,* the first absolutely authenticated text (1655), is a series of "actor's numbers" and, particularly, as René Bray has shown,[3] a "vehicle" entirely conceived to show Molière's talents.

Yet there is more to *L'Étourdi*: it is also a "written" comedy, and well written at that. Combined with Molière's sense of the needs and immediate possibilities of an itinerant troupe was his obvious sense of the *dignity* of comedy. Molière the writer put himself into the service of Molière the actor and his comrades, but without ever stooping: he manipulated the alexandrine; he chose to be a servant in good taste. And doubtless, at heart, he wanted to be known as a good writer, as he was already known as a good clown—having failed to fulfill his early dream of being a good tragedian, an ambition he was wise enough to renounce. He had to survive, to please, to adapt to the possibilities of the material he found, but he did it with esthetic dignity. Son of the manufacturing bourgeoisie, Molière was to try, throughout his career, to reconcile his clients' pleasure with his dignity as a craftsman.

To continue the metaphor, one sees, during those years in the provinces, a dual apprenticeship: knowledge gained of the raw material of comic humor (farce), and an ability to manufacture quality products, although more or less "copies." Molière was never to lose sight of the former, and he was to eliminate the imitative nature of the latter. On his return to Paris, it was with farce that he attracted attention; and it was finally by elevating the element of farce in comedy, by introducing it into great literature, that he produced his "masterwork," in a craftsman's sense of the word: *L'École des femmes.*

We are somewhat surprised today at the great wave of hostility provoked by that comedy. At first sight, nothing could be more innocent than the actual scenario, the tradition of which goes back to antiquity: a young slave girl is stolen away by the young leading man from the old fogy who was keeping her to himself. The play was a pretext for stage effects, with juicy roles for Molière and his best pupil, Lagrange. The ill temper of the minor writers, the prudes' reaction to Molière's private life, the pedants' indignation in the face of some twisting of the rules—all that is not enough to explain the violence of the response. With *L'École des femmes,* a comedy of substance fell on the heads of the Parisian public of 1662, most unexpectedly.

[3] *Molière, homme de théâtre;* see bibliography at end of volume.

First of all, the play was unlike anything ever performed before. Beneath a well-known and respected form (five acts in verse) lurked a content that was very strange indeed—half farce and half chit-chat— with an obvious disdain for the canons of the comedy of intrigue; and such discord seemed like cheating. That portion of the public which likes to come upon the same reliable patterns in the theater has always been shocked by novelty or invention of any kind. On a deeper level the innovation here consisted in displacing the comedy's center of interest: to be sure, the ridiculous mask is a pretext for "interesting action" (the machinations of Horace and Agnès, Arnolphe's counterattacks), but that action is no longer an end; it is a means, a tool to chip the mask and finally shatter it. And that cannot be done without exploiting to the utmost the characters' traits, just as the grotesques of farce were exploited to the utmost, with a kind of relentlessness that is troubling—or astonishing: for what is more astonishing than the fact that Molière creates a victim whom he obviously wants to destroy and whom at the same time he makes particularly tough? On an even deeper level, such an ambition is dangerous. The comedy, of course, remains literature, but it is no longer literature about literature: originally the cuckold of farce or the jealous lover of the comedy of intrigue, Arnolphe no longer reflects his literary sources but, rather, ourselves. Relatively speaking, he is, to his sources, what Ubu would be to Monsieur Perrichon.

The premiere of *L'École des femmes* (1662) was a theatrical event of as much importance as that of *Le Cid* (1636) and certainly more than that of *Hernani* (1830). Its repercussions can be felt in all the good comedies of the eighteenth century and in the bourgeois genres of the nineteenth, and they continued their course from *Ubu Roi* to the theater of Ionesco in the twentieth, with detours by way of the Boulevards and Jean Anouilh. With *L'École des femmes*, a comic synthesis took place. The fixity of the mask of farce, which suddenly becomes three-dimensional, is the comic counterpart of fate or tragic destiny. Not by chance has J. D. Hubert recently called this play "a burlesque tragedy." [4] In other words, instead of being simply an imaginary *romanesque* world (and its charms are not to be disdained) or conferring on the spectator that absolute superiority of witnessing an exhibition of dehumanized marionettes, comedy suddenly assimilates its diverse pasts and, without repudiating them even when it parodies them, makes our life into a farce and farce into our life: the romanesque quality becomes a true poetic solution, not a mere literary device. With *L'École des femmes*, the spectator finds himself in both the imaginary and the real, literature and life; he is torn apart, as he should be in the theater—pulled out of himself toward the innocent delights of theatrical illusion and at the same time thrown back on himself to the reality of his basic instincts. He has

[4] *Molière and the Comedy of Intellect*; see bibliography at end of volume.

to deal with the contemptible masks of the traditional stage, but the *papier-mâché* of the mask has become flesh, while keeping its original shape and colors. Such transmutation is painful for the audience.

Contemporary playgoers often disparage Beckett or Ionesco by saying: "All that's old hat. One can see the same thing in any Parisian music hall or at any Irish or British vaudeville." Or: "The 'absurd' dialogue of that team of American Negro comedians is worth all of Ionesco's dialogues." Or: "The two cronies in *Waiting for Godot* are merely a mixture of all the cronies of English farce." In *L'École des femmes* (and this essay is too short to go back to *Les Précieuses ridicules*), Molière was the Beckett or Ionesco of his time. By fully exploiting the possibilities of the traditional "number," he obliged the spectator to recognize, in the clown on stage, both the convention and himself. He submitted his audience to the transition from entertainment to true theater in an intolerable leap.

This was done by means of a certain realism within the unreality. Enough details are given so that Arnolphe, the hero of *L'École des femmes,* is immediately recognizable as a typical French bourgeois of the seventeenth century, a bourgeois in general, and—still more generally— man, to the extent that he is a possessive creature. Representative of a caste at a given moment of history, symbol of a class at any moment of history, and image of a permanent dimension of man in any class at any moment, Arnolphe justifies certain of Sartre's theories on the meaning of literature: it is through specific and historic embodiments that one reaches, if not absolute, at least lasting, truths.

The "truth" of Arnolphe is a priori that of the masks of farce: fixity. A mask is sculptured once and for all, fixed for the duration of the play. If one removes the mask and transposes the lines of the artificial face to the character's psychology, manners, and human attitudes, one then has what the French call a "caractère." A *papier-mâché* mask is communicated from one generation of actors to another. Harlequin, with his black mask and motley, has been the same for at least three centuries, laying eggs and wielding the bat. The counterpart to that tradition is Arnolphe's snicker when he is certain that he has found the recipe against being cuckolded. But although Harlequin, when he is now revived, remains an esthetic delight and even a reminder of the essence of theater, Arnolphe is truer, while just as stylized: Harlequin speaks to us of theater; Arnolphe speaks to us of man. And many men do not like being spoken about.

Arnolphe and Agnès face to face prove that there is no universality outside a concrete and historic embodiment. Once that point is accepted, the critic can profitably study the play. He finds that it deals with tyranny in the face of natural spontaneity, with a desire to change the world in the face of the need for the consent of others, and so forth. Yet all that, in the abstract, is not new. Moreover, in fictional literature and in farce, what normal spectator does not accept a bias in favor of spontaneity and consent? But when asked to consider a three-dimensional cuckold, he balks because at that moment the cuckold becomes identifiable with the spectator, who himself is, and knows he is, three-dimensional—or more simply, the spectator finds himself cuckolded.

Cuckolded and tyrannical and blind and victimized and, on occasion, unhappy. And, in addition, he is asked to laugh at it all—that is, at himself. It is one thing to ask the spectator to laugh at a masked and hunchbacked cuckold with a false goatee and dressed in tights; it is another to present him, by means of the same comic devices, with a potential cuckold, wearing a quite normal beard and dressed, like the spectator, as a bourgeois (a little out of fashion and with a bit too much green, perhaps), without a mask, and physically "real" (perhaps a little too stocky, but so, after all, was Molière).[5]

No, the attack on *L'École des femmes* was not unjustified. Apart from the vicious or personal details, such as the accusation of incest flung at Poquelin himself, and over and above the vulgarity of the *grand siècle,* it showed that comedy, for the first time, was dangerous: it no longer involved some conventional other person but, in the very terms of the convention, the spectator himself.

Have we spoken at too great length about that "touching little farce?" [6] Not really, for whoever reads Molière's works chronologically, amused by *L'Étourdi,* delighted by *Les Précieuses ridicules,* esthetically satisfied by *L'École des maris,* is struck by the innovation of *L'École des femmes.* Molière had up to then struggled to make a living. From that point on, he was also to struggle for his own identity and for the rights of the comic genre: his literary and theatrical apprenticeship was over.

Of course, Molière continued to write entertainments for the court, which in themselves are admirable, charming, poetic. Modern critics are right to bring them back into high esteem: Molière was an organizer of the pleasures of his century, and perhaps the best of them. All periods, even the most tragic, have their free and easy joys, without which no portrait of them would be complete. But if Molière had not existed, some Benserade would have taken his place, with almost as much talent.

In any case, such entertainments should not be disregarded. In them Molière, a complete man of the theater, gave free rein to his imagination;

---

[5] To be sure, one must not exaggerate the "realism" of Molière. Vedel (*op. cit.*) has emphasized how Molière made use of the details of his time whenever he had the chance, but the playwright-actor worked essentially in the imaginary universe of the theater. Not one of Molière's comedies is an exact copy of reality—even when such an esthetic would have been possible. To consider his works as a group of documents on his times is a gross misconception. On the other hand, to consider them as a pure exercise of dramatic virtuosity is just as wrong. The truth lies in the synthesis of the two.

[6] Roger Gellert, in the *New Statesman* (January 24, 1964), when the eighteenth century translation of the play was revived in London.

besides, they allowed him to rely more or less on royal protection, thanks to which he was able to explore *high* comedy. For while he was creating *La Princesse d'Élide, L'Amour médecin, Mélicerte,* and *Le Sicilien,* he was also writing the first *Tartuffe* (and fighting to have it performed), *George Dandin, Dom Juan, Le Misanthrope,* and *L'Avare,* as well as *Le Médecin malgré lui* and *Amphitryon.* Those were the five years (1664-69) in Molière's career which crowned his life: from forty-two to forty-seven, even though physically ill, he was in full possession of his art, but at the same time had not "hardened" into a specific image of himself. Thirteen plays in five years is not bad. Out of those thirteen plays, nine are still performable before an inexperienced public, and *are* performed, which is still better.

What endures is the element shown by that gift of absorption and transmutation revealed by *L'École des femmes.* To take only the established masterpieces of that period (*Tartuffe, Dom Juan, Le Misanthrope, L'Avare*) or the near-masterpieces (*George Dandin, Amphitryon, Le Médecin malgré lui*), all modern critics are agreed that such plays are based on the farcical and the romanesque: two poles of the imaginary which Molière never forgot. His genius was to bring them together without producing a burlesque *à la* Scarron (which would have meant sacrificing the romanesque to the farcical), and from that conjunction, as if from some electrical apparatus, to generate a spark: that of true comedy. At the meeting point of those two poles of the imaginary, thanks to a twist whose force came from experience of the world, the imaginary, while keeping its own dimensions, became the mirror of life. Essentially unrealistic, like all poetic works, Molière's major plays of that period show that everyone's life is a romance, a farce, a disgrace. Their effect might be compared to what would happen if, in a Mack Sennett movie, when a clown throws a cream pie, that pie—by some miracle of film technique—should splash on the faces of all the spectators. The devout, the well-born, the lovers, the husbands become indignant: they have just been told that they are hypocritical or stupid, ridiculous or cuckolded. Unreality invades reality. The spectator doubts himself—or rather, he is led into a state of bad faith to avoid doubting himself.

For Molière's works of that period are one of the strongest provocations ever presented on the French stage. As their means of expression is laughter, the spectator of the time eased his bad conscience by affecting scorn. Even today one still hears the phrase "l'infâme Molière"; in the same spirit the Vichy government tried to ban *Tartuffe,* and François Mauriac has used questionable documents to confront Molière with God.[7]

Yet there is great generosity in Molière, shown in his gift for laughter, open laughter devoid of hypocritical sentimentality as well as of indul-

---

[7] François Mauriac, *Trois Grands Hommes devant Dieu* (Paris, Le Capitole, 1930).

gence. Arnolphe, Orgon, and Alceste are funny. Even the hateful quality of Harpagon or Tartuffe may provoke laughter which liberates, but which also brings about recognition of man as a creature defined by his passions. The characters are forces, or the meeting point of forces, which live in illusion and mistake their specific determinism for free will. Nothing is funnier than a character in Molière who says "I want . . ." with all the ardor of a Cartesian "généreux," whereas it is not *he* who wants, but *something* in him, something the opposite of his freedom. This misunderstanding with oneself is the source of a drama which goes round in circles—the drama of mania; but such maniacs are quite simply caricatures of ourselves to the extent that we live according to our passions.

One may reject, philosophically, this vision of man. By the same token, one must also reject Racine. But here the question is less one of philosophy than of drama. In repeated meetings of one consciousness with another, each bound by its own mirage, its own desire, and therefore impervious to others, the characters constantly bounce one against the other, and their growing and reciprocal exasperation is paralleled in us. To be sure, there are tormentors and victims, madmen and so-called reasonable men, and we side with the victims against the tormentors, with the reasonable against the mad. But an obstinacy in reason which comes close to mania, despite its defeats, and a stubbornness of the victims in defense of their "normal" appetites, makes them such creatures of passion that it seems no more than a happy chance that their desires are in keeping with the norms of society.

We are alluding here, of course, to the young lovers of Molière's comedies: we find them likable because they consent to each other. Consent can be found in *L'Avare* and *Tartuffe,* but is altogether missing from *Dom Juan,* and exists between Éliante and Philinte, in *Le Misanthrope,* only because of the latter's complete vacuity—as if, at that particular moment in his career, Molière had finally discovered that a man can only consent to another to the extent that he is not a "creature defined by his passion"—that is, to the extent that he stops being a man.

Are Molière's works a comedy of character? A catalogue of unconscious mannerisms, observed in real life or borrowed from tradition, and linked with a conventional or new notion of a "type"? At first sight, yes. But if only that, they would be no more than a dramatized version of La Bruyère. Each of Molière's comedies, going beyond specific failings and obvious ridiculous ways, transcends manners and characters. Each one is a veritable comedy of passion, just as tragedy in Racine is said to be tragedy of passion. The ridiculousness of Molière's characters is not merely an accidental outgrowth of human nature: it is that nature. *Dom Juan* and *Le Misanthrope* prove that the soul is not definable in terms of free will and understanding, modified—disastrously but only on occasion —by the vices of the time; it is essentially vice, accompanied by an illusion of freedom. Molière (along with Racine) is the gravedigger of Descartes.

But the comedy of Molière is not exhausted in that almost Jansenist statement. On the human level Molière clearly desired earthly happiness, an attitude incompatible with Jansenism and related rather to a certain Gassendist naturalism that no one has yet managed to define satisfactorily. The union of Philinte and Éliante, in *Le Misanthrope*, is one of Molière's dreams, a dream that came from his generosity, his love for man—but what a pitiful embodiment! In this realm there is a kind of optimism, but it is a despondent optimism.

Although despondent as a man (that is, the man Molière considered from the perspective of his works, for we have no right to speak of any other), Molière was not despondent as a playwright. By means of the theater, that higher game, he achieved a state of joy. Comedy is probably the only solution for pessimists, for without denying the horror of the human condition, comedy absorbs it to provoke laughter about an illusion that is frankly an illusion. Boileau made his friends laugh by imitating Molière as he snickered during the last scene of Act II of *Le Misanthrope*. In other words, Molière, who had written the part for himself, re-established the superiority of the illusory miracle of theater at the last second: a striking contradiction between his vision of the world as a dead end and a gratuitousness which, despite man's despair as a prisoner, re-affirmed, no doubt unconsciously, a freedom that Molière found in the dual creative act of the poet and actor.

In all probability, Molière was not a happy man in private life. But through the prisoners he created for the duration of a performance, it is equally probable that he experienced something which the world had forbidden him to believe in: his own freedom. Having, as writer and actor, created a parodic universe, he was both God and the creature.

To our mind, *Dom Juan* and *Le Misanthrope* (however successful they were at the time) are at once masterpieces and experimental plays: masterpieces because experimental. After them, Molière was in complete possession of his acquisitions. He invented no longer; he perfected. With *Les Femmes savantes* (1672) he even presented an anthology of his capabilities. The craftsman of the theater, who had achieved his mastership with *L'École des femmes*, now produced a kind of academic exhibition-piece, in which he brought together all the fruits of his experience: themes, devices, recognition of his sources. Tartuffe fuses with Mascarille; Orgon, in changing his sex, cleverly absorbs Magdelon; Arsinoé is satisfied to grow younger, whereas Cathos draws near to menopause, Gorgibus takes on the coloring of Dandin, and so on. Trissotin, Philaminte, Armande, Bélise, Chrysale: what a review of what we already know! And what a conscious repetition of the basic design of all family comedy: the young couple, the obstacle to their happiness in the form of one parent's

obstinacy, the rival whom that parent inflicts on the girl—all too beautiful, too perfect, to be true. At the age of fifty, with *Les Femmes savantes,*
Molière carved out his own official statue for posterity. A fine statue, it
commands respect but teaches us nothing we had not already known. If
it touches us, the reason for it is indirect: one year before his death, the
King's upholsterer was haunted by a concern for the dignity of French
craftsmanship.

After the impasse portrayed in *Le Misanthrope,* Molière directed his
energy to rediscovering a *possible* form of comedy and to re-establishing,
at least fictitiously, the notion of mutual consent. The stroke of genius
was to have put Tartuffe on the side of consent in *Les Fourberies de
Scapin.* Putting the knave in the service of others was no doubt a return
to an old Latin tradition. But that return was due neither to chance nor
to the mere coquetry of a theatrical virtuoso. Here we have a manipula-
tion both magical and highly conscious. True, Scapin is the height of
farce, the intellectualization, by a mature man, of all he had learned
about a certain form of theater. Yet comic illusion also triumphs: evil
finally serves good—good being, in an imaginary Naples, one creature's
consent to another. In this play the clown's "turn," the romanesque
convention, and the crime of knavery are combined (as in *Le Mariage de
Figaro*) to impose, by means of the most frankly imagined artifice, the
illusory solution to man's condition: good and evil merged in the indis-
putable joy of consent.

For after the difficult trilogy *Tartuffe–Dom Juan–Le Misanthrope,*
Molière's theater was indeed to be concerned primarily with joy, without
illusion but not without hope. The lack of illusion can be found in the
ambiguous first scene of *L'Avare.* In the very first lines Molière affirms
that Valère and Élise are lovers, in the modern sense of the word; then
the dialogue turns to the convention of chaste and "precious" lovers. But
the harm has been done: the romanesque element, which Dullin so well
spotted,[8] simply sends both the spectator and the characters back to the
tradition of artificial propriety. The characters put on masks to perform
a comedy according to the rules, but the masks are necessarily transparent;
hence the spectator, who has been made aware of the reality, is obliged
to play the game with them, knowing well that it is a game. Brutally, we
are told that Valère and Élise had consented to one another as far as
consummation and the anguish of infidelity that follows—and once that
has been accepted, the entire play takes on its meaning as a *theatrical*
solution. After three minutes of dialogue, the playwright revirginizes
Élise and restores to the couple a "precious" chastity that fools no one.
The concession to convention allows a salutary escape to a more beautiful world where, thanks to the magic spell of scenic poetry, the miserly
and love-smitten old man pushes the unreal logic of his nature to the

[8] See below, his pages "On *L'Avare.*"

extreme; where he is the ideal obstacle to "honest" loves; where an order is established by the poet despite insoluble or unpleasant realities, leading to a poetic finale which is not a concession to convention but an affirmation. Only the playwright can take the evil of human nature and render it inoffensive.

This theatrical solution seems to be the key to Molière's works at about the time he was finally authorized to perform *Tartuffe*. It takes the forms of the romanesque, breaks out enchantingly in the court plays, underlies the carnival clownery of *Le Bourgeois gentilhomme* or *Le Malade imaginaire*—all plays of consent, but thanks to the intervention of the unreal. Carnival? Yes, for the mask, in its noble form (the extravagant mythological spree of the court plays) or in its popular form (*turqueries* and syringes), is the instrument of salvation and liberation. Hence the comedy of Molière was no longer troubling; except for a few skirmishes, his struggles seemed to be over. There were the unpleasant dealings with the composer Lully, who played some mean tricks on him, but that kind of quarrel did not call into question the very essence of his works.

Yet, for a moralist, Scapin is as much a knave as Tartuffe, Jourdain as dangerously obstinate as Orgon, Harpagon as possessive as Arnolphe (and with even less generosity), Argan as stupid as Sganarelle, and as devout—in medicine—as Orgon is in religion. Moreover, an element of the macabre was added here and there: so many doctors as prophets of death, a few counterfeits of death itself or the death agony (in the case of Harpagon, Scapin, Argan, and in certain respects, in *Psyché*). But, on the other hand, the provocation did cease: the disquieting search was replaced by a peremptory affirmation, that of an art sufficient unto itself which resulted in the free form of *La Comtesse d'Escarbagnas,* in the somewhat cold perfection of *Les Femmes savantes,* and above all, in the theatrical entertainments.

It is difficult to imagine a ballet bringing together Alceste and Célimène at the end of *Le Misanthrope.* But it is a ballet that saves Dandin from drowning himself. This kind of *fête* is more than an ultimate escape, a skillful pretense. It is a manifestation of comedy's role. A mechanism to reveal the true by means of the truer than true, comedy is also a lesson. But this didacticism is, as Pascal would have said, "of another order." Indeed, in *Le Malade imaginaire,* it is not actually Béralde who teaches us how to live well. Argan himself—at the moment that he is admitted among the doctors—instructs us by the spectacle of delirium being absorbed into a super-delirium, of nature being beaten at its own game by an act characteristic of man and called a game, or rather a super-game, involving the wonders of reflection and imagination. The spectacle produces joy precisely because it entails the intense satisfaction of being superior and of knowing that one is superior. So conceived, comedy is not an escape; it is an affirmation.

It was while making an affirmation against death that Molière died.

Suddenly taken ill during a performance of *Le Malade imaginaire* on February 17, 1673, he was brought home and there he died during the night. That day the actor, who was really ill, had joyously played the part of a man who pretended to be ill. The double deceit of actor and character, meeting head-on the truth of death at the end of a double lie, has caused much ink to flow, and continues to move deeply the glorifiers of Molière. In point of fact, chance served Molière well, and that ideal end transformed his life into a destiny.

We are still touched by that destiny, the notion of which has been kept alive by Madame Dussane[9] and many other theater people. But is it enough to give us an understanding of Molière's works? There is no reason to believe that sentimental biography limits our understanding of them. Yet a mixture of divinization of the man and dull moral interpretations of the works had, in the past, worked to fix a rather boring image of the poet. Twentieth century criticism has, on the whole, proved to be more exciting.

We do not take into account here the historical research which, not very long ago, with its established methods of detection, freed Molière from certain tenacious myths: Michaut's fundamental work[10] was published only in 1922-25. We prefer to dwell on that which has led to a better understanding of Molière's theater as theater, and on the perspectives given us by new methods of criticism. For there we have perhaps the two most original contributions of our times.

Since the beginning of the century, scholars and men of the theater have contributed to the real "retheatricalization" of Molière's works. For the general public the director Louis Jouvet has been particularly instrumental in this, not only by his celebrated staging of *L'École des femmes,* but also by his lectures, certain words of which still ring out in the minds of critics and men of the theater:

> Made to please the multitude, Molière's plays have been plucked from their finality by all sorts of exegetists who believed that classicism was their property. The actor was robbed for the benefit of academic storehouses. Having been forsaken by the public and the scholars . . . it is up to the actor to rediscover and recover that heritage; to get at the both simple and complicated dramatic mechanism by which a work of genius was originally set in motion; to rediscover, for everyone's use, its plot, the freshness of its story, everything that charmed the audience and the actors who performed it for the first time. . . . The comedies of Molière must be judged under the stage lights, not in the books of expositors. And although one reads them in the silence of a room, one must realize that he wrote them for the crowd.[11]

[9] See bibliography at end of volume.
[10] See bibliography at end of volume.
[11] *Conferencia,* XVIII (September 1, 1937), pp. 297-98.

Yet, to be fair, we must go back even further: as early as 1901 an article by Gustave Lanson recalled the very sources of Molière's art; at the period of the First World War Jacques Copeau, in his productions and explanations, rediscovered the playwright and the actor of farce by concentrating particularly on *Scapin*, which he brought back into esteem; and although none of the writings of Jacques Arnavon is included here,[12] the "reforms" he suggested did save Molière from a scenic and academic rut—unfortunately, by making use of a naturalism that was salutary at the time but not relevant today. Gustave Lanson, René Bray, and Alfred Simon, on the one hand, and Copeau and Dullin, on the other, represent here the artisans of the retheatricalization of Molière.

The eternal question of the relations between the man and his works has also been stated in new terms. To be sure, certain critics—such as René Jasinski in his very detailed and highly erudite study of *Le Misanthrope*[13]—consider that Molière's works represent, above all, a personal confession, along with the affirmation of a temperate wisdom. But other critics have challenged that kind of interpretation. Many of these (mostly English and American new critics, followers of Will G. Moore) reject almost entirely the "person" Molière; others continue to bring him in, but essentially in terms inseparable from the structure, the dramaturgy, and the problem of poetic creation as such. In any case, a universe of characters will henceforth be dealt with, and if Molière the man happens to be spoken of, it must be less in terms of his relations with his wife, for example, than with his works—including their demands and, if need be, their social and political implications.

Finally, not the least of the twentieth century's contributions, in addition to rediscovering the theatricality of farce (latent in all the works, or frankly asserted, as in *Scapin*), has been the revival, by our critics and men of the theater, of one of Molière's most ambiguous plays: *Dom Juan*.[14] Once no more than a poor and misunderstood relative, the Dom has recently given rise to a profusion of commentaries, often and necessarily conflicting. By virtue of this, a fair share of this anthology is devoted to him; for whether or not he corresponds to certain "heroes of our times," he has become the center of attraction among all the works. This is perhaps the most striking indication of the fact that the Molière of the twentieth century is no longer the mouthpiece of "petit-bourgeois" common sense, but rather the poet of frenzied struggles which the *vis comica* makes every effort to control.

[12] See bibliography at end of volume.
[13] See bibliography at end of volume.
[14] "Dom Juan" is Molière's variation of the customary spelling, "Don Juan." This former is used here for all references to Molière's play and its hero; the customary spelling for references to the legendary figure. Tartuffe, formerly spelled with either one or two *f*'s, will be consistently spelled with two.

PROLOGUE

The Actor

by René Bray

It is evident that nature had not especially designed Molière for an actor's career. His talents were mediocre, at least for the taste of the times. Mlle. Poisson, who had acted at the Palais Royal with her parents, the Du Croisys, when she was very small, put it bluntly: "Nature, which had been so generous to him in the realm of intellectual gifts, had refused him those outward talents so necessary for the stage, particularly for tragic roles. A muffled voice, harsh inflections, and a hurried speech which made him declaim too quickly, all rendered him far inferior to the actors of the Hôtel de Bourgogne."

"He had," she added, "many difficulties to overcome, and only cured himself of this hastiness, so contrary to good articulation, by constant efforts that gave him hiccoughs, which he retained until he died, and even took advantage of on certain occasions." These hiccoughs are confirmed as early as 1663. De Visé, in the *Vengeance des marquis*,[1] drawing a caricature of Molière, has him hiccough at the end of each line, to the

[1] *Ed. note: La Vengeance des Marquis, Réponse à "L'Impromptu de Versailles"* by Donneau de Visé (1638-1710) has been reprinted in Paul Lacroix's "Collection Molièresque."

great delight of the scoffers. Grimarest, like Mlle. Poisson, attributes this unpleasant tic of the throat to the restraint the budding actor had to impose upon his naturally precipitate delivery.

Mlle. Poisson also informs us that he acted with his eyebrows, which were thick and black, moving them in such a way as to make his face comical. De Visé and Montfleury show him contorting his whole body, jerking as if on springs; to imitate his obese rival at the Hôtel de Bourgogne, he puffed himself up completely, bloated his face, and wheezed and frothed. His virtuosity was recognized. "He was all actor, from head to foot," wrote De Visé. "He seemed to have several voices all speaking in him; and with a step, a smile, a lowering of an eyelid, and a tilt of the head, he could give more of an idea of things than the greatest talker could have done in an hour."

So with him gesture had no less importance than diction, and he expressed as much in attitude as in words. It was in acting with his body that he allowed the spectator to enter into the subtleties of a character. Meanwhile, he was not neglecting diction; Grimarest recalls that he did not declaim at all haphazardly, but was careful of the stresses in a sentence, regulated his delivery, and varied his intonations.

At the end of his life the pulmonary disease from which he suffered made acting more difficult by inflicting upon him the torture of an ungovernable cough. Chalussay dwells on this infirmity in *Élomire hypocondre*:[2]

> C'est une grosse toux, avec mille tintouins
> Dont l'oreille me corne.

> [It is a great cough with a thousand reverberations
> Which is ringing in my ears.]

These are the terms in which Élomire complains. In revenge for the gibes Molière had flung at them, his victims had a good time coughing in front of him by turns and in every key in order to make him "cough his lungs out" himself. Molière made use of his cough as he did of his hiccoughs: he incorporated it into his character, thus identifying the man and the actor, and made still another source of comedy out of it.

How one would like to have seen him act! One curses the insufficiency of the language used by the author of the *Vengeance des marquis* in drawing the caricature of the one he calls The Painter: "Ariste goes off the stage and comes back walking like the Painter, and says: 'Do you see that walk? Look carefully and see if he doesn't do the same. This is how he recites, in profile—look closely at this hip, it's something to see. Some-

---

[2] *Ed. note:* Le Boulanger de Chalussay's *Élomire hypocondre* has been reprinted in Paul Lacroix's "Collection Molièresque."

times he recites like this, crossing his arms and hiccoughing at the end of each line!' " This walk, this recitation in profile, this position of the hip, crossed arms, and terminal hiccough—the sketch leaves great freedom to the imagination.

Who taught him this trade, at which he became so clever and of which he certainly knew nothing at the time of the Illustre Théâtre? None of his contemporaries had any doubt: Molière was a student of the actors of farce. Somaize, in 1660, presented him as "le premier farceur de France [the foremost actor of farce in France]"—it was deservedly high praise. It would be useless to assume, as some have done, that as a child he had admired the prowess of Tabarin at the Pont-Neuf, or that of Turlupin, Gros-Guillaume, and Gaultier-Garguille at the Hôtel de Bourgogne. It was not at such a tender age that he was formed. Undoubtedly he profited by the advice of his friends at the Illustre Théâtre and in the Dufresne company, and he had certainly studied the acting of competitors whom he encountered during his provincial wanderings. But we must believe, along with Somaize, De Visé, and Montfleury, and all those who witnessed his first Parisian appearances, that he had gone for his instruction to the Italian comedians.

The Italians had already been established in Paris at the time of the Illustre Théâtre. The company of Tiberio Fiorelli, otherwise called Scaramouche, with its stars Dominique Locatelli, known as Trivelin, and Brigida Bianchi, called Aurelia, was there continuously from 1645 to 1647, and Molière could have already been inspired by their lessons. They came back to France after the Fronde, and one finds them again in the capital from 1653 to 1659. After an absence of three years, they reappear there yet again in 1662, and this time for a permanent engagement. At least three good actors were outstanding along with Scaramouche, Trivelin, and Aurelia: Pantalon, the Doctor, and Harlequin. The company consisted of ten comedians in all. It was a *commedia dell'arte,* or improvisatory, troupe—no memorized texts. There was only an outline for the action, which consisted of little comic scenes alternated in according to a previously arranged pattern. The acting was enhanced by *lazzi.* Until 1668 at least, the troupe played in Italian; and in order to make themselves understood by a public scarcely acquainted with their language, and also through a natural tendency to physical expressiveness, they practiced an extremely physical style of acting. "The Italians," said Chapuzeau, "who claim first place in comedy, make it consist largely of gestures and bodily agility."

These were Molière's teachers. When he got to Paris, he was established at the same theater as they, and since he acted *aux jours extraordinaires* and they *aux ordinaires,*[3] he was free to attend their productions. He saw

[3] *Ed. note: Jours ordinaires:* Tuesday, Friday, Sunday. *Jours extraordinaires:* Monday, Wednesday, Thursday, Saturday.

them rehearse, he watched their exercises; he was on good enough terms with them to join them at gay suppers after their day's work. In May 1659 the two troupes joined forces (that is, Jodelet and Du Parc, representing Molière's company) to put on for Mazarin in Vincennes a burlesque entertainment upon an agreed subject.

This relationship lasted less than a year. When it began again in 1662 in similar circumstances, Molière's talent must have been formed, although perhaps it was still further improved by contact with his neighbors. The experience of Scaramouche was inexhaustible, and Harlequin's was increasing. At all events both would undoubtedly have been of use to the novice actor. His enemies thought to crush him by calling him a plagiarist and counterfeiter, crying that he was imitating Trivelin and Scaramouche—but where could he find better models? "He is the inheritor of Scaramouche," said Montfleury. And Chalussay:

> Élomire
> Veut se rendre parfait dans l'art de faire rire:
> Que fait-il, le matois, dans ce hardi dessein?
> Chez le grand Scaramouche il va jour et matin:
> Là, le miroir en main et ce grand homme en face,
> Il n'est contorsion, posture ni grimace
> Que ce grand écolier du plus grand des bouffons
> Ne fasse et ne refasse en cent et cent façons.

[Elomire wants to become perfect in the art of making people laugh: for this bold plan, what does the fox do? He goes to see Scaramouche day and night, and there, holding a mirror in his hand and facing the great man, this great student of the best of all clowns copies every contortion, posture, and grimace over and over again, hundreds and hundreds of times.]

The frontispiece of Chalussay's pamphlet accurately represents these comic lessons: the resemblance is undeniable. The pupil is shown in the image of the master, with the same posture, same features, and same moustache. Other portraits go so far as to adorn Molière's chin with Fiorelli's saucy goatee.

With the aid of precise details recently provided by G. Attinger,[4] we can get a fairly clear idea of Scaramouche's acting and of what his pupil borrowed from him. This great comedian enriched his improvisations with a studied technique. Acting behind a mask, he developed mimicry, and triumphed in scenes without speech, thanks to the expressiveness of his attitudes and gestures. Until the end of his life, he retained an astonishing elasticity of body. He was a virtuoso of mime.

His originality shows more clearly on comparison with his friend and successor Dominique Biancolelli, who played behind the mask of Harle-

[4] *Ed. Note: In* L'Esprit de la "commedia dell'arte" *dans le théâtre français* (Neuchâtel, 1950).

quin. Scaramouche had a more calculated acting style, more skillful and restrained, while Harlequin trusted more to instinct and relied on many more effects. The former had enough confidence in himself to freeze into silence and immobility on stage; the latter swept the audience along with a frenzied action. Scaramouche depended on gesture and scorned words, while Harlequin threw himself into speeches as torrential as his movements, and never rejected verbal comedy.

Molière certainly took from Scaramouche his liking for study and his care in preparation; and he also owed to him his confidence in the expressive value of gesture. Did he act as restrainedly as the Italian? One may detect, in the burlesque roles of Pourceaugnac, Jourdain, and Argan, and also of Mascarille in the *Précieuses,* an abundance of effects which would be more akin to Harlequin's technique. But perhaps these are rash distinctions. It must be made clear in any case that since it was written down and not improvised, the Molièresque comedy used words no less than gesture, and on this point departed from the *commedia dell'arte,* particularly from the style of Scaramouche.

It nevertheless remains that Molière was an actor of farce, as Somaize said. His name, as an actor, is inscribed in the roster of all artists in laughter whose brilliant memory is recalled in a painting done in 1670 and preserved at the Théâtre-Français. The Italians of course are in it: Scaramouche, Trivelin, Briguelle, Pantalon, Polichinelle, Doctor Balourd, Harlequin. Next to these are the Frenchmen from the first half of the century: Turlupin, Matamore, Gaultier-Garguille, Guillot-Gorju, Gros-Guillaume. Jodelet has his place. And then the two French comedians still alive in 1670: Poisson, of the Hôtel de Bourgogne, and Molière—Molière-Mascarille, Molière-Sganarelle, Molière-Scapin. In this perspective it is difficult to maintain the fiction of an acting that cares for what is *natural*. Finding the best way to make people laugh, rather than copying nature, was Scaramouche's aim and Molière's as well.

Under Scaramouche's tutelage, Molière thus became a buffoon. Neufvillenaine, one of those who saw him act in 1660, remarks in a synopsis of the *Comédie Seganarelle,* that his playing consisted almost wholly in actions. His body did the acting—his art was an actor's and not a poet's. A little later, De Visé analyzes his comic methods: grimaces, buffoonery, huge wigs, and huge trouser ruffles were the essence of them. He exteriorized a character's life and translated the sense of a situation into images. Sound was added to the visual effect, so that a piece of buffoonery might take the form of a shout or a whisper, a verbal vagary or dialectal gibberish. The stammer and the hiccough intruded upon all this. He made use of all the laugh-provoking techniques that had been accumulated by the tradition of farce.

Neufvillenaine has set down all his freshest impressions as a spectator. Sometimes he exclaims over the jealous posturing of the hero behind his wife's back; sometimes he wishes he had the brush of Poussin, Le Brun, or

Mignard in order to render a gesture or an attitude. He is astonished at the nimbleness with which expressions succeeded one another on the actor's features. "No one has ever been so good at rearranging his face," he cries, "and in this play you could say he changed it more than twenty times." Further on: "No better acting has ever been seen." He states that the most worn out tricks seemed new when Molière used them. He doesn't know which he must admire more, the author for having written the play, or the actor for presenting it so well.

Arnolphe was as funny as Sganarelle. In particular, the scene in Act V where he struggles to make the naïve Agnès feel his love left lasting impression. The *Critique* mentions his extravagant eye-rolling, ridiculous sighs, and silly tears. The final *ouf!* although a simple word, was considered a masterpiece: Arnolphe, breathing out the pain that stifles him, put so much artistry into it that one didn't know whether to laugh or cry. If this ambiguity displeased certain intransigent believers in the unity of tone, it was nevertheless the gauge of an unparalleled virtuosity.

Orgon also did not fail to provoke laughter. From the first act to the last, he constantly multiplied his stage effects. Even Alceste's extremes of voice and gesture unleashed gales of laughter: Brossette attests to this after once seeing old Boileau imitate him at Auteuil after the actor was dead, in the final scene of Act II of *Le Misanthrope*. "Molière, in reciting that," he wrote, "used to accompany it with a bitter laugh, so biting that M. Despreaux delighted us when he did it the same way."

The stage business in *Le Médecin malgré lui*, especially that of the bottle; the entrance of Don Pèdre, in *Le Sicilien*, in nightcap and dressing-gown, a sword under his arm; the despairing grimaces of Dandin; the haggard face of Pourceaugnac, and the grotesque way he uses his hat to protect himself from the clysters; Jourdain frolicking in the Mamamouchi costume; the nervousness of Harpagon running into his garden to get back his moneybox, and his frenzy when he searches for the thief right across the footlights into the audience; Argan flinging himself upon the *chaise percée;* all these were landmarks of Molière's genius and of his greatness as an actor, fully as much as they were immensely funny theater.

From *Les Précieuses* to *Le Malade imaginaire,* from Mascarille to Argan, the actor did not change. He never divorced himself from his Italian masters. From them he learned and never forgot the value of movement. He knew that all theater is spectacle first; the spectator participates in the action with his eyes and ears, and the mind can only follow. To act is to make a face or a body move, to make sounds heard, inside a space bounded by painted canvas. The actor is matter, and it is from matter that the spirit emerges.

I

THE ART OF COMEDY

Molière and Farce

by Gustave Lanson

If there was one part of his art that Molière neglected or scorned, it was putting together a plot, manipulating its threads to lead the spectator to the denouement by every sort of detour and surprise. Molière's art was never one to entangle in order to disentangle, to give new impetus to an action whose momentum seems exhausted, to scramble it up the moment it seems clear, and to unscramble it suddenly by a facile trick just when it seems insoluble. He is just a little boy in this domain, compared to Beaumarchais, Scribe, Sardou, or even Corneille. Must we refer to *School for Wives* (*L'École des femmes*), clumsily built on an overlong quidproquo and disentangled by a badly prepared recognition; *The Learned Ladies* (*Les Femmes savantes*) and the naïve and convenient invention of false letters; *Tartuffe* and the miracle of the king's intervention—a *deus ex machina* whatever one says; *The Miser* (*L'Avare*) and its cascade of recognitions that permits marriages needed by the comedy without sacrificing anything of Harpagon's character; *George Dandin* which has no denouement, leaving things hanging after the play, as they ran ahead in the play? Even *The Misanthrope* with its minimal action

"Molière and Farce" by Gustave Lanson. From the *Tulane Drama Review*, VIII, 2 (Winter 1963); pages 144-54 of the article are reprinted here. Copyright © 1963 by the *Tulane Drama Review*. Reprinted by permission of the *Tulane Drama Review* and the translator. The original article, "Molière et la farce," *Revue de Paris* (May 1901), was translated by Ruby Cohen.

cannot attain its denouement without the unexpected artifice of letters suddenly discovered.

But that is enough to prove the point; it is not through plot that Molière's comedy rates high. Everybody admits it. But let us examine the implications of this admission. Plot is precisely that characteristic of literary comedy that the Italian Renaissance derived from classical comedy. It is plot that Italy gave to Spain and France for their modern comedy. Invention consists in scrambling and unscrambling a skein of deceptions and errors; the *inganno* is the inexhaustible source of interest and laughter. The principal theatrical agents are valets, messengers, fools of every kind and every costume; they take triumphant possession of the stage because in them are the springs of action.

Moreover, it is plot that characterizes most French comedy before Molière: *The Gallantries of the Duke of Ossone* (*Les Galanteries du duc d'Ossone*) by Mairet and Corneille's *Liar* (*Le Menteur*), *The Sister* (*La Soeur*) by Rotrou and *The Invisible Beauty* (*La Belle invisible*) by Boisrobert, *The Foolish Spirit* (*L'Esprit follet*) of d'Ouville and *The Foolish Master* (*Le Maître étourdi*) of Quinault. And when young Molière wished to aspire to authorship, he first handled comedy in his own way; he wrote *The Fool* (*L'Étourdi*), a series of deceptions, and *The Chagrin of Love* (*Le Dépit amoureux*), a web of error.

But by the time he wrote *The High-Browed Ladies* (*Les Précieuses ridicules*), and when he offered *The Misanthrope* or *The Forced Marriage* (*Le Mariage forcé*), *Tartuffe* or *Pourceaugnac*, *The Learned Ladies* or *The Imaginary Invalid* (*Le Malade imaginaire*), then, as in the plays in which Trivelin and Scaramouche acted, the plot is only a thread to link comic situations, a framework for witty scenes. It is only a pretext to control the strings of human puppets whose expressive gestures make the comedy.

I do not even mention *The Angry Ones* (*Les Fâcheux*): the insignificant plot serves to put on stage a hunter, a musician, a scholar, a gambler, etc. Is this not the resurrection of our ancient theater's comic monologue? But rather than a single character like the marvelous "Archer of Bagnolet," the masterpiece of the genre, the plot permits a whole series of types to present themselves through their own words.

The Angry Ones is an exception, but all through Molière we find scenes that are scarcely attached to the plot, and yet do not compete with it. The scenes of *Chagrin of Love*, artificially divided into three different plots, can be detached from any of them, and isolated, as the Comédie-Française produces them, make a delightful little farce. Similarly, we find Sganarelle's discussions with his master, and Dom Juan getting rid of a creditor in *Dom Juan*; in *The Miser*, the calculations of the miser who wants to give a dinner and the memorable scene of the flocks that the money lender wants to lend instead of money; in *Learned Ladies*, the conference of wits and Chrysale's quarrels with his wife; in *The Misan-*

thrope, the scene of the sonnet, the conversation of the coquette and the prude. There are many more such scenes, whose resonance goes far beyond the plot, and whose effect does not reside in the help or hindrance that they give to the denouement, to the marriage that is essential to literary comedy. Separated from the plot, they retain their essential value and their full flavor, which lie entirely in the naïve and witty interpretation of manners and character through dialogue. But plotless and expressive dialogue of manner and character is the domain of Italian farce, with its imaginative slapstick, and of French farce, with its coarse platitudes. Molière enlarges the boundaries, multiplies the stock types and the reactions of each type; he does not change the principle, which is always to seek the comic in some relationship with life, not in a relationship to a climax.

It may seem audacious to link farce to the great comedy of character of which Molière alone was capable. Nowhere else was he more truly creative. But where did he get the idea?

Certainly not from literary comedy, dominated by a plot upon which one generalized. From each actor the situation drew feelings adapted to his role in the play. Dialogue was assigned to the characters by a vague classification into humors or tastes, based on age, sex, and profession, and this classification was supported by generalizations from Aristotle and Horace on the four seasons of life, and by the models of Terence. The same situations called for similar feelings in various people, and different situations evoked different feelings in the same person. Facial expressions that could scarcely be distinguished from one another, generally believable moods, but without specific and individual cohesion—that is what literary comedy offered Molière. There were no *characters.*

For Molière a character is a person who is powerfully unified by the domination of a passion or vice that destroys or subdues all other likes and dislikes of his soul, and this quality becomes the motivating force of all his thought and action. Love alone can sometimes resist this tyranny, and the comic springs forth from this resistance, from its partial defeat or its unforeseen compromises.

Nevertheless, there are several works of literary comedy that might have guided Molière in this way. Not *The Liar (Le Menteur)*, which no one today dreams of playing as a comedy of character, but *The Comic Illusion (L'Illusion comique)*[1] with the startling fantasy of the braggart; *The Pedant Fooled (Le Pédant joué)*,[2] with the caricatures of pedant, captain, and peasant; *The Parasite (Le Parasite)* by Tristan, with another captain playing with the parasite; *Don Japhet* and *Jodelet* by Scarron, those monstrous caricatures; and above all Gillet de la Tessonnerie's *The Countryman (Le Compagnard)*, in which the conventional character of

---

[1] *Le Menteur* and *L'Illusion comique:* comedies by Pierre Corneille. (*Ed. note*)

[2] Comedy by Cyrano de Bergerac. (*Ed. note*)

the captain is almost completely transformed into a country gentleman through real observation. Aren't these works, whose plots contain a marked and burlesque figure, sketches and models for comedy of character? Molière might have started there.

He might have, since almost all these comedies take on a distinctive quality through introducing into the plot a stock type taken from French or foreign farce.[3] He might have, but he did not. Otherwise, why did he not continue Corneille's Braggart (Le Matamore) or Gillet's Countryman in verse comedies? Why in his first effort at character did he turn to the limitations of prose, in the style of farce?

If the comedy of character is sketched in *The High-Browed Ladies* and *Sganarelle,* there is proof that Molière first conceived character in the form of the Italian *mask,* which the French actors of farce had made their own.

Masks of the *commedia dell'arte,* for that matter, are nothing but sketches of general characteristics. Originally, to be sure, the *masks* had local and professional traits that particularized them: Pantaloon was a Venetian merchant; the Doctor was from Bologna, and, as his name indicates, knew his law; Harlequin was a peasant from Bergamo; Scaramouche, a Neapolitan adventurer; and the Captain (also Neapolitan vaguely crossed with Spanish), although not the great lord he claimed to be, was a rich gentleman.

But in France these origins and professions were not noticed, and were transformed into general characteristics. The Captain is no more than vanity and cowardice; Scaramouche, roguery and impudence; Brighella, the insolent tricky valet; Harlequin, the naïve and awkward valet; the Doctor becomes a pedant of philosophy and letters; and Pantaloon is melancholy old age, miserly and foolish. Italian authors in France modified the original types, varying them to bring out their general meaning and thus transforming Trivelin and Harlequin. In spite of dialects and costumes that still continued to reveal the local origin of more than one *mask,* the French spectator saw and could see only general expressions of foolishness and deceit, of lasciviousness and avarice—all humanity gracefully individualized by the imagination and personal observation of the actor.

And that is exactly the principle of *character* as Molière uses it. He knew it so well that he first molded his observation and invention into *masks.*

---

[3] Le Matamore and Jodelet are taken from contemporary French farce. Scarron, Thomas Corneille, and others draw upon the Spanish genre called *comedia de figuron,* and these *figurones* seem to be stock types transplanted from popular comedy to literary comedy. In the works of Tristan, his parasite, aside from being a personal satire, is merely a mold for tirades, a theme with variations in the manner of farce. I would say the same about Desmarets' *Visionaries;* its characters are mere labels tacked on to several kinds of literary amplification.

He began by creating Mascarille and Sganarelle,[4] two *masks* of valets that, in the Italian manner, he submitted to various conditions.

Mascarille, *fourbum imperator,* close relative of Scapin, completely Italian in features and costume, helped Molière ridicule *The High-Browed Ladies.* But this valet's mask is narrow. He is only a rascal, he can only *imitate* others by exaggerating their foibles. With him, there could be no true and exact portrayal of French manners; he would remain Mascarille carrying out his duties, Mascarille imitating the marquis, and not what the poet now envisaged, a true marquis lifted from life on to the stage.

Then Molière took up another valet, Sganarelle, from the pageants of his youth. Only his name is still Italian, and if he was masked at first, Molière unmasked him. Valet though he is, he seems to be the heir of Guillot-Gorju;[5] he ridicules doctors. We find him rigged out in doctor's robes three times: in *The Flying Doctor (Le Médecin volant),* in *The Doctor in Spite of Himself (Le Médecin malgré lui),* and in *Dom Juan.* But Molière broadens the mask and transforms Sganarelle. In contrast with Mascarille, who is essentially a valet, Sganarelle is only occasionally a valet. In essence, he is of the people, ignorant, selfish, a drunkard and coward, rather simple except when fear or acquisitiveness sharpens his mind. His gift is for coarse common sense rather than brilliant grace and light verve. He may be mature or old, peasant or bourgeois, husband, teacher, or father, but as any of these, he is robbed, deceived, and beaten. Between 1660 and 1666, having rejected Mascarille, Molière gave us Sganarelle in six plays, but we can see the *mask* disintegrate in his hands. These Sganarelles share little more than their name; the permanence of Italian Harlequin and Pantaloon are gone, and under this one name we now find a whole family of spirits and temperaments.

However, Molière got rid of Sganarelle as well. The Italian *masks* helped him to simplify life, to delineate moral aspects in the physical; when he had acquired the method, he rejected the *mask.* The artificial identity created by a name hampered him. If Sganarelle remains in the drunken peasant whose wife's revenge converts him into a doctor, the old amorous bourgeois of *The Forced Marriage (Le Mariage forcé)* is no longer Sganarelle. There are two men and two lives, no longer a single man in two roles. And Molière broke the last bond that attached him to the comedy of the *commedia dell'arte.* He even strove to wipe out of the

[4] Of these two *masks,* only Mascarille is masked. From *School for Husbands (L'École des maris)* on, Sganarelle is not masked. In various documents of the time, he has exaggerated, pencilled (or perhaps inked) eyebrows and moustache; Ronsard in *The Royal Grove* speaks of "A Janin whose face is marked with flour or ink." This actor without a mask, whose face is made up but not in white-face, belongs more than the masked actor to the French tradition.

[5] 1600-1648. Farce-player at the Hôtel de Bourgogne. *(Ed. note)*

public mind the identity of these Sganarelles; he dressed them differently (as the inventory of his wardrobe shows): here in crimson satin, there in "musk-colored" satin, elsewhere in "olive-colored breeches and coat" and "underbreeches of flower yellow." [6]

Before 1666, he often liberated himself from Mascarille and Sganarelle; after 1666, he no longer returned to these *masks*. How much Tartuffe would have lost in being called Mascarille the hypocrite, and Orgon, Sganarelle the pious! In giving each bourgeois or fool his own name, the author revealed no less of their basis in good common sense and fearful credulity, of ingenious wit and audacious mischief. But he did not allow the abstract, general type to dominate. He permitted himself to individualize that type, to give it characteristics that renewed it. Thus he came closer to life. Sganarelle shows progress over Mascarille; the disappearance of Sganarelle marks a new step in the true imitation of manners.

To arrive at this point, Molière had to go through half his Parisian career. But although he rejected its appearance, he kept the structure of the *mask*. Arnolphe, Harpagon, Tartuffe, Alceste, are made up no differently from the six Sganarelles, from Pantaloon or Scaramouche. They retain the invariable fixity of characters in any situation of Italian *masks*. They are placed before the public, they are allowed to take any positions, to make all gestures relevant to their character. We see the Misanthrope with the flatterer, with the vain wit, the prude, the flirt; with everyone, he says the word, makes the grimace, that characterize him. The *mask*, emphasized by melancholy, contains and makes entertaining the dialogue of the jealous lover;[7] and Alceste, retaining certain speeches from *Don Garcie* and literary comedy, is unique. Everywhere else, the only purpose of the action is not to show a change in feeling, but to bring forth inexhaustibly, by different acts and under different light, that feeling which is the single mainspring of the character. As Harlequin, through all his contortions, invariably expresses his own sly naïveté, so Harpagon is a miser in every syllable of his part—and Tartuffe a hypocrite.

The permanence of their types is dazzling and changeless; for this reason La Bruyère found them coarse and Fénelon forced. For this reason, too, their comedy has no denouement, because they have to be as they are from start to finish; they cannot say *yes* after having said *no,* a *no* which resides in the necessity of their essence; for such characters,

---

[6] Similarly, in his last years, Molière changed Mascarille from his Italian original; the frontispiece of the 1682 edition shows Mascarille of *The High-Browed Ladies*, recognizable in wig and costume, but without a mask; he no longer has one, but shows his face, that of Molière as Sganarelle.

[7] As everyone knows, *The Misanthrope* borrows its strongest scene and its finest lines from *Don Garcie*. But the development of the feeling of jealousy is subordinated to the comic caricature of the man who would speak openly.

denouements would be artificial. Lapses and repentances are as impossible for them as an act of bravery or decency for Scaramouche.

But in Molière's comedy, there is an important part that Italian farce does not contain, at least for the French spectator: the painting of social conditions and relationships.

Molière shows us all the classes and relationships that composed French society in his time: peasants, bourgeois, squires, wits, great lords, servants, middle-class women, young and older ladies. A large part of his gift lies in spreading vices and ridiculous qualities through these different classes.

Already, under the name of Sganarelle, he had created a figure that was well known in our comic tradition. Sganarelle, valet or master, widower or husband, lover or father, resembles the rascal of our farce more than he does Pantaloon or Harlequin of the *commedia dell'arte*. Like him, he is always beaten, robbed, and deceived. Saint-Beuve realized it—Sganarelle contains Arnolphe, Dandin, and Orgon; in spite of his Italian name, he is pure French.

And what was distinctive about our own farce, as opposed to the character sketches of the Italian *masks,* was the witty image of social relationships. Our farce shows not libertines or misers or scoundrels, but a gentleman, a priest, a lawyer, an old soldier, a rascal, a cobbler, a tailor, a hosier. It portrays not love but home life, and love as a disturbance in home life, and a worry for the husband. It displays the details of quarrels and mistakes in the home, but the eternal conflict between feminine ruse and masculine brutality results less from opposition of two moral natures than from a conflict between two social conditions. It is the state of marriage that is revealed to us in this conflict of the two sexes' maliciousness.

In that way Molière reflects old French farce. How did he come to know it? Could its spirit and trends still be seen under its Italianized form in the farces at the Pont-Neuf and the Hôtel de Bourgogne? Did he see it in the provinces, where it was still being played? Could he envision it through the printed text? Did he come upon booklets like those of Oudot, Rousset, and Barnaby Chaussard that chance has preserved for us? He knew French farce—the fact is certain, since he borrowed from it; the path is uncertain. Although there is a marked difference, due to his poetic genius and the refinement of his classical art, the figures of Arnolphe, Jourdain, Dandin, Pourceaugnac recall the Naudet's, George le Veau's, Colin's of old farce, as well as the draper Guillaume, and the lawyer Patelin. These are the germs that Molière developed, the first use of the comic method of his masterpieces. Although his characters are infinitely richer in substance, far less spare in design, they are constructed by the same method. They have no other way of looking at life than these coarse creatures who so easily amused the subjects of Louis XI and Louis XII.

On the one hand are the great characters with conventional names, Alceste, Tartuffe, Harpagon, who are like *masks* of humanity, on the other hand are characters with real and probable names, Pourceaugnac, Dandin, Jourdain, Arnolphe (or Arnould), deriving from a more purely French tradition. The first are more abstract and moral, the second more localized and social.

What they share, and what unites them in the theater, is their naïve expression in dialogue. Comedy is *active conversation;* dialogue is all, if we mean that expressive and mimed dialogue of which I have spoken, that copious dialogue spilling over the plot so that the internal originality of a vigorously characterized nature reveals itself without reservation or hesitation, with candid passion.

And finally old French farce, differing from the pure artistry of Italian farce, contains a social moral which is usually low and coarse. The farce evokes a judgment about the character and situation. *The Wash-Tub* (*Le Cuvier*) or *The Bridge for Asses* (*Le Pont aux ânes*) contains an implicit ideal of what relationships should exist between husband and wife; *Georges le Veau,* a statement about bad matches; *Master Minim the Student* (*Maître Minim Étudiant*) or *Pernet Who Goes to School* (*Pernet qui va à l'école*), judgments on the practical usefulness of knowledge. Naudet applauds the vengeance of the thief over the gentleman; this is the morality of Figaro wishing to serve his master with what he fears to receive from him. Both "The Archer of Bagnolet" and Colin who "goes to Naples and brings back a Turkish prisoner" judge the brutal, pillaging soldiers by portraying them. In other words, many farces are expressions of popular conscience, of its way of looking at domestic and social relationships. There is an infinite distance between this rudimentary morality and the profound philosophy of Molière's comedies, which contain a seriousness, force, and personal freedom of thought that are unique. Nevertheless, the conception of life of these comedies is also not that of Corneille's *Liar,* nor of Rotrou, nor Scarron, nor Machiavelli, nor Aretino, nor Rojas, nor Moreto; consciously or not, Molière followed in the path of French farce, where what is laughable is what shocks the moral judgment and social prejudice of the public.

No matter how much we pay homage to Molière's genius, to his creative powers, to the suggestions of classical, Italian, French, and Spanish comedy, it is here that we have his true roots. He began with farce, and there he formed his true and expressive style. There he found the principle of *pantomime,* of *active gestures* that freed him from seeking witty words and brilliant dialogue. There he found a tendency that he could develop, and a method that he could use, the principle of concentration on a general character or on the socially ridiculous, there above all he found the habit of situating the source of laughter outside of the plot and entirely in the relationship that his people bear to people in real life.

Let us therefore accept the title thrust upon him by his malicious contemporaries: Molière is "the first jester of France." [8] This is truer than the criticism of his friend Boileau, who reproached him with having been too close to the people. Boileau dreamed of an academic Molière, but the true Molière is seen in a picture of the Comédie-Française, where he stands amid other illustrious actors of farce, both Italian and French. In this picture of *farceurs,* Molière figures in the company of Harlequin and Gros-Guillaume, of Scaramouche and Guillot-Gorju. These are his masters, these are his origins. And he is great enough not to blush at them.

He is the best farceur, and for this reason he is the best creator of comedy. That is why he has not dated in two hundred and fifty years. Whereas Corneille and especially Racine are practically inaccessible except to the educated who are trained to appreciate their intelligence and beauty, mass audiences without instruction or training respond at once to Molière; Molière enters their minds and goes right to their hearts. He appeals to the people, because he springs from the people; because his works, having assimilated all the learned and witty inventions, take their main form and their essential flavor from popular Italian or French comedy; because popular comedy revealed to him that in the "strange enterprise of amusing decent people" and others as well, nothing is more effective than holding "the mirror up to nature."

[8] The phrase in French is "le premier farceur de France." It is difficult to translate, meaning at once "the greatest creator of farce in France" and "the greatest farce actor in France." (*Trans. note*)

The Elementary Rites of
Molière's Comedy

by Alfred Simon

In its boldest thrusts, Molière's comedy acknowledges its fidelity to
the elementary rites of farce. Molière is not a thinker: rich in truths, he
does not encumber himself with theories. Rather than an observer, he is
a contemplator: otherwise would his creatures risk their human density
(which appears to be carried to the most direct realism) in the corrosive
zones of poetry? But the contemplator himself gives way to the skillful
artisan who handles and shapes the stuff of theatricality. Theater is a
game which shakes the body and the mind with the same jolt, com-
municating from one to the other the secret lie, image, or mime through
which the performance ends in a signified truth. It is important that this
artisan of laughter not be forgotten.

Academic gravity has weighed upon him for too long, forming in the
mind of the average Frenchman the gloomy image of a deep thinker, the
common-sense moralist, and the character portrayer. After Copeau, the
reaction went to the other extreme of giving an exaggerated preponder-
ance to the early unsigned farces and the grossest aspects of Molière's
humor. Many young professional or amateur actors do this.

But the point is neither to deny Molière's ideas, nor to disavow the
moralist that, cautiously agreeing with his times, he wished to be, and
still less to deny the existence of the visionary who was able to find the
man beneath the puppet, and the universal beneath the particular. But
the point is rather to show how farce definitely structures comedy, provides it with the four elements which are to the principle of its very
existence as air, water, earth, and fire are to the principle of natural
dynamism. Elementary and ritual, farce infuses its poetic dynamism into
all the roads by which Molière approaches his profound truth. The studied presence of noise, movement, mask, and object haunts those of his

"The Elementary Rites of Molière's Comedy" by Alfred Simon. From *Cahiers de la
Compagnie Madeleine Renaud—Jean Louis Barrault* (Paris: Julliard), No. 15 (January
1956). Translated and reprinted by permission of the publisher and the author. The
pages printed here were translated by Stirling Haig.

comedies that seem the most realistic and literary. These elements mark the intervention of the comic *fatum,* of theatrical destiny in its most opportune or gratuitous, most expected or surprising, form.

From Gesture to Posture

Theater, playing upon appearance—body, face, forms, and colors— does not cease being a spectacle in order to become a game until appearances come alive, until bodies, forms, and colors begin to move. It becomes a game, then action—that is, a game endowed with significance. Then intelligence takes a hand and high comedy begins. But appearance and movement are still the mainstays. This is why the actor's gesture is the principal agent of comedy. It is more effective than words, for its success is more related to the spontaneity of theater, and the actor is always the master and inventor of the gesture, whereas words remain within the author's power, irremediably written down and defined by their automatism (intonation being less flexible than the parabola of the gesture which the poet prescribes or describes, but does not write out). The extent to which Molière, actor and poet, emphasized the harmonious divergence of laughter and smile has not always been adequately noted. His evolution does not go from laughter to smile, since it is at the end of his career that he integrates the *commedia sostenuta* with the bursts of laughter of *Le Bourgeois gentilhomme, Les Fourberies de Scapin,* and *Le Malade imaginaire.* Rather, this evolution leads from separated laughter and seriousness (as in his first farces and dramatic experiments) to their total integration. A single play escapes this dialectic of pure comedy to do homage to what Donneau de Visé called "inner laughter": *Le Misanthrope.* And even here, the marquis scenes, Oronte as a whole, and Dubois' brief appearance are pure bodily stage business. It would be pointless to deny that Molière felt tempted by the dramatic and even the despicable in *Tartuffe, Dom Juan,* and the fifth act of *Les Femmes savantes.* But he had nothing to fear from it and he was marvelously successful in maintaining the balance between humor and seriousness which the sentimentality of bourgeois comedy was deliberately to break.

The smile alone braves the ridiculous, for in order that the evidence of its attack on human dignity subsist, the ridiculous must keep its human depth and warmth. When the ridiculous is provoked to the point of becoming grotesque—that is, when smiles give way to laughter, and intellectual restrictions give way to the liberation of the instincts, which is the supreme victory of the comic actor—one passes the bounds of what is human. There is no place left for nuance, either psychological or moral. The character, a pure appearance offered to our view, is dismantled, mechanized, and, puppet of cogs and sounds that he is, literally explodes in the audience's guffaws, to fall to earth in droplets of absurd and unsubstantial poetry. And gesture, with its extensions, is the principal agent of that explosion.

Gesture is fragile, it is barely touched upon in the history of the theater. In the absence of any cinematographic or even photographic documents, only two engravings by Chauveau and posthumous illustrations attest almost without a doubt the features, but not the gesturing, of Molière the comic player. On the other hand, Molière's contemporaries emphasized his art of the grimace, which they called "scurrility." To quote Neufvillenaine on Sganarelle: "His face and gestures so well express his jealousy that it would not be necessary for him to talk in order to seem the most jealous of men. . . . No one has ever been heard to speak so naïvely, nor to appear with such a silly face. . . . Never did anyone know how to put on a face so well, and one can say that in this play, he changes it twenty times or more." And Donneau de Visé: "He was all actor, from head to toe. He seemed to have several voices. Everything about him was expressive, and with a step, a smile, a wink of the eye, a shake of the head, he suggested more things than the greatest speaker could have said in an hour." Very precisely, Molière based the essential part of his acting on mime. His knowledge of pantomime, at least perfected in the company of the Italian actors, and among them particularly Tiberio Fiorelli (called Scaramouche), is fully utilized in the characters that he invented for himself, and he tried to inculcate it in the members of his troupe.

If his theater escapes being bourgeois comedy, he owes it to the gesture as a manifestation. Molière decomposes life into a mechanical ballet, he schematizes and puts rhythm into the visual development of the action by means of a particularity which is formal, invented, utilized, or prolonged; he firmly sketches out a silhouette, starts a gag, and literally dazzles us. The false dignity that textbooks have conferred upon the classics still keeps us from admitting the inspired mime in Molière, the dancing buffoon that he was. And yet the works themselves, despite their director's silence, sufficiently demonstrate that our imagination is in great danger of missing the whole truth. The great comedies especially are the ones to suffer from this basic lack of understanding. Thus *Tartuffe* becomes dismally bourgeois, *Dom Juan* is disquieting without being amusing, *L'Avare* drags, and *Le Misanthrope* languishes. Naturalism and academicism kill Molière in the same way, by not recognizing that Tartuffe, Dom Juan, and Alceste, in order to attain all their truth, need to have their share of visual humor—the gesture—confirmed, which the silhouette stabilizes and the posture totalizes. And heaven knows that Molière, with consummate art, made use of silhouette and posture. Why should we not be able to re-invent the most fleeting of the gestures which condition and crown them? We must, because ultimately the Molière whom we most admire creates a character by hypostasizing a silhouette, develops a situation by exploiting a posture. Whence the strange fraternity between Sganarelle and Alceste, between the jealousy of the Barbouillé and the misfortunes of George Dandin.

From Word to Discourse

Viewed from the stage, theater begins with silence prior to the performance. Then comes the noise (the three raps and musical overture) and movement (the raising of the curtain or stage lighting). The spectacle starts with the metamorphosis of the setting, brought about by sounds, quickly identified with words, which together become an exchange of dialogue. The meaning of the dialogue does not command attention at once, and the void of silence is what is first broken. This is why the theater sometimes feels the need to speak meaningless words, in order to check its voice and hear itself make noise, to start up a system of noises, various incidents, romps, falls, and blows—until one of them, transcending its own theatricality, provokes the collective burst of laughter from which the buffoon gathers impetus to spring to the height of his fantasy.

The words spoken by the player therefore fulfill the triple function of material noises, intellectual signs, and harmonious sounds. Farce is preferably based upon the first function, pressing the two others into its service, as if to prolong its echo. The clown inseparably blends words and noises, speaking in bursts of horns, tympani, whistles, and sawing of fiddles, or imitating the noises of matter by volleys of words with ludicrously twisted meanings and accents which invert the order of things. The Italian players, unable to make themselves understood by their Parisian audience except by gestures, began introducing some French words into their original dialect, and in the end based a part of their comic effects on the very strangeness of the sonorities. Language then lost its value as a sign, the gesture being substituted in its place so as to establish communication, and became purely material sounds.

Molière also used the resonant shell of language. By crystallizing it, just as he crystallized attitudes, feelings, or ideas, he transformed it into a mechanism for provoking laughter in ways other than witticisms or puns. In his first attempts, and following the itinerant tradition, he left whole scenes to the actor's discretion. The words themselves are of little importance, and the tangled skein of quarrels is what elevates the philosophers of *La Jalousie du barbouillé* or the professors of *Le Bourgeois gentilhomme* to the peak of comic *hubris*.

Various stages mark this freeing of language, starting with the mutterings in which nonverbal language draws its effectiveness from intonation and rough assonances, then gibberish or jargon which outrageously deform familiar phrases, and finally the galimatias which pushes to the limits of the absurd the language of doctors, scholars, *précieuses,* or bumpkins. And this is the trap. A thesis recently defended at the Sorbonne showed how Molière took "verbal fantasy," whose tradition harks back to the Middle Ages, and by submitting it to the movement of his dialogues and the theatrical requirements of action, led it to its apex and made it almost impossible to use. Now as the dramatic art of the playwright progressed, and as his aims rose, verbal fantasy acquired virulence and audacity, and did more to strike down the ridiculousness in question than a thousand theoretical elaborations. It is a long way from peasant or Swiss accents, or imaginary languages borrowed from Italy, Spain, or Turkey, whose lunar apotheosis is reached in *Le Bourgeois gentilhomme,* to certain traits which strain the fundamentals of human speech. One can still allow that Pourceaugnac's delirium is a pure laughter mechanism.

"Des médecins habillés de noir. Dans une chaise. Tâter le pouls. Comme ainsi soit. Deux gros joufflus. Grands chapeaux. Bon di, Bon di. Six pantalons—Tara ta ta. [Doctors dressed in black. In a chair. Feeling the pulse. So be it. Two fat chubby-cheeked men. Big hats. *Bon di, bon di.* Six pantaloons—Tara ta ta]." But in the end the most usual methods of enumeration or repetition give out a strange sound. When Lubin, in *George Dandin,* tells Claudine: "Si tu veux, tu seras ma femme, je serai ton mari, nous serons mari et femme [If you like, you'll be my wife, I'll be your husband, we'll be husband and wife]," it is impossible not to compare this to certain speeches of the defenders of common sense and average reason. The tireless harping of the Aristes, the Philintes, the Cléantes, with their ponderousness and self-satisfied wisdom, has something mechanically laughable about it. Elsewhere, Orgon's "le pauvre homme" and Harpagon's "sans dot" so pitilessly highlights the clearly circumscribed folly of the human puppets who say those words that it would be worth studying, from this viewpoint, the use Molière makes of language, and the ways in which he moves from jargon to discourse, from verbal frenzy to doctrinal exposition. The problems of expression are more or less fully propounded everywhere in his works, in a more or less burlesque perspective. The mutes whose speech must be restored, the pedagogues at grips with technical language, the *femmes savantes* with verbal elegance, and above all Monsieur Jourdain, the man who does not know how to talk with the philosophy teacher, a theorist of speech; these are the important milestones of this exploration.

Is *Dom Juan,* so rich in fecund ambiguities, not in a certain sense, from beginning to end, the struggle of Sganarelle to provoke a debate with Dom Juan, to have it out with him? "Oh! Dame, interrompez-moi, si vous voulez. Je ne saurais disputer si on ne m'interrompt [Oh! Well then, please interrupt me. I can't argue if I'm not interrupted]." The first time he begins his argument he bases his speech precisely on total gesture. He mimes his discourse. "Je peux frapper des mains, hausser le bras, lever les yeux au ciel, baisser la tête, remuer les pieds, aller à droite, à gauche, en avant, en arrière, tourner . . . [I can clap my hands, raise my arms, life my eyes, lower my head, move my feet, go to the right, to the left, forward, backward, turn . . .]." Thereupon Sganarelle trips and falls. Gesture has undercut speech. "Bon, voilà ton raisonnement qui a le nez cassé [Fine, now your reasoning has a broken nose]."

We could apply Dom Juan's remark again and again. If the "reasoners" do not break their noses, it is because they have an easy time of it. Their speeches forge ahead with no concern about being convincing, because they are attacking folly, foolishness, and the ridiculous. Sganarelle has to deal with a complex being who is none other than dangerous liberty in person. When Dom Juan's audacity has passed all bounds, freeing Sganarelle from his scruples and even his cowardice, the valet in turn crosses the line, and enters into a state of "utterance." He undertakes to define his wisdom. Gesture no longer hampers him. He indulges in words and phrases, as Ariste or Philinte do, and the language is more crystallized, more mechanical than ever.

"Sachez Monsieur, que tant va la cruche à l'eau qu'à la fin elle se brise; et comme le dit fort bien cet auteur que je ne connais pas, l'homme en ce monde est ainsi que l'oiseau sur la branche, la branche est attachée à l'arbre, . . [Note, Sir, that the pitcher goes so often to the well that at last it breaks; and as that writer whom I don't know puts it so well, man in this world is like a bird on a branch, the branch is attached to the tree, . . .]." In that "hodgepodge" found in *Dom Juan,* in that extraordinary mixture of Ariste and Pancrace, Molière surely challenges all the speeches and all the sages of his comedies, and perhaps a certain side of himself.

From Mask to Face

It was quite a shock the day it had to be admitted, on the unimpeachable evidence of one of Chauveau's frontispieces, that Molière played the Mascarille of *Les Précieuses ridicules* wearing a mask. A choice had to be made: either *Les Précieuses* is a farce that must be played as such, under penalty of seriously betraying Molière, or else the mask has its place in high comedy. The truth is that mask, farce, and comedy contracted a poetic marriage, and one that is in no way a misalliance.

Like gesture and elementary language, the mask tends to impose a stereotyped image of man. It is something hollow that is filled by a face in flesh, and at the same time an alien relief superimposed upon personal traits: the inert upon the living, the rigid upon the pliable, the fixed upon the moving. Intensity of expression depends upon the exact correspondence between them. One cannot say what is more singular about the mask, its inertia or its strangeness. Whether just stiff cardboard or an alien face, the mask awaits. It awaits its look, its grimace, it awaits life from someone else's life. It is interposed between the actor and the character. It conceals the actor, but reveals the character. And most of all, it trusts in the actor's body, for hereafter it is in the way he holds his head, moves his hands, muscles, and legs that the actor can hope to animate a character who can no longer count on the detailed expressiveness of his face. But the most striking characteristic of the mask is its inhumanity. The masked actor is no longer a man, nor the character he embodies. He no longer entirely embodies the character but rather its mask —that is, a concealed face as well as a set face, a misplaced face. He becomes a hybrid being, real and imaginary, fleshly and material, a "monster." This is why neither the ancient comedy nor the *commedia dell'arte* masked its young and handsome characters.

In his first plays, Molière accepted this inhumanity of comedy which no doubt increased the comedy's poetic import. But he felt the temptation to rediscover the individual man behind the type. The mask conceals the face, but in turn the face conceals the soul, and the soul conceals itself. Everything becomes a mask. The universe of the theater, like the theater of life, then becomes a vast play of masks which the contemplator cannot accept as such. He must rip away these disguises, these masks of flesh in cardboard faces. Technically, however, grotesque and monstrous masks continue to appear in Molière's theater, in farce or in *comédie-ballet*: the doctors of *L'Amour médecin* or *Le Malade imaginaire*, the philosophers of *Le Mariage forcé*, the Turks of *Le Bourgeois gentilhomme*. And when there is no thin cardboard, make-up comes in: florid faces, flour-whitened faces, false beards, monumental wigs, and all the accessories of theatrical magic. Often, as René Bray has shown, Molière confronts mask and antimask in the same scene, the man and the monster, Orgon and Dorine, Purgon and Béralde. Molière's success lies in the equilibrium of this play between the dancing mechanism of masks, handed down from the legendary past of the theater, and the naked truth of characters already facing toward a future theater. The complexity of the great comedies rests upon this effort of the masks to humanize their own petrified mugs, and upon the hesitation of the others between the enormous candor of the mask and the subtle hypocrisy of the real face played upon one's feelings, and the soul which has become its own screen.

To suppress through staging this obsession of the mask, which is properly the interplay of the theater and life, is to unbalance things, to initiate the fall of comedy into bourgeois naturalism, and to make Molière principally responsible for the immense poetic loss which has struck the French theater since the end of the Golden Century. The dialectic of the mask, which makes all disguised faces into the true protagonists of Molière's farces—the *précieux*, the pedants, the prudes, the impostors, the courtiers—no doubt achieves its high point in *Le Misanthrope*. Alceste has set out to tear off all the masks in the world, believing that

everyone has chosen the mask which would permit him to dodge himself
and others. He does not understand that in the end the face itself, assuming all the tics of the soul, stiffens, hardens, and becomes in turn a mask.
Touching and ridiculous, his maniacal passion creates the mask of truth
for him.

From Object to Annoyance

The study of the relationship between Molière's comedy and the object which in the theater has the very precise name of prop can only be
touched upon here. The famous *Mémoire des décorateurs de l'Hôtel de
Bourgogne* enumerates the list of props for *L'Avare*: "Two smocks are
needed, spectacles, a broom, a bat, a small chest, a table, a chair, a writing desk, paper, a gown, two candlesticks on the table in the fifth act."
With these, the photographer Agnès Varda composed a still-life that was
expressive in its starkness. The role of the object begins with farce; we
are familiar with the use clowns make of it, and its ambiguities which
Charlie Chaplin plays upon with such subtlety. The prop moves between
the setting and the character, sometimes becoming part of the former as
furniture or curio, sometimes becoming part of the costume as trinket or
tool. It accompanies the action and occasionally provokes surprises by
means of its potential in visual gags.

The bourgeois theater transforms the object into a curio, and out of a
concern for realism, multiplies it and deprives it of any character. The
poetic theater, on the contrary, confers upon it an intense presence and
quite often a sign value. Certain objects are thus privileged.

Among those which most often appear in Molière's comedies, the
following are significant:

Objects that stand for possession: the chest, the purse, the key ring.

Those which stand for enjoyment: the snuff-box, the bottle, the dish of
food.

The signs of frivolity (mirrors, ribbons, jewels), denunciation (letters or
portraits), and repression (stick or sword).

In Molière's theater, these props are always thrown into relief with
particular sharpness.

Dom Juan begins with Sganarelle's monologue on the benefits of
tobacco. The gesture of taking snuff, the sneezes, the fellow's talk and
grimaces radiate from the tiny box, which represents the ultimate material residuum of theatrical business. There is also the gold *louis* that Dom
Juan dangles before the Poor Man's eyes, as one of the most audacious
scenes that Molière wrote is played out.

Molière himself indicated or suggested most of these stage effects. Some
of them have been handed down by tradition. In *L'École des femmes*, at
the height of his anger and jealousy, Arnolphe used to arrange his hat

and coat on the ground, and Molière found the source of a real gag in this. Others have been invented or re-invented by great actors faithful to the poet's spirit. Can we now imagine the Géronte of *Les Fourberies de Scapin* without the parasol that Louis Jouvet used as an all-purpose tool in the Vieux-Colombier's production? He himself reports that Jacques Copeau had thought of having Sylvestre chew and spit sunflower seeds, but that he never met an actor capable of carrying it off!

We must remember that when he has the help of the object, the director can do away with any equivocal emphasis. The object is the occasion and the obstacle at the same time. Reduced to its pure appearance, it is nevertheless irreducible. The only way to ignore it is to make it vanish. And in fact the objects of Molière's comedies have the magical presence of props on the table of a vaudeville magician, or of the acrobatic fittings that mysteriously shine at the top of a circus tent. They come into play as soon as they are made to vanish. But they are never suppressed. And the stick crashes down on the back of Sganarelle or Géronte, Célimène's note provokes Alceste, the quacks' syringes assail Pourceaugnac, the ludicrous hat on Monsieur Jourdain's head not only anoints him Mamamouchi, but makes him the lunar puppet in the eternal comedy. The object is an irreducible obstacle that stands between the character and his madness. He stumbles over it, and the prop's cunning materiality captures certain characters, whose only role—their gestures are so stiff, their language so mechanical, their mask so set—is to be present at the least convenient moment: such are the notaries, the doctors, the pedants, and the bumpkins who trip up the protagonist, unless through his own foolishness he has already set these inevitable robots in motion. Sometimes a character supremely "juggles" the object as well as the character-object. See Dom Juan and the gold *louis,* Dom Juan with Charlotte and Mathurine, and compare the elegance with which he "annihilates" the *fâcheux-type,* Monsieur Dimanche, and Sganarelle's clumsiness in becoming entangled with him. Here again Dom Juan is exceptional. He escapes the comedy of the *fâcheux,* the trap of the character-object that haunts Molière's comedies and totally victimizes Alceste. All the confluence of importunities and the succession of *fâcheux* prevent him from reaching Célimène for a decisive coming to terms.

Scapin

When Molière produced *Les Fourberies de Scapin* in 1671, he was coming to the end of his career. He had a funny sketch in reserve: *La Comtesse d'Escarbagnas,* was working on what he believed to be the great work of his life: *Les Femmes savantes,* and had projected the final macabre burst of laughter: *Le Malade imaginaire.*

There is no other equivalent to *Scapin* in his works except the far-off

Étourdi, and this reminder allows us . . . to measure the distance covered. Apotheosis of actor and acting, *Scapin* is a kind of homage by Molière, already tapped by death, to the *commedia dell'arte,* which had already reached its decline. We must grasp the significance of this ceremonial affiliation of the greatest comic poet of all time to the highest comic tradition.

It is ritual ceremonial, and its rites are the very ones which save the theater and whose recurrence in Molière's works I have just pointed out. *Les Fourberies de Scapin* is their *summa.* In this *commedia sostenuta,* for it is not simply a farce, all the theater's primary forces breeze through. Gesture, word, mask, and object have been distilled and bound together to call forth the great master of acting: Scapin.

Scapin is farce transcended, and *commedia dell'arte* perfected; but it must be admitted, however heretical the assertion may seem, that it also constitutes a transcendence of *Tartuffe* and *Le Misanthrope;* not only because it comes at the end of Molière's long struggle against the deceptions of his times, but because the gaiety that penetrates it is rich in all the bitterness and audacities, past and surpassed. Molière was therefore coming to an end, and he chose to emerge in this Neapolitan scenery, fresh as a water color, abstract as a diagram or a mountebank's platform, and here he met his double and witness in the company of the great puppets of the burlesque escapade, from Harlequin to Charlie Chaplin's tramp. Here the hideous Gérontes walk about masked, stupid, or avaricious. The young fops are dandies whose frivolity, inconsistency, and egotism are weighed. The young ladies display sardonic fright and tearful kindness. All these people barely stand up, and they are fine skittlepins for the nimble dancer who is put into action at the least chance for mischief. Everyone thinks that he is his valet, but fooling everyone, he serves the theater alone. Through gesture and speech, he creates his universe where the pawns assume positions according to his whim, while he alone is involved in the situation. It is he, more than Molière, who relegates all the others to the rank of silhouettes and marionettes, while he himself accedes to the dignity of the great leading role.

I am not trying to prove anything with *Les Fourberies de Scapin,* since I had to go, beyond farce, into the complexity of the great masterpieces. But Scapin alone, from one end of the comedy to the other, offers this ecstatic image of bodily acting driven to its limits. And its paroxysm comes in Scene 2 of Act III.

Scapin, the character-actor, master of the situation, reduces Géronte, the mask and character-object, to the derisory posture of a man caught in a sack. Two objects intervene, thanks to which Scapin can juggle the order of the world: the sack and the bat. He surpasses gesture through dance, and discourse through unbridled dialogue, multiplies his face and voice, and counterfeits all the possible events of the world. While he exalts himself in dancing, and annihilates the foul burden in the sack by beating it, he arrives at a truly Dionysian intoxication. Here he is in the perfectly harmonious world of acting, where he forgets the materiality of the object, and the very object of his action. Lost in the vastness of his fantasy, Scapin could only have tripped himself up. The character-object recovers life, catches Scapin unawares, and unmasks him in turn. But Scapin always knew that his acting was the most dangerous.

Speech

by Will G. Moore

Whereas psychology, character drawing, and satire might lead to an intellectual use of language, to precision, distinction, and differentiation, the concentration of dramatic energy in person and situation leads to the opposite. Excitability of any kind, be it irritation, mania, gaiety, anger, or fun, leads to incoherence, which is that state in which one's power of intelligent expression in words is defeated. Language in Molière shows with almost infinite variety this clash of man and speech. The gift of speech is the mark of the intelligent or civilized man; natural man, animal man is frequently speechless. He might, if he could, say with Dandin: "Je ne dis mot, car je ne gagnerais rien à parler [I say nothing, for I'd gain nothing by speaking]." Or even more frequently his utterance escapes his control: he says what he does not mean, or less, or more, than he means. Here for a dramatist dealing chiefly in words was a wide field of evidence of human behavior under the pressure of emotion. Molière has, as I hope to show, exploited it as no other artist has done.

To do this at all implies a firm understanding of the social function of language. At its simplest, language is communication and in normal intercourse language obeys the single condition that both parties understand what is said. Samuel Butler had it that the essential ingredients of language were three: a sayer, a sayee, and a convention. Someone must speak, someone must hear, both must understand more or less the same thing by what is said: what the one emits the other must admit. When this is not so, language fails in its social function; it is, we say, unintelligible, it is misunderstood, or in more pictorial explanatory phrase, it does not get across. Many rudimentary comic situations are no more than interferences with this structure of three-point relationship. Suppose, for instance, that the speaker is not sure who is at the other end of the chain of communication, or that he thinks the hearer is someone other than he really is. Suppose again that what he says is not heard, or not grasped, or misinterpreted. These elementary cases occur in Molière. Horace betrays the whole story to Arnolphe because he mistakes his identity. But what would in real life give rise to an amusing remark or incident is screwed up, so to speak, by the dramatist in order to produce its maximum comic potential. The situation is arranged so that Horace does not merely give the show away, but relates to Arnolphe, as if he were a third party, the discomfiture of Arnolphe, and not only so but expects Arnolphe to be as amused as he is, and comments on the fact that he is not laughing enough. The mock soldier in the *Fourberies* asks Argante if he has seen "ce faquin d'Argante" and describes in blood-curdling terms (to Argante) what he would do to him if he should happen to find him. The effect is due to nothing more than mistaken identity and consequently misdirected language. Its more philosophic development will be noticed later.

A similar everyday case is that of being misheard. Of this, too, there are cases in Molière, but intensified again to a degree that rarely occurs in life. La Flèche (deliberately?) mishears the most suspicious of men, thus: Harpagon: "Ne serais-tu point un homme à faire courir le bruit que j'ai chez moi de l'argent caché?—Vous avez de l'argent caché?—Non, coquin, je ne dis pas cela [Are you not the sort of man who would spread the rumor that I have money hid in my house?—You have money hid in your house?—No, you rogue, that is not what I said]." A variant of this is Sganarelle's (deliberate?) misunderstanding of the doctors' verdict on his daughter: "Nous avons vu suffisamment la malade et sans doute qu'il y a beaucoup d'impuretés en elle.—Ma fille est impure? [We have sufficiently examined the patient, and have no doubt that there are many impurities in her.—My daughter impure?]."

One of the basic assumptions and intentions of social speech is its comprehensibility: it conveys the mind and intention of the speaker. Speech that does not do this is comic; we laugh, for example, at a man who speaks and yet has nothing to say. But such a man is not often so funny as Molière makes Sganarelle. As a doctor, called to pronounce on a case, he cannot appear tongue-tied, he has nothing relevant to say; his speech, therefore, is nonsense, clothed in the forms of sense: "Hippocrate dit . . . que nous nous couvrions tous deux.—Hippocrate dit cela?— Oui.—Dans quel chapitre, s'il vous plaît?—Dans son chapitre . . . des chapeaux [Hippocrate says . . . that we should both put our hats on.— Hippocrate says that?—Yes.—In what chapter, please?—In his chapter . . . on hats]."

A parallel case is incoherence, that of a man who has something in his mind but cannot express it. The seventeenth century admitted that language did not suffice to express all that men wished to express. The quality too rare or precious to admit of precise definition was known as "je ne sais quoi," which is possibly one of the many *précieux* expressions which have justified their invention. But Molière is alive to the comedy of the position of having to define the indefinable. Alceste, when asked what is wrong with him, cannot, for excellent reasons, say what it is: "J'ai ce que

sans mourir je ne puis concevoir [I have something that I couldn't conceive of without dying]." It is perhaps fitting that a Frenchman should
have given such delightful expression to this incapacity to express. The
most dramatic case occurs in *Tartuffe*. Orgon, attempting to describe
Tartuffe, cannot find words to do so:

> C'est un homme . . . qui . . . ah . . . un homme . . . un homme en-
> fin . . .

> [He's a man . . . who . . . ah . . . a man . . . well, a *man*],

a line which appears to mirror exactly the stuttering of a man who has
the will, but not the capacity, to speak, but which is fuller, rounder, more
intense than life, since it embodies a triple statement: that Orgon cannot
describe him, that he is indescribable (which is true, but in a different
sense for Orgon and for us), and finally that any attempt to describe him
can only say that he is . . . a man, which in fact he hardly is. For Orgon
he is almost the perfect man; for the others he is almost inhuman. Thus
can language, under a guise of helpless incoherence, unite in a single
expression allusion to widely differing states of mind.

What might be called a complementary phenomenon is even more impressive. A man may be incoherent because he has too much in his mind
to say. The artistic parallel to this is speech, in a moment of intensity,
that says far more than is meant. Again, the logical function of speech is
broken, we should perhaps say broken through, by nature, by emotion
that ruins the intended effect of speech and conveys not the meaning of
the speaker but his real state, possibly against his will. The language of
Molière's maniacs and fools is no longer the vehicle of their intention,
but conveys in its sweep and force their condition also. Argan, for example, at the end of a long duel of repartee admits, as he never would
wittingly do, his own evil nature. (The situation had been already worked
out in similar fashion in the *Fourberies*.)

> Voici qui est plaisant. Je ne mettrai pas ma fille dans un couvent si je
> veux?—Non, vous dis-je.—Qui m'en empêchera?—Vous-même.—Moi?—Oui.
> Vous n'aurez pas ce coeur-là.—Je l'aurai.—Vous vous moquez.—Je ne me
> moque point.—La tendresse paternelle vous prendra.—Elle ne me prendra
> point.—Une petite larme ou deux, des bras jetés au cou, un mon petit
> papa mignon, prononcé tendrement, sera assez pour vous toucher.—Tout
> cela ne fera rien.—Oui, oui.—Je vous dis que je n'en démordrai point.—
> Bagatelles.—Il ne faut point dire: Bagatelles.—Mon Dieu, je vous connais,
> vous êtes bon naturellement.—Je ne suis point bon, je suis méchant quand
> je veux.

> [Well, that's nice! You mean to say that I can't put my daughter in a
> nunnery if I will?—No, I tell you.—And who will stop me?—You your-

self.— I myself?—Yes, you won't have the heart.—Of course I will.—You're
joking.—I am not joking.—A father's love will take hold of you.—It will
not take hold of me.—A few tears, her arms around your neck, "my cute
little father" in a tender voice, will be enough to bring you round.—Not
at all.—Oh yes.—I tell you that I am determined.—Rubbish.—Don't say
rubbish.—Go on, I know you, you really have a kind heart.—I don't have
a kind heart, I am nasty when I want to be.]

The same kind of situation occurs in *Tartuffe,* showing the same pastiche of realism, but only a pastiche; surely no people ever quarreled with
this remorseless logic, getting nearer and nearer to the absurd as they get
more excited, until the wire-puller produces the final unmasking absurdity. This is no realism, but a sovereign exercise of dramatic irony. In the
first love scene the hypocrite ardently pleads his case, but at the same
time provides, for those who overhear, the admission of his own rascality.
The lady claims to be shocked at his "déclaration tout-à-fait galante"
coming from a man of piety, and thus provokes him to say:

> Ah, pour être dévot je n'en suis pas moins homme. . . .
> Je sais qu'un tel discours de moi paraît étrange;
> Mais, Madame, après tout, je ne suis pas un ange.

[Ah, I may be pious, but I am still a man. . . . I know that such words
coming from me must seem strange; but, Madame, after all, I am no angel.]

His meaning is clear, but so also is that grosser meaning that he did not
intend to convey but which his words would carry to the audience. One
might paraphrase his intention thus: "My piety does not make me any
less a man," which also means that his piety does not affect his humanity,
because it is only skin-deep. And with the confession that he was "no
angel" would not Damis and Dorine boisterously agree, reading into it
the most joyful litotes? No angel, that was a rich way to describe him.

As a variant of this dramatic trick of forcing a man to say two things
when he thinks he is only saying one, the famous monologue of Harpagon
shows case after case of statements pushed beyond their meaning and
exaggerated to absurdity by the passion of the utterance. The equivalent
in word does not seem strong enough, so the speaker embroiders on the
concept and pushes it beyond the credible, thus:

> Au voleur, au voleur, à l'assassin, au meurtrier. . . . Je suis perdu, je
> suis assassiné, on m'a coupé la gorge. . . . C'en est fait, je n'en puis plus,
> je me meurs, je suis mort, je suis enterré. N'y a-t-il personne qui veuille
> me ressusciter en me rendant mon cher argent? . . . Je veux aller quérir la
> justice, et faire donner la question à toute la maison. . . . Allons vite, des
> commissaires, des archers, des prévôts, des juges, des gênes, des potences

et des bourreaux. Je veux faire pendre tout le monde, et si je ne retrouve
mon argent, je me pendrai moi-même après.

[Thief, thief, assassin, murderer. . . . I am lost, I am murdered, they
have cut my throat. . . . It's all over, I can't stand it any more, I am dying,
I am dead, I am buried. Will nobody bring me back to life by giving me
back my dear money? . . . I will go for the police and make them put the
whole household through torture. . . . Quick, officers, archers, provosts,
judges, racks, gallows and hangmen. I want everybody hung, and if I don't
find my money, I will hang myself after them.]

To talk like this is certainly grotesque; it is also the mark of a lunatic,
but the exaggerating method is clear enough in each case for us to realize
that the force behind the words is striving always to surpass them, to find
the impossible, that is, words to equal his horror at the theft, a horror
which is strictly and soberly speaking indescribable: it goes beyond words.
But this is a feature of other "possédés" in Molière's comedies. Alceste
had perhaps no idea of how much he was giving away when he said:
"Personne n'a, Madame, aimé comme je fais [No one, Madame, has loved
as I do]," until the phrase was out and capped immediately by the cool
rejoinder: "En effet, la méthode en est toute nouvelle [Indeed, the
method is quite new]."

Perhaps Orgon's famous repetitions are to be accounted for in similar
fashion. Here again criticism has yielded perhaps too easily to the assumption that what is not deep and serious psychology is a blemish, a
lazzo of farce introduced to catch the gallery or to lighten the tone. The
scene is unreal, but so is all fantasy. And it is surely a plausible fantasy
that the master of the house should inquire about what is going on, that
the servant should speak only of Madame, about whom he can find out
for himself, that he should therefore interrupt her with his "Et Tartuffe?"
and after each of her taunts against the holy man should ejaculate "Le
pauvre homme!" This is comic, not as pointless repetition but as the
language of absorption. The fact that his sole reflection should fall so
faultlessly in place means nothing to him and much to the audience.

Let us now see how the rogues use language to their own purposes.
Language is as comic when designedly misused as when it unintentionally
betrays. The source of comedy lies in the fact of interference with the
normal process of communication; in the one case the man's nature or
passion interferes with his intention; in the other his intention deliberately obscures or twists or abandons normal speech in order to attain a
particular end. The clearest example of this procedure is professional
jargon. Words are used for an effect other than that conveyed by their
meaning. They convey perhaps no actual sense at all but an aura of
authority. One can watch the gap widen between their meaninglessness
and their effect. This makes nonsense into an effective form of language:

what is without meaning can impress fools. Sganarelle, delighted that none of the company knows Latin, reels off a meaningless string of words at which his audience gapes with admiration: "Ah, que n'ai-je étudié?—L'habile homme que voilà.—Oui, ça est si biau que je n'y entends goutte [Ah, why didn't I study?—There's a clever man.—Yes, that's so beautiful I don't understand a word of it]." Diafoirus finds Argan's pulse "duriuscule pour ne pas dire dur." He gets over a diagnosis directly opposed to that of a colleague by equating the two with a great show of authority: "Eh oui, rôti, bouilli, même chose." The curses of Purgon are in the same category; like much of Molière's irony, they are effective on the man who sees magic power in them; they are joyously ridiculous for the audience who see there is no meaning in them.

And there are, in the same play, superior cases of this irony. Authority is perhaps less dramatic when it replaces argument than when it confirms bad argument. Thanks to his authority, to his professional standing, to his use of the right academic jargon, and to his undoubted skill, Diafoirus is able to prove that black is white. In the very presence of his slow-witted son, described in stage directions as having "une mine tout-à-fait niaise," he undertakes to convince Argan that the boy is a desirable marriage partner. His speech is a masterpiece of specious argument. Studiously moderate, admitting that appearances are against him, and all the while insinuating points that each tell for something against the appearances, he almost succeeds in reversing the firmest judgments of sense impression. He admits what others might call a certain quietness, dullness, and slowness in the boy, whom none who know him would describe as given to devilry. "Il n'a jamais eu l'imagination bien vive, ni ce feu d'esprit qui se remarque dans quelques-uns"; even as a child he played no games, was always "doux, paisible et taciturne," and only learnt his letters at nine. But his father reflected that late fruit is rich fruit: "On grave sur le marbre bien plus malaisément que sur le sable [It is harder to carve on marble than it is on sand]," and thus he felt confident that "cette lenteur à comprendre, cette pesanteur d'imagination" was the sign of a ripening judgment, and indeed "à force de battre le fer il en est venu glorieusement à avoir ses licences." Is not this as good as Flaubert in its remorseless "pondération"? The technique is so faultless that one finds oneself gazing apprehensively at the stupid boy, and reflecting that perhaps his looks belie him; "there must be something" in what his father says. Joseph Prudhomme is pilloried here, along with the whole of modern "fumisterie," the gullibility of the public and the adventitious methods of the advertiser.

A companion piece in its deliberate use of language as a means of mystification is the tactic of Tartuffe, when in his tightest corner. He uses words which are true, but which he would not for the world have accepted by others as true; he uses them because, and only because, they will be disbelieved. The trick is one that only a hypocrite can play, but it is important to see why it adds to the esthetic enjoyment of the audience. When discovered by Damis in the act of making love to the wife of his host, Tartuffe admits his guilt, in general terms so sweeping that they appear, not as fact, which they are, but as the fruit of humility. Thus by describing himself (to the joy of the audience) the rogue convinces the fool of the opposite. His dangerous tactic succeeds completely.

> Oui, mon frère, je suis un méchant, un coupable,
> Un malheureux pécheur, tout plein d'iniquité,
> Le plus grand scélérat qui jamais ait été,
> Chaque instant de ma vie est chargé de souillures. . . .

[Yes, my brother, I am a wicked man, a guilty man, an unhappy sinner, full of iniquity, the worst scoundrel that ever was. Each moment of my life is burdened with the stain of sin. . . .]

These statements are true, but they are the reverse of sincere. They overturn the universal assumptions of language; they are uttered not to persuade but to hoodwink. From this kind of man the truth is heard only when he can be certain that it will be taken for the opposite. With relentless dramatic skill Molière forces his rogue into a situation where he can and must show forth this paradox. And he pushes that situation to the extreme of tension. The hypocrite, sure of his case, dances on the tightrope of his own astuteness. They must not be deceived, he says, by his appearance:

> Vous fiez-vous, mon frère, à mon extérieur?
> Et, pour tout ce qu'on voit, me croyez-vous meilleur?
> Non, non; vous vous laissez tromper à l'apparence,
> Et je ne suis rien moins, hélas, que ce qu'on pense.
> Tout le monde me prend pour un homme de bien;
> Mais la vérité pure est que je ne vaux rien.

[My brother, do you trust my appearance? And because of what I seem, do you think I am a better man? No, no, you are taken in by the way I look; I am, alas, nothing like what people think I am. They all take me for a good man; but the whole truth is I am worth nothing.]

Can the mastery of irony go farther than to convict a criminal out of his own mouth and by his own tactic and desire? Is not this a new discovery in dramatic ambiguity? Molière here attains, it seems to me, that razor-edge of language which (*pace* Mr. Empson) it is not quite right to call ambiguity. For this statement cannot be taken in one of two or more ways; it has different meanings to different people, and in particular one meaning for the dupe and another for the audience. But the clarity is perfect; neither of the receiving parties is likely to understand it the wrong way: Tartuffe is sure of Orgon, and Molière is sure of his public.

The principle at work here is dramatic irony. This is used with remarkable consistency throughout Molière's comedy and no definition of his art can fail to include it as an ingredient. The dramatist makes his puppets say what, on reflection, they would not say. All of us are funny when we say what we do not mean, or when our speech, intending to convey definite meaning, conveys something more, or conveys precisely that which we would hide. This does not happen nearly so often in life as in Molière's plays. He puts his characters systematically, so to speak, into corners, situations where their speech, intending to be intelligent, is in fact instinctive, where they say more than they mean, or where they are not conscious of what they are saying. Does not comedy largely consist of this use of language against the intention of the user but obeying the intention of the dramatist? "Je ne suis pas bon, je suis méchant quand je veux" is extracted from Argan, unwittingly, by a long process of contradiction. It is not what he would ever want to say. It is, however, a deeply true statement about him, and about all of us. Comic drama elicits the utterance of what in most of us is buried, suppressed, unutterable.

By such brilliant use of ironic language Molière was the liberator of his age. The practice of the society in which he moved covered the normal content of language with a social coating of convention. The phenomenon of politeness turns around this question of speech. In normal speech we should all maintain that we mean what we say, or at least that we say more or less what we mean. But social speech does almost the opposite. It conceals meaning and thus is a tyranny. Men have to say they are "delighted" when they are not; they have to praise those whom they do not admire; they have to conceal their real feeling. Molière's drama, by exposing this tyranny, relieves us of its strain and shows us countless situations in which conventions of speech break down. He situates his characters so that the veneer of politeness peels off like a crust, so that their animosity may have free play. We have seen how Jourdain's teachers quarrel, and just so do Vadius and Trissotin, Célimène and Arsinoé. Even Alceste's courtesy is not proof against the fatuousness of Oronte, who asks point-blank whether his sonnet is a bad one, and thus forces Alceste into the series of excuses that begin with "Je ne dis pas cela." In other words, direct speech must be disavowed; one must say that one has not said it, or meant it. "What do you mean?" becomes a key question. "What should I mean," answers Angélique, direct and nettled, "but what I say?" There is comedy, as Molière suggests in more than one place, in the very expression "Je veux dire," in the necessity of saying what you say. Neither Alceste nor anyone else can tell when a society lady is sincere: "De tout ce que j'ai dit, je me dédis ici [Everything I said, I take back now]." Alceste is comic in that in such a society he admits no criterion but nature:

> Ce n'est que jeu de mots, qu'affectation pure,
> Et ce n'est point ainsi que parle la nature.

[It is mere playing on words, pure affection. Nature does not speak so.]

For a seventeenth century gentleman this was an impossible position, and the fact that it is less so now means that the comedy loses something of its point.

Part of the comedy of Alceste lies in his use of the social language of his day. He adopts the clichés, but puts meaning into them. In this as in other respects he is individual, personal, refusing to conform to the social pattern. The gallants of his day spoke of "mon faible," "la chaîne qui m'attache" as almost meaningless clichés. For Alceste the same language will do, and it becomes, comically, meaningful. The intellectual, or doctrinaire, part of him actually does regard love as a weakness and fondness for the lady as a chain. In his mouth "l'attachement" is no longer a cliché, but a description.

How is it that speech is thus so much more meaningful in Molière than in life? Do we not here approach one of the secrets of his art, something that is not merely superficial grace but the sign of a dynamic quality? Molière has left no treatise on language. We must assume the subtlety of his imaginative penetration into speech by his artistic use of it in character. One odd reference, however, suggests that he was perfectly aware of the delicacies and even of the philosophy of language. In a completely serious and personal piece of writing, the preface to *Tartuffe,* we find him making the statement that "on doit discourir des choses et non pas des mots . . . la plupart des contrariétés viennent de ne pas entendre et d'envelopper dans un même mot des choses opposées . . . il ne faut qu'ôter le voile de l'équivoque [We should argue over things and not over words . . . most arguments come from not understanding and assimilating in the same word contrary things . . . all we have to do is to remove the veil of ambiguity]." This is not only a description of the accomplishment of his own dramatic irony; it is an admission that should be placed where I think it belongs, beside the arguments of Pascal in the fragment on *L'Esprit géométrique.* Both men discerned the fatal flaw in reasoning that originates in the fact that the same thing may be understood in different ways. Language as disguise: Molière could not remain blind to this while he unmasked so many social disguises. Does not "la dévotion" in his play mean different things to different people? What was a *libertin?* Cléante complains that "c'est être libertin que d'avoir de bons yeux [As soon as you have good eyesight, you are called a freethinker]." It is all a question of what you mean. What you intend to say and what you do say are often quite different. In speech as in act there may rise to the surface with or without our knowledge fragments of the subterranean world in every man. As another contemporary said: "Il s'en faut que nous connaissions toutes nos volontés [We are far from knowing all the impulses of our will]."

The Comedy of Will

by Ramon Fernandez

Through the mechanics of our reaction to comedy, the easiest way to reveal the comic element in a character is to make him unaware of what makes him ridiculous. Striken with mental blindness and deafness, his communication with other humans is totally disrupted. A comic character par excellence is solitary. His is an artificial and stylized solitude, but one which is only the exaggeration and solidification of a natural tendency. The double awareness that provokes laughter stems from the fact that the words and actions of the comic character have simultaneously one meaning for him and one meaning for the spectator—and both these meanings are incompatible.

What is the meaning attributed by a character to his actions? The comic character lives a life without measure, without suppleness, without shadings, wholly engrossed in himself and his petty level of existence. His isolation results, on the one hand, from his refusal to adapt to life and to accept the language of a common understanding, and, on the other, from his total concern—as though bewitched—with the satisfaction of his desires, to the exclusion of everything else. The mechanism of comedy is the unfolding of the plot in such a way as to make all the action of the character automatically work against himself. In this sense, a comic character is wholly willful. His will is exercised in complete disregard for the condition of life, and comic punishment reminds us that the man who considers himself the most independent and most self-willed is only the plaything of natural forces. In addition, the comic hero, around 1660, is naturally a caricature of the Cornelian hero. When Arnolphe, in *L'École des femmes,* recites the line from *Sertorius*[1]—which instantly conveys a derisory meaning—"Je suis maître, je parle, allez, obéissez," he considers himself lordly at a moment when he appears to the spectator as the slave of passion and circumstance.

[1] *Sertorius,* tragedy by Pierre Corneille. (*Trans. note*)

The degree to which a comic hero is aware of what makes him funny determines his level on the human ladder. The early Molière characters, the *précieuses,* the Sganarelles, like the later Bélise, Orgon, and Monsieur Jourdain, are wholly unaware. Their perception of themselves and of others never coincides with that of the spectator. Whoever pulls the strings easily manipulates them. Their comedy is candid and mechanical.

With Arnolphe, things change. In the plot Arnolphe is informed by Horace of all the unconscious betrayals of which he has been and will be the victim. He is not manipulated like the Sganarelle of *L'École des maris,* or as is Orgon by Tartuffe. Nonetheless, all of his desires work in his disfavor. He is the victim of forces infinitely greater than his will— the romance of the young lovers, and even his own passion that works on him like a charm. Orgon is hypnotized by Tartuffe, Arnolphe by himself. His situation is comical, but he cannot see it as such since as a result of it he suffers the tortures of hell. The comic type of an Arnolphe —subtler and more intense than a Sganarelle type—heightens the quality of the comedy.

The comedy of Alceste is even more refined. Aware of the situation that makes him comical, his famous lines: "Moi, je veux me fâcher et ne veux point entendre," and "Par la sambleu, Messieurs, je ne croyais pas être si plaisant que je suis," are extremely meaningful. Not only is he unwilling to remain ignorant of the situation inflicted on him, he denounces its ridiculousness, he wars against the society and the so-called justification that unjustly render him comical. Alceste, in fact, would alter the literary genre of the play in which he is the hero. Like Arnolphe, he has to admit to the failure of his will, but more subtly and more profoundly than Arnolphe, since he reveals, at the end, that in him as in everybody else, "il est toujours de l'homme," that reason "is not what governs love," that his heroic heart is a captive heart. Arnolphe is aware of the mechanism that governs him but has not deduced the governing law. Alceste is aware of this law—which is none other than the law of comedy—and in his revolt against it (a revolt which his constitution and his times prevent from becoming revolutionary) he has no alternative but self-imposed solitude.

And so the awareness of the superior comic type is no more favorable to personal will than the unawareness of the inferior type. Alceste no more escapes the law of comedy than does Monsieur Jourdain. The world of reason once penetrated by comic reason is no longer a Cartesian world. In order to understand the spirit of comedy, one must distinguish between pragmatic reason and ideal reason. Pragmatic reason is concerned with knowing the world as it is, with all its densities and incoherences. Ideal reason seeks to achieve a harmony between the world and all its norms, among which unity is on the highest level. The need to unify the world, and in consequence, to find its innermost movement, is the very essence of ideal reason. The theme of the comic spirit is precisely the impossibility of this unification. The comic vision of the world amounts to saying: "The world is false and absurd and is therefore incompatible with reason. We no sooner become conscious of the world than our consciousness disintegrates and collapses. But this world does not cease being penetrated by reason and dominated by it in some way, however makeshift. Reason will continue to indict irrationality by portraying it with the features of error and incoherence." The comic vision of the world is the revenge of the mind. One thus understands how Molière, the interpreter of comic reason, marks the transition between Corneille and Racine, between a world hospitable to ideal reason and one in which passion completely eludes reasonable will.

Is Molière, therefore, totally pessimistic? One would think the opposite to read his commentators. Molière, they tell us, denounced those errors and faults—social and individual—which are redeemable, and which were furthermore redeemed with the help of his genius. If one were to make an experiment and read Molière with the idea of raising nature to the sphere of reason, this might easily be achieved on the level of *précieuses,* parvenus, libidinous misers, hack writers, and charlatan doctors. On the level of Arnolphe, it becomes more difficult; even more so when we arrive at Tartuffe; and improbable when we reach Dom Juan and Alceste, in fact utterly hopeless, since will, by turning against itself, becomes comic in turn. In effect, the reason that triumphs in Molière's comedy is pragmatic reason. "There," he tells us, "that is how nature operates. It is you who must adapt to nature, not nature to you. Otherwise, you are ridiculous." Molieresque reason, in essence, is the lucid acceptance, whenever possible, of things as they are, which necessarily implies a weak character. As soon as a man's character takes on stature and becomes complex, he finds on the upper rungs of the comic ladder the disharmony which, on the lower rungs, makes us laugh at Monsieur Jourdain. Molière wrote a ballet whose title demonstrates his vision of life—*Le Ballet des Incompatibles.*

On the subject of nature, which we are ordered to accept on pain of falling into ridicule, let us beware of one frequent mistake (furthered by the success of Bergson's highly penetrating work),[2] that of seeing in comedy a stiffening of life, and opposing the mechanical to the living as that which is ridiculous and that which is not.

I must say that this judgment strikes me as fairly confusing. In what way is the love shared by Agnès and Horace less "mechanical" than Arnolphe's? Is it because Arnolphe is twenty years older than Horace? What, after all, is this "life," whose blind laws are to be accepted, if not a machine hostile to anyone who would modify its workings? Arnolphe's efforts are futile, precisely because they are undertaken against an automat, because he wants Agnès not to be Agnès, like Don Quixote who

[2] Bergson, Henri, *Le Rire.* (*Trans. note*)

wants the windmills not to be windmills. Poorly adjusted, agreed, but poorly adjusted to a determinism whose course is prearranged. In what way is Alceste more "mechanical" than Célimène and the society that jeers at him? Is it not instead society, through its inertia and automatism, that bestows on him this rigidity? The inability to adapt to life, I grant, produces "mechanical" effects, but life on its own produces equally mechanical ones. The fresh, distraught prisoner does not notice his chains; they tighten and make him fall. The older prisoners who laugh at this, because they carry their chains more adroitly, draw no illusions about "life" and "liberty" from this. Noble or ignoble, the comic hero is a man who vainly struggles against the determinism, the automatism of nature. What is comic in him emerges at the precise moment when nature, imposing on him her forms and laws, reveals the inherent automatism of his so-called will. On one side there is the world of freedom and childhood where everyone dwells in his dreams; on the other side is the world of willing servitude, the prison made livable through practice and habit. Laughter is the crossing of the equator that takes us from one world to the other.

World of Imagination

by René Bray

With Molière as with every great dramatist (but more with him, since as an actor he had spent his life on the stage), imagination prevailed over observation. Molière's imagination has no less potency than Shakespeare's; it has the power to merge reality with artifice and truth with convention. Imagination does not proceed by means of clever combinations of these, nor does it seek to balance the one with the other in order to satisfy two contradictory tastes; rather, it effects a transmutation in which neither gold nor lead keep their metallic identities. It is poetic, which is to say, creative. One might quote for our poet's benefit what François Mauriac recently said about the great novelists: "There exists a planet Balzac, a planet Dostoievski, inhabited by monsters with the heads of both men and women, at least as alive and perhaps more so, and in any case less ephemeral than the inhabitants of the planet earth, but who are not like them, or only superficially resemble them."

A Molière character, whether Scapin or Alceste, whether inspired originally by a *mask* of pure convention or by a flesh-and-blood model encountered in a salon, no longer retains any link with his origins. From the moment of conception he is enclosed in an imaginary frame, he is made of canvas and painted in *trompe l'oeil* with color and light; he dresses according to a code which is not the world's; he makes up with cosmetics suitable only to the glare of the stage; he walks and gesticulates according to the demands of comedy and not of the action in which he is supposed to take part; his language is dictated by the law of the theater, which is not that of real life but of illusion, upon which actor and spectator are agreed. Comedy is directly established in artifice. Not that it may slide into incoherence and lack of logic—the theater has its own logic which is as different from the logic of life as is non-Euclidean mathematics from Euclidean. The comic imagination is not absolutely free. Rather, it obeys rules which are strict but proper to it, and which free it from those of reality.

Criticism is too often still obsessed with the classic notion of verisimilitude. The theoreticians of classicism founded almost their whole doctrine on this alleged rule and gave it a narrow significance. Applying it tyrannically to the theater, they praised plays in which they thought they found a picture of reality and condemned those which made sacrifices to fantasy. D'Aubignac[1] prescribed that the dramatic action should take place during the same time and in the same space as the action it represented, and according to him, reason could not credit a representation which did violence to the habits of daily life.

He was not wrong in supposing that the spectator must have faith in the reality of the spectacle: if he doesn't believe in it he won't enjoy it or participate. But this belief does not mean submission to the same strictures d'Aubignac imposes on him. From the moment he passes through the doors of the theater, he enters the kingdom of illusion. The child listening to the fairy tale of Tom Thumb knows very well that he will never meet an ogre himself, but that certainty does not in the least prevent him from believing in the story. The spectator hearing the voices of the witches generating the doom of Macbeth does not refuse credence to the tale Shakespeare unfolds upon the stage. His imagination follows the poet's, without being disturbed by any judgments his reason may bring up about the reality of unreality of what he sees and hears. Verisimilitude is thus nothing but a meeting between the poet's power of suggestion and the spectator's power of belief. The first has no limits other than those of genius, of which it is the attribute; the second depends on multiple factors of a social as well as a personal kind, depending on the period, the environment from which the audience is drawn, the shape of their culture, their theatrical experience, and depending also on what might be called the spirit of the "house," which varies from evening to evening, even for the same show and the same audience. At all events, in this matter the dictates of reason have only a small influence.

The seventeenth century critics would have done better, in assessing the value of a play, not to use the idea of *verisimilitude,* but rather the notion of *propriety.* If they had, they would have provided for the creative power of the imagination. A play is a creation of the imagination, dominated in its structure by an inner propriety—that is, by a coherence established among the elements of the action; and in its effect by an external propriety—that is, by the desired agreement between show and audience. If this agreement is reached (which happens without recourse to rational confirmation based on comparison with any reality going on outside the theater), the play moves with one leap into that harmony which is created by obedience to the laws of the enchanted world of the stage. The place where *Le Misanthrope* unfolds is not a salon in the

---

[1] L'Abbé d'Aubignac (1604-1676): critic and theoretician, author of *La Pratique du Théâtre.* (*Ed. note*)

Marais, but that illusory room the poet sees in his imagination as clearly
as the one he actually saw yesterday, and which he tries to bring to life
with the help of the means at his disposal at the Palais-Royal. Alceste and
Célimène have no reality other than that given them by this force of
illusion which dwelt in Molière, and which he made the audience share.
Pourceaugnac, Scapin, Jourdain, Argan, Harpagon have no more nor
less. Wise or foolish, all the characters thus created live the same imaginary life. They are all animated by that power of expansion proper to
dramatic genius, which gives birth to a reality truer than the real.

The young Poquelin left the tapestry-worker's shop at twenty because
his imagination too vividly conjured up the marvels of the stage. All his
life this seduction was in operation; and all his life Molière remained
under the spell of the enchantment which had fallen on him. He was
a fanciful man, but this never prevented him from managing his or his
troupe's affairs. Orgon is sensible about everything that is not concerned
with Tartuffe; Argan manages his household very well and is unreason-
able only when his health is involved; if Jourdain is rich, it is because
he has not lacked good business sense, and his folly arises only from his
vanity. "It is not incompatible," says the poet, "for a person to be ridiculous in some things and a gentleman in others." Molière was like his
heroes: a gentleman in town but possessed by the demon of the theater
as soon as he arrived at the Palais-Royal.

Or rather, his heroes were made in his image. Jouvet said: "Behind
Molière, who is the first of them all, all his heroes are prey to their
imagination, men at the mercy of themselves, irrational men who are
reasonable in unreason." Sganarelle and Argan are both victims of their
imagination—one about illness, the other about cuckoldry. In support
of Jouvet, W. G. Moore remarks that Tartuffe, Arnolphe, and Dom Juan
all strive equally to be taken for what they are not: Tartuffe wears a mask
of religion to hide his sensuality; Arnolphe is a timid man who pretends
to be a tyrant: Dom Juan has a generous heart in spite of his profession
of faith in calculation; Jourdain has certainly forgotten his tradesman's
past and does not doubt his gentleman's rank; Mascarille and Jodelet
have enough imagination to persuade themselves of the reality of their
"bravery"; the doctors dissimulate their ignorance and greed beneath the
pride of pedantry. They have all constructed masks for themselves in
order to live as they please if only for a day or a moment. Whether they
wear them consciously or unconsciously, they are all living in their
imagination.

Some go further in these subtle games. Tartuffe is a perfect actor: how
artfully he tosses off his order to his valet as soon as he notices that he
is observed:

> Laurent, serrez ma haire avec ma discipline.

[Laurent, put my hair-shirt away along with my scourge.]

Célimène joins with intense pleasure in the game the marquises propose to her and sustains with mastery her character as slanderer; a little later, when Alceste wishes to confound her with the letter Arsinoé has shown him, she shifts with hauteur into a new part—the role of outraged virtue. Dom Juan before Elvire is just as good an actor as is Angélique before Dandin. Argan, for the benefit of his wife and daughter, does a dying act. Frosine feigns admiration for the fine bearing and health of the wretched, coughing Harpagon. Is there a better stage-director than the first Mascarille, the one in *L'Étourdi*, except for the ingenious Scapin? The galley scene is a little comedy within the comedy, and so is the one where Sosie acts the heroes with such virtuosity, to prepare for telling Alcmène about Amphitryon's victory. "To act within the action, to play a character who in turn plays another," said Vedel, "This is what satisfies the theater-demon in Molière."

To gain access to a girl he desires, the lover will take on the most diverse disguises: he becomes a doctor, a singing-master, a painter, a son of the Grand Turk, or an Armenian merchant. Jupiter himself takes the shape of a Theban general. Does Elmire hesitate much in the face of the deception she must stoop to in order to trap the hypocrite? Although Sganarelle obstinately refuses to allow himself to don the doctor's gown and claims that he will remain a wood-cutter, the blows of the stick have an admirable effect upon his nature—he comes to the point of curing the sick with as much impudence as Purgon.

What a swarm of fantasists, in this theater which is called realistic! Alceste himself would be a victim of the confusion which destroys the boundaries between the real and the unreal. He is scandalized, said W. G. Moore, at how the world fails to run as it should, and in his doctrinaire idealism he confuses truth and reality. We are on the stage, and anything is possible there. Illusion dwells in the hearts of creatures lit by the footlights. They are at the mercy of demons which no reality allows them to annihilate or quell. For reality does not cross the footlights, it does not even enter the doors of the theater: it remains in the street waiting for the audience to come out. These beings whose presence is thrust upon us are not real at all; they have the essential truth conceived by creative genius, which is still more imaginative than its characters and draws them all into the saraband of illusion.

How can we still give credit to this myth we have often evoked, and from which criticism obstinately refuses to free itself—the theory of a rational Molière?

La parfaite raison fuit toute extremité.

[Perfect reason flees everything extreme.]

This line has given rise to infinite deductions about the poet's moral nature, ideas, and philosophy. Alceste exaggerates his need of frankness, Orgon carries his religion to the point of bigotry, Chrysale is altogether too much attached to the material, Philaminte to the spiritual. It is deduced from this that Molière disapproves of them: since these characters he uses to make us laugh are irrational, he must be rational himself.

As we have said, this is a moralistic viewpoint, and to speak thus is to trample on everything which is essential to a show, particularly a comedy. The function of a comedy is to make people laugh, and what would they laugh at if not ridiculous characters? And where are they found but among people who wander off course, people whose behavior expresses folly? And when, as with Molière, all one's energy is devoted to laughter, should not the ridiculous be carried to extremes? It is not then by reason of personal choice that the poet makes Alceste a madman and Orgon blind, submerges Chrysale in materialism and refines Philaminte's sentiments into contempt for all contingency: Comedy demands it.

Arnolphe, Jourdain, Argan, Harpagon, as well as Sganarelle, Mascarille, Dandin, Don Pèdre, Pourceaugnac, and the Gérontes, Orontes, Gorgibuses, all the ones we laugh at so freely, are filled with unreason, and all are fond of *extremes*. If Molière comedy gives certain people the impression of being a comedy of reason, it is simply because laughter affords a kind of retrenchment. The laughing spectator detaches himself from responsibility for what he laughs at: he implicitly refuses to be Harpagon or Jourdain. He establishes himself at a distance from Chrysale as well as from Philaminte, in a rational central position equidistant from both extremes, equidistant from both kinds of folly. But this impression which some acquire through the effect of thought, a thing the true spectator rejects, leads to an erroneous conclusion if it brings with it the notion of any desire in the author to moralize.

To go back to Jouvet: "Molière, who has been labeled a man of reason, is the man who best felt and understood what irrationality was, and his theater, which seemed the triumph of reason in the eyes of his commentators, is in fact the realm of that wonderful unreason called poetry." The man who conceived the characters of Jourdain and Argan could not have done it without entering into their derangement. He was the imaginary invalid and the bourgeois lost in a dream of noble rank; he experienced the obsessions of Orgon; he felt with Harpagon the loss of his wits. The power of his imagination gave him kinship with the vagaries he put on the stage. To create them, he had to sympathize with the irrational beings who populated his theater. He was a poet: his creation is the proof.

The seventeenth century set *fantasy* and *verisimilitude* in opposition. The theoreticians considered perfection in art to be the conciliation of these two exigencies. Ordinarily they only applied the notion of fantasy to the noble genres of epic and tragedy. But fantasy is not in the least absent from Molière's comedy: it is the soul of the machinery in *Psyché* and *Amphitryon*; it rumbles at the denouement of *Dom Juan*; it provides the chief charm of the court comedies; it glides through the ballets. Would there not be something even more generally "fantastic" in all the scenes which unleash an irrepressible laugh? The fantastic is "everything contrary to the ordinary course of nature," said P. Rapin.[2] Nothing could be more contrary to nature than Molière's comic world, and nothing more riddled with fabrication. "Dramatic poetry must have marvels to be perfect," wrote Chapelain,[3] and this may be applied to comedy as well as tragedy. The universe of marvels where Alceste, Jourdain, and Sganarelle all dwell is not ruled by the laws of reason. It is an enchanted kingdom under the sway of the irrational and the fanciful.

[2] Père René Rapin (1621-1687), Jesuit, poet, and author of *Réflexions sur la "Poétique" d'Aristote*. *(Ed. note)*

[3] Chapelain, Jean (1595-1674), epic poet and theoretician. *(Ed. note)*

The Anti-Bourgeois

by Paul Bénichou

One of the most common tendencies of Molière criticism, as soon as it attempts to *situate* Molière's works in some precise way, is to find in them the commonly held ideas of the bourgeoisie. How many times, particularly in the last sixty years, has this been stated in order to define his characters or his philosophy! Common sense and bourgeoisie are two notions so hopelessly confused in the minds of most people that anything in Molière that is found to mock excess passes these days for bourgeois. A partial examination of his works, limited to a few plays (whose interpretation is furthermore open to question), particularly *Les Précieuses ridicules* and *Les Femmes savantes,* confirms this viewpoint. The practice, in force since Brunetière, of separating the first half of the seventeenth century—imaginative and idealistic—from the era inaugurated by Molière, Racine, Boileau—an era of naturalism and positivistic ideas—only reinforced the idea of a middle-class Molière, interpreter of the non-aristocratic, well-adjusted, and down-to-earth aspects of the reign of Louis XIV. Although it was not Brunetière's intention to make of Molière a simple bourgeois, but rather a moral revolutionary, the intermediary between Rabelais and Diderot, he contributed greatly to the bourgeois image of Molière by contrasting Molière's work with the general current of aristocratic idealism. Faguet went so far as to represent the author of *Dom Juan* as the Sancho Panza of France.[1] This conception is sufficiently widespread today, and has sufficiently eclipsed the evidently erroneous idea of a pathetic and suffering Molière in the romantic style, to warrant first place in any discussion of Molière. . . .

One need only glance at the plays of Molière to see that the bourgeois appearing in them is almost always mediocre and ridiculous. There is not a single bourgeois in Molière who provides, insofar as he is a bourgeois, some manner of elevation or moral values. The very idea of

[1] Faguet, *En lisant Molière,* 1914, p. 98.

a strictly bourgeois virtue would be sought in vain in any of his comedies. The sense of measure or *juste-milieu* is characterized in Molière by the gentleman, the man of society, noble or commoner, who is formed in the ideal of aristocratic civility—not the bourgeois as such. Even in those works that are seemingly most hostile to aristocratic thought and behavior—as in *Les Précieuses* and *Les Femmes savantes*—the type of the good bourgeois gets his share of caricature. Gorgibus is as poor a paragon as the *précieuses*. The candor of the one contrasted with the pretentiousness of the others makes us laugh and may even encourage a momentary solidarity. But when Molière wanted to develop the subject in *Les Femmes savantes,* he indicated two forms of good sense by incarnating one in Chrysale, in whom it is prosaic and derisory, and one in Clitandre, in whom it is synonymous with good breeding. Good sense, whenever it is worthy of polite society, has lost all association with the bourgeoisie. As to the *précieuses* or the *femmes savantes,* their comedy stems in large part from the disproportion between their station and their aspirations. Gorgibus and Chrysale, defining their true background which is wholly ordinary, make them look above all like middle-class women aping great ladies. This was a comic element even more perceptible at that time than today. Not that Molière didn't ridicule in the *précieuses* certain characteristics borrowed from an unquestionably aristocratic philosophy, and particularly, a literary spirituality. But he makes these ideas bourgeois in order to render them comical. He saturates them with middle-class mediocrity, presents them as antiquated and badly imitated by an inferior world, and thus appears himself to be the champion, not of middle-class good sense, but of aristocratic good taste. The solidarity established by Molière in *Les Femmes savantes* between *préciosité* and pedantry is no less worthy of comment. The pedant was one of the types most incompatible with the manners of high society, and all of the commentaries of the period indicate that a horror of pedantry was one of the characteristics of the *précieuse* who, according to the Abbé de Pure, "is in perpetual combat against the Pedant and the Provincial." [2] This is also true of the *précieuse* in Boileau's *Satire X* who, far from allowing herself to be embraced "for the love of Greek," "scorns the frivolous lovers of Greek and Latin."

Molière has thus multiplied the characteristics which distinguish his *précieuses* from those of society. Not that he unreservedly admired the latter, but his way of ridiculing their imitators in no way reveals any pro-bourgeois prejudice. The true spirit of *Les Femmes savantes* must be found in the vehement apology of court taste made to the pedants by Clitandre, the son of a gentleman and the "honnête homme" of the play.[3] This very Clitandre, who "allows that a woman be enlightened in

[2] Abbé de Pure, *La Précieuse,* Part 1, Book 1, p. 193.
[3] *Les Femmes savantes,* IV, 3.

all things" but does not wish her to become obsessed with knowledge or display what she knows, has exactly the same opinions as Mlle. de Scudéry.[4] The *femmes savantes* of Molière are thus inferior to what they read, just as the literary milieu itself, too accustomed to its habit of glibness, was inferior to genuine wit.[5] The anonymous *Portrait de la Précieuse* found in Mlle. de Montpensier's *Recueil*[6] shows that the *précieuses* rarely went to court "because they are not welcome." However vague this information, it proves at least that *préciosité* could be repudiated from a non-bourgeois point of view.

The two plays on which Molière's bourgeois good sense is so often founded are in inspiration very similar to *Le Bourgeois gentilhomme*. Lower class pretensions, its laborious effort to ape the upper class, are smitten with mockery in these plays. If Molière seems at times to approve of bourgeois good sense, it is in a very particular way, one not at all flattering to the bourgeoisie. In fact, the judgments of a Chrysale or a Gorgibus are valid only in their function of preaching to middle-class ladies the virtues of modesty and fidelity to a lower station. This is bourgeois good sense, if you like, but only insofar as it acknowledges the inferiority of the bourgeois.[7] In Molière, the bourgeois appears attractive only in this form, as witnessed particularly by *Le Bourgeois gentilhomme*, which has no meaning other than this, and in which the caricature of the merchant who pretends to be a man of quality is not compensated but is rather heightened by the wisdom of his wife—a kind of feminine counterpart to Chrysale. The misfortunes of George Dandin suggest the same lesson as do the follies of the bourgeois gentleman. True, the aristocracy is not always represented flatteringly—neither the Sotenvilles

[4] This similarity, already noted by Victor Cousin, who quotes several passages from the tenth part of *Cyrus,* becomes striking if one compares Clitandre's remarks (I, 3) with the portrait of Alcionide in the third part, third book, pp. 1111-1112, of the same novel: "She speaks with equal ease on all subjects, but remains so admirably within the proper limits prescribed by tradition and good manners for ladies that they not seem too knowledgeable, that one might say upon hearing her speak of the loftiest things that it is only through simple common sense that she has any understanding of them."

[5] See what Boileau has his interlocutor say in *Satire X:*

> De livres et d'écrits bourgeois admirateur,
> Vais-je épouser ici quelque apprentie auteur?

[Like a bourgeois admirer of books and writings, am I now going to marry some apprentice-author?]

This is *bon ton* looking down on *bel esprit*.

[6] Published in 1659.

[7] Note the ease with which Chrysale fraternizes with a peasant girl as coarse as Martine. Chrysale represents a bourgeoisie without ambition that still feels itself close to the common people.

nor Dorante in *Le Bourgeois gentilhomme* are appealing models. But this is not the point. What does matter is that the social inferiority of the bourgeois be represented forcefully, and that at no time does Molière dream of arousing us against those who take advantage of the differences between the social ranks. This indifference borders on the scandalous in *George Dandin*. The matrimonial difficulties of a commoner married to a noblewoman and overshadowed by a young courtier are represented as a natural and highly entertaining event. One may find this deplorable and immoral, but Molière was clearly not concerned with this aspect of the problem.

One must not forget that in the seventeenth century the middle class enjoyed very little prestige in society. In the following century the balance was redressed, but the bourgeois under Louis XIV is above all—in the view of most—the draper, the notary, the shopkeeper, and he is considered with mere disdain by polite society. It is inconceivable that Molière, who so often addressed the audience of Versailles, thought to preach to it the philosophy of the Place Maubert. Middle-class thinking and tone were deemed disastrous for an author. Others than Molière have been accused of this, Boileau for example, and with good reason. For it was really he who introduced into literature—by making them sound impressive—the spirit and moral maxims of the middle class. And for twenty years he was subjected to the sarcasms and humiliating reminders of the *beaux esprits* of society.[8] No such thing in the case of the numerous critics who assailed Molière. He made them laugh so hard at the expense of the bourgeois that they could not throw up to him his bourgeois origin or accuse him of resembling the bourgeois. Furthermore, though we know little about his way of life, his tastes or his interests, it is quite certain that by electing in his youth to join the theater, when he could have looked forward to a comfortable bourgeois inheritance, he indicated the little esteem in which he held the background which is mistakenly used to explain his plays.

The caricature of the bourgeois was traditional in comic literature. The bourgeois provided comedy with a clearly defined type endowed with characteristic faults and foibles: avarice, cowardliness, jealousy, the oft-foiled inclination toward domestic tyranny, grotesque complacency,

---

[8] One should compare *Satire V, Sur la noblesse,* and the sarcastic violence that occasionally explodes in it, with the conformism of *Le Bourgeois gentilhomme.* Not a single one of his enemies neglected to reproach Boileau with his origins, his inspiration, his bourgeois style. See Coras, *Le Satirique berné,* 1668 (particularly the epigram on *Satire V*); Carel de Sainte-Garde, *Défense des beaux-esprits de ce temps contre un satirique,* 1675 (articles III and XVIII); Desmarets, *Remarques sur les oeuvres satiriques du sieur D . . . ,* 1675 (in particular, the remarks concerning the *Discours au Roi* and the first *Epître*); Pradon, *Le Triomphe de Pradon,* 1684 (an examination of *Satire III*); *Nouvelles remarques sur les ouvrages du sieur D . . . ,* 1695 (remarks on *Satires VI* and *IX,* and *Epître VI*); *Réponse à la Satire X du sieur D . . .* (preface and *passim*).

egotism, and naïveté. This type, distinct both from that of the gentleman
—or more broadly, from the man of society—and from that of the valet,
was frequently used by Molière and occupies an important, perhaps even
first, place in Molière's theater. The Sganarelle in *Le Cocu imaginaire*,
the one in *L'École des maris*, Arnolphe, Sganarelle again in *Le Mariage
forcé*, a last Sganarelle in *L'Amour médecin*, finally Harpagon, constitute
a lineage along which one finds—to the great embarrassment of the
bourgeoisie—the same family resemblance, alternately burlesque and
repulsive, stemming from a basic mixture of possessiveness and pusillanimity. These are indeed the two primary traits of the character, differing to a greater or lesser degree but present in all the variations of
the type that finds itself congenitally afflicted with the failings that the
consummate aristocratic cynicism still considers beneath its class—avidity
and cowardice. These two faults unquestionably constitute, in the general opinion of the time, the theoretical dividing line between the two
social classes.

If it is in love that Molière's bourgeois most commonly manifests his
inferiority it is not only because the domain of love and pleasure is the
one in which Molière's values most readily come into conflict; it is that
the bourgeois character was by tradition incompatible with gallantry.
Bourgeois manners and elegant love hardly went together. To return
to the significant example of Boileau, the reproach leveled against his
origins and his bourgeois mind, and the condemnation of his inaptitude
for love poetry,[9] are one and the same. The usual characteristics of the
merchant mentality were considered fatal to love, to which courtly
tradition—even when reduced to simple gallantry—attributed a nobility
and excellence unattainable to middling souls. This is not to say that the
bourgeois is unsusceptible to love. On the contrary, Molière liked to
present his Sganarelles and Arnolphes in love, even providing them with
passionate insistence in their ardor and painful vulnerability in defeat.
But they don't know how to love; they put the same jealousy and the
same instinct of possessiveness into love that they put into all things.
They speak to their beloveds like Harpagon to his cash box, as proprie-
tors: "You will no longer have the right to refuse me anything, and I
shall be able to do what I wish with you without shocking anyone. You
will be mine from head to foot, and I shall be master of it all." [10] This
ingenuous egotism, far from the procedures of noble and expert gal-

---

[9] See Coras, *Le Satirique berné*, parody of *Epître IX*; Bonnecorse, *Lutrigot*, 1686,
chant II and note; Perrault, in his *Apologie des femmes*, 1694, written in response to
Boileau's *Satire X*, draws a portrait of the "werewolf," enemy of the fair sex and
friend of the rubbish of antiquity, which, while applying to Boileau, reproduces, in
certain of their aspects, Molière's old fools; and finally, Pradon, in the beginning of
his *Réponse à la Satire X du sieur D . . .* , 1694.

[10] Sganarelle in *Le Mariage forcé*, scene 2.

lantry, is ridiculous in proportion to the self-satisfaction that accompanies it:

> Hai! hai! mon petit nez, pauvre petit bouchon,
> Tu ne languiras pas longtemps, je t'en répond:
> Va, chut! Vous le voyez, je ne lui fais pas dire:
> Ce n'est qu'après moi seul que son âme respire.[11]

[Hee! hee! my little nose, poor little mouth, you won't yearn for long, I promise you: come, come, shh! As you see, I don't make her say it: her soul longs for me, and for me alone.]

The proprietary mind has illusions and blind spots that are no less obdurate, or less laughable, than its anxieties, from which arises the frequent comic theme of the jealous lover betrayed. Sganarelle, in *L'École des maris,* at the moment he pronounces the lines quoted above, is in the process of facilitating a meeting—unbeknownst to him—between his lady love and his rival.

Even under the guise of egotism and complacency, pusillanimity is readily discernible. It is not merely this aspect of cowardice that paralyzes the hero of *Le Cocu* before his rival. The terror of a duel over his loved one is accompanied by no less weakness before the lady herself. There is at the heart of all these characters a burning sense of ill-disguised inferiority beneath the apparent euphoria. And so, in *L'École des maris,* Sganarelle's defeat reveals a basic fear of women, barely distinguishable from his inability to love:

> Malheureux qui se fie à femme après cela!
> La meilleure est toujours en malice féconde;
> C'est un sexe engendré pour damner tout le monde.
> J'y renonce à jamais, à ce sexe trompeur,
> Et je le donne tout au diable de bon coeur.[12]

[Unhappy man, who trusts women after that! The best of them are always ripe with malice; it's a sex created to damn everyone. I renounce forever that deceitful sex, and truly, may the devil take them all.]

Deep within themselves, these characters do not feel made for love or for success, and that is why they seek their security in a tyrannical conception of marital life; or conversely, their limitless egotism, which denies them any true communication with the object of their love and constantly

[11] Sganarelle in *L'École des maris,* II, 9.
[12] *Ibid.,* III, 9.

robs them of the security they seek, makes them nervous and anxious about failing.

Arnolphe, in *L'École des femmes,* is without doubt the most accomplished figure created by Molière of the bourgeois in love. An entire play is devoted to him, and not just any ordinary play at that. One would have to quote everything he says to show his alternate roles of pompous bogeyman, lecherous old goat, and above all, niggardly proprietor:

> Je me vois riche assez pour pouvoir, que je croi,
> Choisir une moitié qui tienne tout de moi,
> Et de qui la soumise et pleine dépendance
> N'ait à me reprocher aucun bien ni naissance.[13]

[I see myself as rich enough to be able, I think, to choose a better half who owes everything to me, and whose submissive and total dependency can never reproach me for my wealth or my birth.]

The perfected descendant of numerous characters previously sketched by Molière, Arnolphe combines in equal proportion assurance and anxiety, which are the two basic traits—contradictory in appearance only —of this human type. Humiliation in his case, instead of cropping up from the beginning, as in *Le Cocu,* or not emerging until the end, as in *L'École des maris,* is slowly elaborated as the character is progressively revealed, and ends by appearing under its true colors of inferiority and defeat. The very obsession with cuckoldom betrays a profound fear of women which Arnolphe naïvely expresses in the first scene. When disgrace has progressively stripped him of his fake air of despotic superiority, all that remains is impotent rage and empty supplications. Molière, in the last two acts, exhaustively and brutally explored all the convolutions of his despair.

---

[13] *L'École des femmes,* I, 1. It is quite evident that the spirit of domination can arise—in the relation between the sexes, as elsewhere—from the fear of being dominated. The brilliant characters of aristocratic literature know nothing of hounding jealousy, which is reserved for lovers ill-suited to inspiring love. On the other hand, since true love can only be conceived of as exclusive, a certain embarrassment results in love literature, which in any event clearly sets down the rules of noble jealousy: this jealousy, stemming from an excess of love, can be vulnerable and painful, but never aggressive. The essential thing is not to treat the "object" as a possession, but as a person, and as a person cherished. Subtle discussions of jealousy abound in fictional and erotic literature. That which is termed *préciosité,* and which is frequently no more than the gallantry common to the whole period, rejects as odious the possessive type of jealousy. Molière himself, who had already evoked this traditional debate in a scene of *Les Fâcheux* (II, 4), gave jealousy two different shadings in the two successive portraits (the second of which, however, is drawn from the first and copies it in long passages of dialogue) of Don Garcie, unjustly but respectably jealous, and of Alceste, violent to the point of being despotic in his jealousy. The first wins out; the second loses. On this subject, see Baumal's book, *Molière auteur précieux.*

All the portraits of bourgeois lovers that people Molière's theater only transpose to the order of gallantry those traits commonly attributed to the bourgeois as a social being. Harpagon, insofar as he incarnates bourgeois behavior in its economic aspect, is the almost chemically pure type who engenders and explains this family of characters. The hunger to possess finds its veritable object—money, and its consummate form—frenzy. One of Harpagon's most powerful speeches which best reveals this temperament, in which instinct feeds on the object, wants it to be tangible, and yearns to *hold* it, is the one concerning the supposed dowry attributed to Marianne by Frosine:

> C'est une raillerie que de vouloir me constituer sa dot de toutes les dépenses qu'elle ne fera point. Je n'irai pas donner quittance de ce que je ne reçois pas, et il faut bien que je touche quelque chose.[14]

> [You must be joking, wanting me to accept as a dowry all the money she won't spend. I will not give a receipt for what I don't receive, and I have really got to collect something.]

This desire to hold is the foundation and also the illusion of all avarice. There is certainty and real pleasure only in relations of reciprocity and exchange with the living world. In the end, Harpagon enjoys none of the things he *holds on to*. Arnolphe too wanted so much to hold on to Agnès that he prevented her from thinking about love. The misery of such a state destroys reason itself. Everywhere, Arnolphe sees cuckolds and diabolical women; Harpagon imagines himself surrounded by enemies. Molière pushed this trait in Harpagon to the extreme of madness. Wherever he looks, he says himself, he seems to see a potential thief. Harpagon thus combines the extreme stylization of caricature with the most direct psychological truths. Molière, through Harpagon, gave the abstract formula of a real mentality which can be called bourgeois, designating by this term—in accord with the whole of the seventeenth century —a form of morally inferior existence incapable of achieving a noble human character.

Molière's theater, thus viewed from the outside, with the readily discernible apportionment of its values, the manner in which he immediately distributes, for the mind and the eye, the attractive and the dismal, the brilliant and the mediocre, far from defending the bourgeois, places all prestige in the norms of sentiment and behavior of noble society. Molière did not do this systematically. He merely represented the bourgeois and the gentleman as commonly conceived, dominated as always by the traditional views of the highest social class. It is precisely in this that his works are significant—they attest to a particular set of commonplace ideas.

[14] *L'Avare*, II, 5.

Furthermore, these commonplace ideas did not completely exclude criticism of the aristocratic character. The manners of society also condemned certain ridiculous noblemen who were freely portrayed by Molière among the country squires and provincial ladies. The Sotenvilles, Pourceaugnac, and Mme. d'Escarbagnas caused laughter among the audiences of Paris and Versailles, where satire, even of ridiculous courtiers, was not considered an offense. Molière's enemies tried relentlessly to prick the sensitivity of courtiers by pointing out his portraits of the marquises. But they bitterly confessed that Molière's victims seemed amused by the attacks. In any event, none of them, except in a unique case—one completely personal and unsubstantiated—ever succeeded in inflaming any of the high personages at court against Molière.[15] What Molière does is to attack the marquises in the name of the very principle of "honnêteté," as understood by the court. By ridiculing them, he does not at all attack their class; on the contrary, his calling on the audience of the pit, in *La Critique,* to bear witness against the marquises' lack of taste does not question the prestige of the court. It is only to protect it further that Dorante, courtier, *honnête homme* and spokesman for Molière, denounces "a half dozen gentlemen who dishonor the court by their extravagant manners, and make the people believe that we are all like them." [16] A man of quality is not necessarily an *honnête homme,* and the lower classes are sometimes a good judge. Nowhere does one see that an axiom such as this was ever considered subversive under Louis XIV, nor that it forced the person who propounded it to give up the commonly held ideas of the categories of the nobility and the bourgeois and their respective values.

[15] See especially, Donneau de Visé, *Zélinde,* 1663; Boursault, *Le Portrait du Peintre,* 1663. The same Visé wrote, in the same year, a comedy entitled *La Vengeance des Marquis,* and in his *Lettre sur les affaires du théâtre,* took the matter more seriously, accusing Molière of mistreating the intimates of the king—"Those bastions and ornaments of the State"—in the persons of the marquises.

[16] *Critique de L'École des femmes,* scene 5.

The Comic Hero and His Idols

by Lionel Gossman

We tend, occasionally, to think that some of Molière's comedies are gay and light-hearted, whereas others are more somber and ambiguous. A Jourdain or a Magdelon presents audiences with no problems, but an Alceste leaves them perplexed and uncertain. Jourdain and Magdelon are figures of unalloyed fun, according to this view, pure fools as anyone can easily discern; Alceste, on the other hand, does not seem very funny and to some he even seems almost tragic. Oddly enough, Molière's contemporaries do not seem to have entertained these uncertainties. We hear, of course, of opposition to *Dom Juan* and to *Tartuffe,* but we know that there was also opposition to *Les Précieuses ridicules* and to *L'École des femmes.* Most people appear to have laughed at *all* the comedies. As for ambiguity, there is, as we shall see, a good deal of it in *Le Bourgeois gentilhomme.* A very sentimental reader might find Monsieur Jourdain almost as pathetic and as misunderstood as Alceste.[1] Romantic interpretations of *Le Misanthrope* can easily be extended to all the plays. While it must be recognized that there is a difference between two types of comedy in Molière, between the comedies of the *Bourgeois gentilhomme* type and the comedies of the *Misanthrope* type, if we may make a loose initial distinction, this difference cannot be perfunctorily attributed to the fact that one group is funnier than the other or less mysterious and ambiguous. We should rather try to elucidate it by examining the more or less complex form of the comic hero's relation to the world.

The final judge and the transcendence to which the tragic hero of Racine looks for the ground of his being and the value of his existence is God. The comic hero, on the other hand, looks to others to give him his value and his being. The sign of recognition that Phèdre expects from God, the Jourdains, the Cathoses, and the Alcestes expect from the world.

[1] In Pirandello's *Henry IV,* Molière's Jourdain does indeed appear in a new and deliberately tragicomic guise.

Whereas one group of Molière's characters make no attempt to conceal their idolatry, however, another group of characters affect to despise the idols whose recognition they desire, postulating instead their own superiority and setting themselves up as idols for others to worship.

With the notable exceptions of Dom Juan and Jupiter, the majority of Molière's best known characters are bourgeois of one degree or another. Within this bourgeoisie it is nevertheless possible to distinguish an upper and a lower range. While Alceste obviously belongs to a social class very close to the nobility, perhaps even to a long-established family of *noblesse de robe,* Jourdain is a very ordinary, if rather well-off, merchant, the son of a draper. Corresponding to this hierarchy of ranks, there is the hierarchy of Paris and the provinces. While it is not possible, as it would doubtless be in the work of later writers like Balzac or Stendhal, to identify absolutely attitudes and modes of being in Molière with social class, it is broadly speaking true to say that the "open" comic heroes, those who recognize their models and superiors without shame, are characters of the lower bourgeoisie and the provinces. The "closed" comic heroes, those whose resentment of their idols, precisely for being idols, leads them to deny their recognition of them, belong rather to the upper bourgeoisie and the aristocracy, to those groups that are close to social equality or who have social equality with their idols. The vanities and illusions of the first group, being openly avowed, have a quality of naïveté that makes comedies like *Le Bourgeois gentilhomme* or *Les Précieuses ridicules* hilariously funny. It is not hard for us to discern and transcend the folly of Jourdain. The vanities and illusions of the second group are less easily discerned as comic, for they resemble those we ourselves conceal, those of "in-groups," courtiers, artists, professional people —"tous ces métiers dont le principal instrument est l'opinion que l'on a de soi-même, et dont la matière première est l'opinion que les autres ont de vous [all those professions whose primary instrument is the opinion one has of oneself, and whose raw material is the opinion that others have of you]," as Valéry describes them (*Teste,* "Lettre d'un ami," 23rd ed., Paris, 1946, p. 82).

In the first case the desire *to be distinguished* is a desire to be distinguished from one group by being recognized as a member of a superior group, the superiority of which the aspirant himself necessarily recognizes. "Mon Dieu! ma chère," exclaims Cathos, "que ton père a la forme enfoncée dans la matière! que son intelligence est épaisse, et qu'il fait sombre dans son âme!" "Que veux-tu, ma chère," Cathos answers contritely. "J'en suis en confusion pour lui. J'ai peine à me persuader que je puisse véritablement être sa fille, et je crois que quelque illustre aventure, un jour, me viendra développer une naissance plus illustre (*Précieuses,* sc. 5) [My God! my dear, in the case of your father, how form is crammed into matter! how thick his intelligence is, and how dark it is in his soul! . . . I am so embarrassed for him. I have trouble convincing myself that I am really his daughter, and I believe that some illustrious adventure will one day reveal to me a more illustrious birth]." "Lorsque je hante la noblesse, je fais paroître mon jugement," says Jourdain to his wife, "et cela est plus beau que de hanter votre bourgeoisie *(BG,* III, 3) [When I frequent the nobility, I bring out my good sense, . . and this is finer than frequenting your bourgeoisie]." A little later he accuses his good wife of having "les sentiments d'un petit esprit, de vouloir demeurer toujours dans la bassesse *(BG,* III, 12) [the opinions of a little mind, of wanting to remain always in the lower ranks]." There is nothing secret about the reverence these characters have for their idols, and they seek quite openly to elicit from their silent or masked or absent divinity the sign of recognition that for them is a sign of salvation. "Pour moi," says Mascarille ironically, "je tiens que hors de Paris, il n'y a point de salut pour les honnêtes gens." "C'est une vérité incontestable," answers Cathos *(Précieuses,* sc. 9) [For me, . . I claim that outside of Paris, there is no salvation for *honnêtes gens.* . . . It is an unquestionable truth]." "Est-ce que les gens de qualité apprennent aussi la musique?" asks Jourdain. "Oui, Monsieur," says the Maître de Musique. "Je l'apprendrai donc," Jourdain rejoins without hesitation *(BG,* I, 2) [Does the nobility also learn music? . . . Yes, Sir. . . . I'll learn it then]."

More complex and less immediately comic in their desire to achieve distinction are those who will not share it with anybody, who refuse the models that everyone else accepts and who, far from recognizing their idols, go to great lengths to conceal their mediation by others. They make a point of loudly scorning the ways of the world, those very ways that a Jourdain and a Cathos revere so unquestioningly. Madame Pernelle in *Tartuffe* refuses the courtesies of her daughter-in-law: "Ce sont . . . façons dont je n'ai pas besoin (I, 1, 4) [I have no need of all that fuss]." Harpagon likewise condemns the manners of the world. He reproaches his son with the very imitation that is the butt of Molière's satire in *Le Bourgeois gentilhomme*: "Je vous l'ai dit cent fois, mon fils, toutes vos manières me déplaisent fort: vous donnez furieusement dans le marquis. . . . Je voudrois bien savoir, sans parler du reste, à quoi servent tous ces rubans dont vous voilà lardé depuis les pieds jusqu'à la tête, et si une demi-douzaine d'aiguillettes ne suffit pas pour attacher un haut-de-chausses? Il est bien nécessaire d'employer de l'argent à des perruques, lorsque l'on peut porter des cheveux de son cru, qui ne coûtent rien *(L'Avare,* I, 4) [I have told you a hundred times, my son, that I find all your manners most displeasing; you are trying madly to act like a marquis. . . . I should really like to know, not to mention the rest, what use there is to all those ribbons with which you are decorated from head to foot, and whether a half-dozen aiguillettes are not enough to attach your breeches? It's surely necessary to spend money on wigs, when one can wear one's own hair, which costs nothing]." Arnolphe has his own taste in women and it is not that of everyone else:

> Moi, j'irois me charger d'une spirituelle
> Qui ne parleroit rien que cercle et que ruelle,
> Qui de prose et de vers feroit de doux écrits,
> Et que visiteroient marquis et beaux esprits!
> > (*Éc. femmes*, I, 1, *87-90*)

[Do you think I would take a wit as a wife, one who would speak of nothing but circles and coteries, who would write sweet prose and sweet verse, and who would be visited by marquises and wits!]

Sganarelle, like Harpagon, refuses the fashions of his contemporaries. His brother, he complains, would have him ape the manners of the "jeunes muguets." But he will have none of

> . . . ces petits chapeaux
> Qui laissent éventer leurs débiles cerveaux,
> Et de ces blonds cheveux, de qui la vaste enflure
> Des visages humains offusque la figure.
> De ces petits pourpoints sous les bras se perdants,
> Et de ces grands collets, jusqu'au nombril pendants.
> De ces manches qu'à table on voit tâter les sauces,
> Et de ces cotillons appelés hauts-de-chausses.
> De ces souliers mignons, de rubans revêtus,
> Qui vous font ressembler à des pigeons pattus . . . etc., etc.
> > (*Éc. maris*, I, 1, *21-34*)

[. . . those little hats, which let their weak minds evaporate, and that blond hair, so puffed up and abundant that it hides the human face; and those little doublets disappearing under the arms, and those big tippets hanging down to their navels; those sleeves that at table dip into the sauces, and those petticoats called breeches; those cute shoes, covered with ribbons, that make you look like feather-legged pigeons, . . .]

No, Sganarelle will follow his own fashion in complete indifference to everyone else—"Et qui me trouve mal, n'a qu'à fermer les yeux (*ibid., 74*) [Anyone who thinks I look bad has only to close his eyes]."

   The rejection of society is not, clearly, confined to articles of clothing and a few superficial customs. It is the entire way of life of everybody else that these characters ostensibly reject. People enjoy company, entertainment, balls, receptions, conversations? Madame Pernelle will have none of them. On the contrary she will make a virtue of solitude, abstention, and even brusqueness. Money is spent on carriages, fine clothes, amusements? Harpagon will not spend it at all. Instead he will treasure and revere it for itself. Everybody wants an entertaining, witty, and sociable wife? Arnolphe and Sganarelle will choose a "bête," and they will value precisely that in her which nobody else seems to admire, her ignorance and simplicity. The world is full of flattery and soft with compromise? Alceste will be brusque, frank, and scrupulously uncompromising. Society observes certain codes of behavior, of decency, and of propriety? Dom Juan will flout them and will be blatantly indecent and immoral. These characters—Harpagon, Arnolphe, Sganarelle, Alceste, Dom Juan, Madame Pernelle, Orgon—refuse to recognize that they are mediated by others; the almost childlike guilelessness of Jourdain's fascination with the nobility gives way in them to a subtle concealment by the character of his true desires, and of their source. Far from recognizing their mediators, these characters pretend they have none. Several of them appear to be in thrall to idols; Orgon and Madame Pernelle to Tartuffe, Philaminte and her daughter to their Trissotin, Harpagon to his *"cassette."* The last example reveals these idolatries for what they are, however. Orgon is bent on using Tartuffe as much as Tartuffe is bent on using him. The *femmes savantes,* like the *dévot,* see in their idols an instrument for asserting their superiority to the world around them, and it is on this world that their eyes are really turned. "Nul n'aura de l'esprit hors nous et nos amis" declares Armande: "Nous chercherons partout à trouver à redire, / Et ne verrons que nous qui sache bien écrire" (*FS,* III, 2, 924-26) [No one will be clever but us and our friends. . . . We shall look everywhere for something to criticize, and will consider ourselves the only ones who know how to write]." Likewise Orgon sets himself up *against* society as the only true Christian in it. The function of Tartuffe is to guarantee Orgon's superiority to *everybody* else. In the case of Harpagon the idolatry of the instrument has reached its climax in total alienation and fetishism. In all three plays the idol is used to assert an opposition to society, a distinction from it and a superiority to it. Philaminte and her daughters do not really care about science, Orgon and his mother do not really care about religion (both texts illustrate this amply), and Harpagon does not really care about wealth—on the contrary, his wealth is used to keep him poor. What these characters want above all is *to be distinguished,* but they refuse to adopt the usual method of social advancement and privilege, since this method offers only a *relative* superiority to others, whereas the superiority they desire is *absolute.* They are comic not only because there is a constant contradiction between what they are and what they affect to be, but because their attempt to transcend all social superiorities and to reach an absolute superiority misfires. *La Cour et la ville* will not be convinced that stringent devoutness or erudition are more desirable than social advantage and worldly success. They are no more envious of the spiritual insights of Orgon and the telescopes of Philaminte than they are of Harpagon's beloved *"cassette."* Philaminte, Orgon, and Harpagon do not see this of course. Harpagon imagines that everyone is after his *cassette,* that there is a vast plot to deprive him of this mark of his superiority. Likewise Orgon imagines that his whole family is plotting to remove Tartuffe out of jealousy. Arnolphe and Sganarelle, convinced that the eyes of the entire universe are upon them and that everybody desires to corrupt the virtuous young persons, in the possession of whom they find the mark of their superiority, shut them up and guard them as jealously as Harpagon guards his *cassette.*[2] While choosing to be *different* from everybody else, while turning away from what they castigate as the vain ambitions of the world in order to devote themselves to "authentic" values, these characters nevertheless have to believe that they are envied by everybody else. Thus while Orgon raves that the world in its corruption does not appreciate the saintliness of his Tartuffe, he also imagines that everyone is jealous of his special relation with Tartuffe; while Arnolphe prefers *une bête,* who will interest no one, to an elegant society girl who would be the object of everybody's attention, he still imagines that the entire universe is pursuing his Agnès.

Underlying the apparent indifference of the Arnolphes and the Orgons there is in reality the same fascination with others that we find among the Jourdains or the Cathoses. Orgon could after all practice his devotions quietly, without ostentation. Arnolphe and Sganarelle could avoid being made cuckold by remaining bachelors. But they never entertain this notion. The true object of their craving is not a faithful wife—or in Orgon's case salvation through Christ—but the recognition by others of their superiority. The goals which they choose to pursue are not after all pursued for themselves, nor do they themselves select them as they imagine they do. They are determined for them by their very opposition to society. Arnolphe and Sganarelle are not content to do without a wife; on the contrary; but she must be the opposite of all other wives. Orgon is not content to withdraw inwardly from public life; on the contrary, he continues to live a remarkably public life, but one which is the opposite of the life everyone else leads. Harpagon is not content to renounce material riches; he continues to pursue them but he gives them a meaning and a value absolutely opposed to the meaning and value they have for everyone else. All the posing of the Orgons and the Arnolphes and the Harpagons—though in this last instance it must be admitted that the pose has become truly the only reality of the man; Harpagon has so completely alienated himself that he can even run after his own body (cf. *L'Avare,* IV, 7)—cannot conceal that they are as dependent on others and as mediated by them, whatever claims to independence they may make, as

---

[2] In the same way Rousseau believed, rightly or wrongly, that all his friends were trying to seduce Thérèse.

simple fools like Jourdain and Cathos or Magdelon. Their basic folly is the same and all their cleverness is used not to eradicate it, but to disguise it from themselves and others. This becomes particularly clear in *La Comtesse d'Escarbagnas*. At the end of this play the Countess, having failed to distinguish herself in her little provincial society by aping the noble ladies of the Court, decides to distinguish herself by inverting this imitation, by seeming to reject it in favor of a superiority all her own. She marries Monsieur Tibaudier just to prove her absolute superiority to everyone. "Oui, Monsieur Tibaudier," she says, "Je vous épouse pour faire enrager tout le monde" (sc. 9) [Yes, Monsieur Tibaudier, . . . I shall marry you to infuriate everyone]." Unable to attract the gaze of the world by acting *with* it, the Countess resolves in desperation to attract the attention she craves by acting *against* it. The world and not Monsieur Tibaudier remains, however, the object of her fascination.

In fact, of course, the world is not the least bit *enragé*. The play closes with the Viscount's ironical: "Souffrez, Madame, qu'en enrageant, nous puissions voir ici le *reste* du spectacle (italics added) [But do allow us, Madame, as infuriated as we may be, to see the rest of the show]." The Countess has failed absolutely to fix the world's attention on herself in the way she wanted. On the contrary, it has watched her as it would watch a comedy—which the Countess' behavior *in fact is*—and it is now off to watch another comedy, another stage play. The truth is that it is not the comic heroes who are indifferent to the world, it is the world that is indifferent to them. It is not they who fascinate the world; they are fascinated by it.

The world, indeed, has to be forced by the hero to give him its attention. It is only when Harpagon tries to impose the rules of his crazy universe on others that they begin to be seriously concerned with him. It is only because Philaminte, Armande, and Bélise are not content to be "blue-stockings" quietly on their own, but insist on organizing the lives of Chrysale and Henriette around their own obsessions that father and daughter find themselves forced to take note of them. If Arnolphe had not forcibly embroiled Agnès in his plans, Horace and everyone else would simply have regarded him as an eccentric mysogenist and would not have given him a second thought. This seemingly inevitable imposition of themselves on others is a revealing characteristic of the comic heroes of Molière. It confirms that their professed indifference to others is a sham. Far from seeking to live the good life himself, Alceste is concerned only to impress on others that they are not living it and that they do not have his superior moral vision. The hero's withdrawal to his desert at the end of the play is itself a *spectacular* gesture, and it is for this reason one that will constantly have to be renewed and revived. It is by no means final. Dom Juan is not simply indifferent to the world: he has to arouse its wrath—and thereby its attention—by perpetually flouting its rules, seducing its virgins and wives, blaspheming against its God. The sadism of Orgon has already been alluded to; it is in no way exceptional in the work of Molière. Orgon's relation to Mariane has its counterpart in the relation of Harpagon to Élise or Cléante, of Argan to Angélique or little Louison, of Monsieur Jourdain to Lucile.

In the comedies of Molière the hero's transcendence is the world of others. The silence of this world is intolerable to him, but he is obliged to *force* it to speak and recognize his existence. In the early tragedies of Racine, the hero's transcendence is also the world of others and he too has to resort to violence in order to have himself recognized. It is not surprising, therefore, that sadism is a characteristic shared by comic and tragic heroes alike. This parallel of the early Racinian heroes and of the comic heroes of Molière can be pursued in some detail.

Almost all Molière's comedies oppose ruse to ruse, hypocrisy to hypocrisy, violence to violence: how are we to choose between Jupiter and Amphitryon, Alceste and the two *marquis*, Orgon and Tartuffe, Dandin and Angélique, Argan and Béline? Likewise how are we to choose between Pyrrhus and Hermione or between Hermione and Oreste or between Nero and Agrippine? That salvation and purity are impossible in the world forms part of the tragic vision of Racine. In Molière also participation involves compromise. In a world in which fathers brutalize their children, mothers are jealous of their sons, guardians stultify their wards, no one who participates can be innocent. The only weapon against violence and blackmail is ruse and hypocrisy. "La sincérité souffre un peu au métier que je fais," Valère admits; "mais quand on a besoin des hommes il faut bien s'ajuster à eux; et puisqu'on ne sauroit les gagner que par là, ce n'est pas la faute de ceux qui flattent mais de ceux qui veulent être flattés" (*L'Avare*, I, 1) [Sincerity suffers a bit because of the job I have taken on, . . . but when one needs men, one has to adapt to them; and since that is the only way one can win them, it is not the fault of those who flatter, but of those who want to be flattered]." Lamenting the fact that sons have to get into debt on account of "la maudite avarice des pères [the damnable stinginess of fathers]," Cléante protests: "et on s'étonne après cela que les fils souhaitent qu'ils meurent (*L'Avare*, II, 1) [and some are surprised that, after that, sons hope that they die]." Covielle in *Le Bourgeois gentilhomme* mocks his master for the naïve honesty of his dealings with Jourdain: "Ne voyez-vous pas qu'il est fou? et vous coûtoit-il quelque chose de vous accommoder à ses chimères? (*BG*, III, 13) [Don't you see that he's mad? And would it have cost you anything to adapt to his fantasies?]." In a world in which the only law is willfulness and the only authority is tyranny, no one can remain pure without becoming a victim. Elmire, Horace, and Valère do not seek out ruse and hypocrisy, but they cannot escape them either, for these are the instruments of survival. Even little Louison in *Le Malade imaginaire* has to learn how to deal with her father's tyranny and violence by cunning and deceit. Those who remain pure and innocent risk becoming victims, like Mariane in *Tartuffe* or Angélique in *Le Malade imaginaire,* and if they escape this fate it is only because someone more energetic and less scrupulous has intervened in their behalf. Sometimes they do indeed become victims, as Alcmène does, and sometimes they preserve their innocence through an enigmatic absence or abnegation of desire which places them outside the world, like Éliante in *Le Misanthrope* or Elvire in *Dom Juan,* after her conversion. These characters are as peripheral in Molière's comedies as Racine's Junie, whom Goldmann adjudges the sole tragic character in *Britannicus.*[3] Goldmann saw—rightly it seems to me—that the *innocent stratagème* by which Andromaque hoped to foil Pyrrhus' attempt at blackmail seriously compromises her tragic stature. A similar problem was encountered by Molière in *L'École des femmes,* where Agnès has to be at the same time desiring, active, and innocent. If we look closely at the text, we find that Agnès never *consciously* disobeys Arnolphe. Both her desire for Horace and her active participation in the plot against Arnolphe are conceived entirely on the level of instinct. Only in this way could Molière preserve the innocence of his heroine, while at the same time allowing her to act in pursuit of her own desires.[4]

In both Molière's comedies and Racine's early tragedies the main characters are moved primarily by their desire to force the world to recognize them. In both, the instruments of this desire are imposture and sadism. In both, the heroes fail to make the world break its silence. Racine's characters find themselves refused in the very suffering they inflict on those whose recognition they demand. The comic hero's victims defend themselves against his tyranny by ruse and hypocrisy, and he thereby becomes for them not the transcendent subject of his intention but an object to be tricked and manipulated. The mock-recognition of Jourdain at the end of *Le Bourgeois gentilhomme* or of Argan at the end of *Le Malade imaginaire* has its counterpart in the mock recognition of Oreste by Hermione in *Andromaque* or in the scenes between Nero and Agrippine in *Britannicus.* If we look up the scale in *Andromaque* from Oreste to Andromaque herself we find that for every character the character above is a transcendent subject who is adored and yet at the same time resented precisely on account of this transcendence, which negates the transcendence that the idolator desires and claims for himself. If we look down the scale, we discover that for every character the character below is an object to be manipulated and used. The refusal of the "upper" character to

---

[3] Goldmann, Lucien, *Le Dieu caché,* Paris: Gallimard, 1955. (*Ed. note*)

[4] This aspect of Agnès' behavior was pointed out to me by Mr. Eugenio Donato in a paper he prepared for one of my graduate seminars. I am very happy to acknowledge my debt to him.

recognize the "lower" one confirms the "lower" character in his adoration and at the same time intensifies his desire to reverse the positions. The same pattern is found in the comedies of Molière, though in less schematic form. The verbal battles that make up almost the whole of *Andromaque* have their counterpart in innumerable scenes in Molière's comedies.

II

ON *DOM JUAN* AND OTHER PLAYS

Dom Juan Revisited

by André Villiers

The problem of Don Juan, postulated according to tradition—or according to the myth that evolves with the successive metamorphoses of the Don Juan tradition—invites us to formulate our own hypotheses on the reality of his adventures, on the origins of man's powers of seduction. This involves all of literature, the richest and most abundant there is, since love is its theme; all of psychology, from sympathy to passion, with its deeper roots in the sexual instinct; and the whole question of libido, which means a mountain of human concerns prettied up by art or dissected by the scientist, and which we touch on when we investigate the mysteries of the seducer. Molière does not really open this debate. He does, however, propose another subject of debate which does not seem to be of concern if one limits oneself to attesting, in the traditional manner, that Don Juan is both a seducer and a libertine. One thus casually juxtaposes the two with a most remarkable lack of curiosity. Even stranger is the acceptance of the unity of the character. One is content to think that this is as factual a matter as a photograph: it is thus because the model, a libertine nobleman of the seventeenth century, presented this double image of libertinism. One accepts it as one is forced to accept the testimony of an authoritative document. If one is a critic or inter-

"Dom Juan Revisited" by André Villiers. From *Le Dom Juan de Molière, un problème de mise en scène.* Copyright 1947 by the Société Générale d'Editions, Paris. Translated and reprinted by permission of the author. The pages printed here, and translated by Beth Archer, are the chapter entitled "L'Essence profonde du drame."

preter and happens to question this double image of the character, it turns out to be most disquieting.

This is precisely what brings us to the thought: Molière's Dom Juan, a skirt-chaser indeed, is also a systematic denigrator of established faith and morality. The characteristics of each mingle, as though skepticism, the negation of recognized values, necessarily resulted in a disorder of the senses—unless it works the other way around. What interests us is not to learn how Dom Juan, carried away by his untamed desires, is wedded anew each month to fresh and wondrous conquests, but rather, whether his behavior is the consequence of his skepticism or whether, on the contrary, his skepticism is the consequence of his debauchery. If we were to look at Dom Juan the adventurer as one particular type of man, would he necessarily be a freethinker? And conversely, is the atheistic sensualist predetermined to free love?

This concern exists in Molière. To the preceding questions, the Christian moralist replies that these are two aspects of the same truth: the corruption of the flesh and the evil mind exult in the atheist. There is nevertheless room for further development, and justification of even this particular viewpoint demands some explanation. Nor can the remark often made by libertines themselves, that many believers are of questionable morality and many nonbelievers of virtuous mores, be accepted any more readily. *Dom Juan* calls our attention to this relationship between the two kinds of libertinism, in support of which one can easily find living examples from the seventeenth and eighteenth centuries, to limit ourselves to these distant periods.

If Molière had devoted himself first to the examination of amorous exploits, we would never be able to occupy ourselves with this philosophic curiosity. In so doing, he would have placed less emphasis on the philosophic aspect of libertinism and developed further a type highly distinctive in character, unusual, perhaps even abnormal, and thus excluded the possibility of generalizing from our observations. However, the Don-Juanesque quality of his Dom Juan, stated at the outset like a postulate because it is maintained within the limits already seen, permits one to extend the viewpoint to the amorous behavior of man in general, not merely the seducer.

It is easy to understand that Dr. Marañón, committed as a psychologist and doctor to the destruction of the Don Juan myth, should have stopped along the way to note the almost clinical exactness of Zorilla's characterizations. This he could not have done with Molière's Dom Juan, whose interest lies elsewhere. The Don Juan of the legend that produced (for the revery of a certain kind of man or woman) a literature of affectation and bedroom gossip corresponds to a well-determined mental structure associated with a specific psycho-physiological type. In spite of the prestige surrounding it, this type is far from deserving admiration. Far from being a superman, or more simply an individual extremely talented in the art of love, he appears more like an indifferent exploiter of his own weaknesses and aberrations. In order to benefit from the legend, as Dr. Marañon points out, he requires the enhancement of a myth, aggrandized in the hospital climate of religion and tradition, nurtured by the legion of women whose sexual type corresponds to Don Juan's and who have as little cause for pride over their femininity as Don Juan over his virility. There is in this myth a kind of embezzlement of the true psychological and physical values of man and woman which Dr. Marañon has rightfully denounced (but which in no way diminishes the myth). For such as it is, and nourished by permanent human types who are naturally attracted to it, this myth will always find a climate suitable to its conceptualization and its glorification in literature. There are so many troubling nuances within normalcy which normalcy does not reject within the game of existence! So that even if the myth were to fade, one can always dream of love à la Don Juan as one imagines love à la Werther.

Not being an archetype of normal man, this Don Juan, with his clearly defined characteristics, can therefore not be taken as a model in the examination of amorous behavior. This specialist in love teaches us nothing of a general nature; he only acquaints us with his own case. The lessons we can learn from him are only of auxiliary or parallel interest, just as abnormal psychology contributes to an understanding of normal psychology. Nonetheless, the problems of choice, fidelity, passion exist quite apart from the Don Juan myth. We know that love has a physiological substratum, that determining factors of sexual hyperesthesia exist, that inclinations are intellectualized and sentiments are spiritualized. Psychologists and physiologists, sociologists and moralists analyze the biologic and social conditions of love; philosophers and writers classify and describe them. Stendhal distinguishes four types of love: physical love, passion, inclination, and love that satisfies vanity. After complicating the problem to an excessive degree, one simplifies it out of existence; one overlooks the pressures of society, of habits and mores, of literary tradition and esthetic distortion: and so, discarding civilization, one returns to instinct. Then once again one notices that inclinations are intellectualized and the cycle starts all over again. These detailed analyses generally give a fair picture of the antagonizing, exciting, and moderating effects of society; however, the success and failure of society only creates a perfect order within the framework of hypocrisy or lies. These analyses examine basic inclination for its own sake, or else focus on the genesis of love, "crystallization," jealousy, abandon, etc., but for the most part with regard to one love in particular, leaving aside such questions as the simultaneous longing for more than one person of the opposite sex, which is highly important and cannot be abstracted from the question of pure and simple inclination. All of this concerns men and women who make little or no use of the Don Juan myth in their search for a state of equilibrium—a very difficult undertaking.

Molière did not stress the lonely mythical nature of his character. The portrait of the hero is not inadequate; what we learn from Sganarelle and from a few well-chosen traits satisfies us. But his role as seducer insofar as we see him is fairly moderate. There is no excessive manifestation typical of a Don Juan—impenitent narcissism, for example—that irresistibly fixes our attention on his case, his problems, and that inhibits us, through a slight shift of the imagination, from leaving the seducer in question and going on to man in general, forgetting the licentious libertine and concentrating on normal man, who is equally familiar with the ardor of love.

In his defense *pro domo,* Dom Juan confesses to a generous temperament and a love of variety. Nothing in his development refers to sentiment, only to the intellectualization of inclination, which is treated with considerable grace and distinction. We are obliged to admit that his remarks are not without interest or force. From these simple factors it is possible to construct a code of behavior. Let us recall the declaration made by Oron to the Confessor in *Le Supplément au Voyage de Bougainville*:

> Can anything be more absurd than a rule which proscribes the change native to us, which commands a constancy that cannot be, which violates the freedom of the male and the female by forever chaining them to each other; or more outrageous than a fidelity which limits the most capricious of pleasures to one individual. . . .

In Diderot's Tahitian paradise, Nature is the "sovereign mistress," and whatever is in harmony with her cannot be blameworthy. The precepts to be condemned are those that are "contrary to the general law of living creatures" and "contrary to nature," which means they are at the same time contrary to reason. And we know that the poor Confessor, riddled with remorse, after having slept the first three nights with Oron's three daughters, allotted the fourth night "out of decency to the wife of his host." The ardent and sensitive *Philosophe* did not express himself in these words out of any desire to be shocking. The author of *Le Neveu de Rameau* was very much a moralist, and one cannot deny the master of the *Encyclopédie* (in spite of oscillations of thought that wavered between decided materialism and an evident desire for idealism) the merit of definite coherence and true philosophic penetration. Diderot believes in the excellence of nature. That is why he exalts it in his paradisiac Tahiti, and why his plea for true instinct freed from prejudice does not dispense him from searching, throughout his entire lifetime, for the domain of virtue. His aim is to integrate in a general philosophy of true elevation those natural factors whose excellence is guaranteed as much by reason as by sentimental impulse and sensuous revelation. We know, for he has not concealed it, what the response of his nature was to generous endowments.

His philosophy reflects his temperament. It has even been suggested that [1] the inspiration of his temperament was responsible for the weaknesses of his philosophy, although it is supported by solid reason and ingenious intuitions. Whatever the case may be, there exists in this meeting of a materialistic dialectic and a specific temperament a kind of choice or reciprocal determinism that justifies our hypothesis concerning *Dom Juan*. The double face of the libertine of the senses and the libertine of the mind is no accident: this is not a case of juxtaposition but of correlation.

After the characteristic example of Diderot, it would be easy enough to find others that would lead us to identical thoughts. The example of Luillier comes at once to mind. This pleasure-seeker, this voluptuary addicted to the senses and even to debauchery, with supreme contempt for prejudices and rules, becomes the most devoted protector of Gassendi. What bond can possibly have attached him so faithfully to the provost of Digne, so unlike him in nature and habits, unless, as Monsieur Pintard remarks, it was the hope, while serving the inspired work of Epicure, of conciliating his cult of pleasure and sensuality with the cult of wisdom and reason? In the often naïve justification of their excesses that emanates from erudite skeptics, one must see something more than a banal excuse, something that is more like a quest for a philosophy in which the moral ideal is in agreement with natural demands. Molière's *Dom Juan* represents such a quest, more or less consciously, of course. It is probably because of this that the sophisticated escapades of the philanderer are left in the background and along with the action of the play a discussion ensues which constantly exposes the moral libertine in general—and not merely from the viewpoint of Dom Juan—and the philosopher libertine. The conversation carried on in the background is somewhat like the one between the Confessor and the Tahitian in *Le Supplément au Voyage de Bougainville*.

Out of this our own questions also emerge. The subject is well worth the effort and it should be admitted that it is not often discussed. The efforts of Catholic morality to maintain within certain limits a nature tainted by original sin and diabolically corrupted are an obstacle to the freedom of man endowed by nature with liberal temperament. Each one of his drives, which in themselves do not seem blameworthy, is denounced as indicative of inherent evil. From such a vantage point, man is necessarily libertine. Dom Juan is not alone in rebelling against these imperatives, in wanting to break the narrow framework in which natural inclinations, though intellectualized and civilized, are mocked by painful and heavy shackles. Dom Juan's great tirade smacks of libertinism, but how many others share his views who are not Don Juans? At least his revolt can assail a solid object when man becomes aware of the disharmony of his nature pricked as it is by desires whose satisfaction destroys his health and psycho-physiological equilibrium: alcohol and opium procure pleasures damned only by hygiene; here the evil is evident. It is annoying to think that such excellent and pleasant substances are the source of so many ills—stomach, liver, nervous system. But that's how it is. In what way, however, is variety in love detrimental to health? Is there anything detrimental to one's physical well-being in seeking out the favors of a young woman when fidelity binds one to an aging wife? Why this reprobation of the healthy satisfaction of an inclination when it is the denial, on the contrary, that causes the worst disorders? Diderot's Tahitian is a handsome, honest man; his Tahitian women are in the pink of health. Convinced of the excellence of nature and driven by it, man logically declares war on morality. If he is a believer, and endowed with an ardent temperament, he has the choice, with all the degrees of relativity, between asceticism and hypocrisy. A saint or a Tartuffe. Between the two there are doubtless many shadings. With some indulgence, one might even remove the infamous epithet of Tartuffe when man struggles in a sympathetic way (and with the further help of definite values) to find an equilibrium between his drives and the different norms of moral or religious life. This equilibrium most often, we must admit, entails some degree of untruth. One comes to terms with absolute morality. The hushed-up scandals of bourgeois life and the frequent concessions of marriage provide only compromises which are not stressed.

Our libertine of the senses, even without being abnormal or perverted, without being a Don Juan, applies his critical mind in a most dangerous way to the imperatives of Christian life. His intellectual intemperance is commensurate with his sensual intemperance. He discusses the spirit and the tenets of religion: he is a freethinker.

One can reply to this that there are countless people in whom the most imperious compulsions do not cause a loss of faith. And this is true for ascetics and Tartuffes, as we said earlier. It is possible to imagine that our libertine is tempted neither by mortification nor by hypocrisy.

The questions asked by the libertine on constancy, love of change, the excellence of his inclination are certainly not without answers. But the contradictions between theory and practice endanger these questions when they are confronted with reason. If reason is exercised, the first replies are those of society: children, family, sentiment, tenderness, all of the literature given over to it and that has become a gain, an advantage. Beginning with the known factors of his instinct and the unknown factors of his physical life, the libertine comes first of all into conflict with the demands of social life and with his own spiritual and intellectual acquisitions that lie outside of metaphysics. The sensualist questions and becomes a rationalist. The libertine of the senses tends toward the philosopher. His atheism goes hand in hand with his materialism.

In spite of the absolute coherency of this, it still warrants reflection, since a philosophy like Diderot's or an intellectual movement like that of the libertines can be deeply influenced by the natural, the psycho-physio-logical bent of the initiator.

This brings us a long way from the traditional dissertations on the spicy adventures of the seducer, but Molière's play raises these more significant problems. Dom Juan's rebellion appears, first of all, to be the revolt of an intelligence unable to establish absolute norms of conduct. In order to alter the course of his action, it would have been necessary to stop him from the beginning when he sets up the beguiling image of his pleasures in love. The game is lost when, having asked Sganarelle—who berates him for his monthly marriages—if there is anything more delight-ful, Sganarelle admits that it is indeed delightful and amusing, that he would also partake if it were not wicked, and that the wickedness stems from the mockery of a sacred mystery. The whole of moral structure rests on religious dogma. Heaven, always heaven (one might say parody-ing the exasperated Dom Carlos) is opposed to the actions of Dom Juan. For the atheist, what significance can there be in these threats of punish-ment that he rejects as "faux-jour" or "vapeur," good only for disturbing one's vision and making one believe that the statue of the Commander nods his head? Can one offer anything in response to his objections, based on his nature as a man, his needs, his desires, other than the supernatural? The symbolic line on which the fourth act ends properly situates the drama: "On a pas besoin de lumière quand on est conduit par le ciel." What torch, however, can guide Dom Juan? If he renounces "heavenly grace," the transcendental truth that he cannot conceive, that his reason cannot accept, is there then no moral code? The rejection of the rela-tionship between religious dogma and morality is not a rejection of moral-ity. What is morality? It is not merely a matter of individual salvation, but the order on which the whole of society is based.

Skepticism casts aside the moral ideal or social structure founded in religion, restitutes to man the principle of liberty whose abysses it has not fathomed, proclaims the rights of nature whose limits it has not per-ceived, without knowing for certain the power and value of nature. In this upheaval all notions are re-evaluated: freedom, justice, happiness, social order. Does freedom of mores lead to corruption? Can the sover-eignty of man adapt to the power of a sovereign? Is an ignorant man capable of ruling himself? If the rights of the Sovereign do not issue from God, are they founded in reason? There is much questioning, at the end of the seventeenth century, on the laws of nature and the reasons of state. It is doubtless improper to suggest that an immediate need was seen for the founding of a new order; the thinking of the time is more critical than constructive. It is audacious thinking that, often impressed with logical consequences, takes refuge in prudent waitfulness. Or further still, lost in the complexity of the problems raised, it is thinking that wanders off into uncertainty and paradox. However, the maturation of philosophy looms imminent. It will be necessary to wait some fifteen years after *Dom Juan* for Bayle to be known, twenty-five years before Locke publishes his *Essay on Human Understanding*. But Hobbes has already published, in France—*De Cive* and *The Leviathan*, and Sorbière's *Discours sceptiques* has already appeared. The libertines now have the heritage of Montaigne. From diverse philosophic horizons arise the subjects that will soon be of concern to everyone.

At the risk of creating a misunderstanding based on romantic distortion, one might say that *Dom Juan* reflects an anxiety. Molière's character is certainly condemned for his irrefutable corruption, for his clearly defined dastardliness. But it is evident that this lengthy moral debate in a number of acts demonstrates, in a broader sense, man's bewildered search for an ethic liberated from the postulates of religion and agreeing with a naturalistic conception of values. This lends great importance to the scene of the poor man. The "love of humanity" that Dom Juan tosses at the poor man in rags and at the coarse valet, both of whom are unable to comprehend its meaning, is a hope that reaches out toward a new order, an ideal held up that might prove worthy of love and, founded in man, be made for man.

In appearance, any digression from the character of Dom Juan is out of place if it strays from the reality of his actions, if it embroiders on the myth and neglects the simple realities of the plot. But the meaning of the play goes beyond the first impression of the plot. An idea haunts the play, runs through the speeches of the characters, opposes one to the other and confronts their reasoning, leads the action—in short, it is the idea of man's freedom. A man loosed from the chains of his beliefs and his superstitions, who estimates his obligations, those of his own nature and those of other men. Molière's creation is weakened if one denies this underlying and persistent preoccupation. It would seem instead that the indifferent speculations on the adventures of a seducer are the more banal digressions. *Dom Juan,* through its example of one outrageous case, reasoning as it were through the absurd, and carrying the hypothesis to its extreme, constantly interrogates and postulates on the subject of man in general. To have presented a new ideal in Dom Juan is no mean achievement, even considering the destructive power of a libertine work at that time, which might later have reconstructed into something new the ideal it destroyed. The skeptic idealizes; and along with the audacity of the militant libertine, one must admire the elevated thinking of the moralist, the genius inspired with a future truth.

The spectacle of mores provided the observer with the material for Dom Juan. It offered him, along with the character of a debauched and atheistic libertine nobleman, all kinds of possibilities for the discussion of that world teeming with ideas in ferment. Molière clearly saw the reciprocal relationship between spiritual problems on one side, and social and moral problems on the other. The pretext of a fable allowed him to seize the subject in its most vital spot.

Love serves in effect as the chopping board for questions regarding the excellence of nature and the freedom of man. Many other developments are possible, but the relations between man and woman, which aliments the most incendiary literature, pose in themselves the whole problem of individual freedom and social pressures. The behavior of a man in love points to his inclination and the value he places on it, to the limits he assigns to it and those imposed on him. This is the most pressing of concerns, the one that in the absolute is translated by defeat, and in practice, by all the compromises of everyday morality and the liberties taken in marriage.

Molière might have moralized, as has often been done, in the name of good sense or of some vague postulate on the laws of nature. In *Dom Juan* he expressed himself in the manner of a thinker concerned with the core of the issue. It is no exaggeration to say that he proves himself a philosopher.

Much has been written on the philosophy of Molière—a bit in order to exalt it and much to laud it, but often the praise has demeaned it. Perhaps his more serious adversaries are to be found among those who praised it while confining it within the limits of a harmless mediocrity rather than among those who attacked it bitterly.

In his writings Molière was a philosopher, just as he was a libertine in the orientation of his thinking, by dint of his relations and his resolutely libertine position. His philosophy remains unchanged from *L'École des maris* and *L'École des femmes* to *George Dandin,* works in which he seeks to establish through reason the founding of a morality that is in harmony with the simple laws of nature, and from *Les Précieuses ridicules* to *Tartuffe* and *Dom Juan,* in which he militates against moral, social, and religious hypocrisy. In *Dom Juan* he appears as a sensualist and a skeptic, while at the same time affirming his faith in the ideal of humanity and confining man's freedom within his duties to society.

Social equilibrium such as is found in *L'École des femmes* and in *Le Bourgeois gentilhomme,* toward which the lessons of all his plays tend, is in fact not an ideal proposed for its own sake, as though it were the exalting, transcendent, ultimate aim. It is a just ideal, and one that is, above all, indispensable. The limits imposed on the free exercise of our natural rights are not prejudices or religious beliefs, but the duties "necessary for human survival," as Locke was to say later on—the rights of Society. There is no other rule of virtue. However, this moral principle is equally valid for the inspiration of a love of humanity.

Molière looks upon the dispositions of nature with smiling favor, and when its exaggerations joggle established conventions, he looks upon it with indulgence. One guesses that he is more amused than admonishing when consecrated virtue is rapped across the knuckles. He assumes an air of complicity and amusement in *George Dandin* and *Amphitryon,* as he does in *Dom Juan* when the Don extolls the joy of amorous conquest or courts the giddy village girls. Nature is what it is, and Molière does not deify it. He rejoices when nature is pleasurable and salubrious; it is only fair then to let nature flourish. In any event, it is useless to try and force nature, as can be seen in *L'École des femmes.* Such is life, and to resist nature, as La Mothe Le Vayer said, "is to try to row against the current." In respecting nature, the essential thing is not to let it go astray or endanger the family and society. What must be found is an equilibrium.

If one attributes all of Molière's importance to his good sense, his defense of the family, and his apology for marriages between people of the same ages and conditions, his philosophy certainly does not soar very high. If he is no more than this moralist of middling virtues, his generosity of spirit appears to be little more than an impediment to pure conformity and betrays an absence of somewhat deeper spiritual concerns. This, however, is how Molière has often been praised for his solid lessons in bourgeois morality, while it has been regretted that he was given to vulgar materialism, evidenced by Chrysale's "bonne soupe." Peace is signed over *Tartuffe*; Veuillot's incendiary remarks have not reignited the quarrel of the false bigots; Molière the comic actor-writer has been completely vindicated by certain members of the Church. Everyone is more or less in agreement as to the meaning present in *L'Imposteur* and concedes that *Le Festin de Pierre,* taking its place in the history of the Don Juan myth, is a masterpiece . . . that is never performed. In return, and all the while proclaiming him the greatest comic genius in any age or land, Molière is maintained in a down-to-earth realm of prosaic virtues. His genius is affirmed at the same time as his grandeur is denied. He is allowed to rest on the unanimity of flat praise that borders on oblivion and injustice.

This is a strange kind of homage to pay the only author of the seventeenth century who made a metaphysical shudder go across the stage while presenting within the theater the audacious and disturbing problem of human liberty; who alone translated the philosophic anxiety of his time, whose entire literary production is an insurrection—in the sense implying conspiracies, attacks, libel, torch burials—for the emancipation of man and his triumph over prejudices and untruth; who alone, and ahead of his times, proposed as an ideal—intuiting some future age— that magnificent love of humanity which abounds in his works. One cannot close one's eyes to marks of such pre-eminence unless one is blind; and if all one wants to see in it is good sense, then one should recognize it as the good sense of Montaigne or Bayle. The indulgent smile Molière has for the spectacle of the world is not a pallid understanding for the infractions of a bourgeois morality whose purely relative value he knows. Aware of his obligations as a man in society, he tries to arrange the rights of human nature into a harmonious order in which everyone finds his place. But he does this with the serenity of the stoic who dominates his trials and with the tenderness that he inspires in us for his Alceste—a sage whose reason has not dried up his heart.

There is in Molière's attitude, as there is in his philosophy, this very important lesson which his works reveal to us, and it is a truly elevated philosophy, one worthy of the appellation. *Dom Juan* is not a dispensation from rules of conduct, nor is it a course in practical morality; but the wealth of ideas that its five acts suggest is considerable. It is a play that offers us ample material for meditation that is not limited to the problem of a particular period, and that leaves us marveling over so unique a work.

The Humanity of Molière's *Dom Juan*

by James Doolittle

Dom Juan has behaved like a Scudéry hero in order to overcome Elvire's resistance. Elvire has given herself not to Dom Juan but to a lover who exists only in an imagination formed upon the ideals of a pretty fiction. Against the visible facts, against her better judgment, Elvire has striven to preserve her illusion; she will not surrender it without the final evidence of Dom Juan's words and aspect. Undeceived, outraged, convinced of betrayal, she speaks her bitterness in a sarcastic regret that Dom Juan will not reconstitute the marionette, that he will not allow her to recreate the form of her departed illusion: "Que vous savez mal vous défendre pour un homme de cour, et qui doit être accoutumé à ces sortes de choses! . . . Que ne vous armez-vous le front d'une noble effronterie? Que ne me jurez-vous . . . que vous m'aimez toujours avec une ardeur sans égale? . . . Que ne me dites-vous que des affaires de la dernière conséquence vous ont obligé à partir sans m'en donner avis . . . et qu'éloigné de moi, vous souffrez ce que souffre un corps qui est séparé de son âme? Voilà comme il faut vous défendre, et non pas être interdit comme vous êtes (I. iii) [How bad you are at defending yourself, you a courtier, who must be used to this kind of thing! . . . Why don't you bear on your brow some noble insolence? Why don't you swear to me . . . that you still love me with unequaled ardor? . . . Why don't you tell me that matters of the utmost importance forced you to leave without giving me notice . . . and that far from me, you suffer what a body suffers when it is separated from its soul? That is how to defend yourself, and not to look taken aback, as you do]."

Elvire is trying to humiliate Dom Juan not for his infidelity but for his seeming inability to hide it; not for an action which she evidently finds common enough among men of his station, but for his silence ("interdit"), for his failure to cloak his action in a set of conventional phrases.

"The Humanity of Molière's *Dom Juan*" by James Doolittle. From *PMLA*, LXVIII, 3 (June 1953). Reprinted by permission of the author and *PMLA*. The pages reprinted here are only part of the original article. The excluded passages are primarily concerned with the obviously ridiculous or comic characters: Sganarelle, Gusman, the peasants, and Monsieur Dimanche.

Face to face with the fact that Dom Juan is not her hero, she would like to keep the latter at all costs.

Dom Juan just as tenaciously persists in successively destroying her illusions. Not having acquiesced in the social gesture, he alleges a religious one to account for his conduct: "un pur motif de conscience . . . j'ai ouvert les yeux de l'âme sur ce que je faisais [purely motivated by my conscience . . . I opened the eyes of my soul on what I was doing]"— not intending to deceive her, but knowing that his allegation will prevent her from resorting to religious arguments. Elvire, thus deprived of recourse to these institutions, has nothing left but herself to fall back on: "C'est une lâcheté que de se faire expliquer trop sa honte; et, sur de tels sujets, un noble coeur, au premier mot, doit prendre son parti . . . Le Ciel te punira, perfide, de l'outrage que tu me fais; et si le Ciel n'a rien que tu puisses appréhender, appréhende du moins la colère d'une femme offensée [It is cowardly to ask for too many explanations for one's own dishonor; and, on such matters, a noble heart must, from the very first word, make a decision . . . Heaven will punish you, traitor, for the offense that you inflict upon me; and if there is nothing in Heaven that you fear, fear at least the anger of an outraged woman]." "Un noble coeur," "la colère d'une femme offensée"—she sees herself in the third person; unable to appeal to any other institution, she comes finally to herself, but, so to speak, to herself institutionalized. Faced with what ought to be an agonizing reality, she wraps herself in a veil of impersonality and abstraction.

When she returns to the stage (IV. vi), she is actually wearing a veil, possibly to conceal her identity in public, or to suggest her coming retreat, or to symbolize her flight from reality, or perhaps all three. No longer the noble wife whose sense of the fitness of things has been outraged, she is now the emissary of the cult. Her love is no longer "terrestre"; it is a "flamme" purified of all traffic with the senses, a holy tenderness, a love "détaché de tout." It is pure and perfect, completely abstract. Or so she says.

The beginning of this scene, in other words, presents her as an abstraction still, but now the servant of a different illusion. It puts into her mouth the language of a director of conscience, forcing her to stress the distinction between the passion which made her consent to her abduction and the celestial love which has been substituted for it. Since the latter, by institutional definition, is pure, it need not be referred to by circumlocution. In I. iii Elvire had mentioned love only three times, calling it first "tendresse," then "sentiments," finally "ardeur." In IV. vi the terrestrial variety is "indignes ardeurs," "transports tumultueux d'un attachement criminel"; finally the word itself is pronounced: "amour terrestre et grossier." This love becomes immediately "détaché de tout . . . ce parfait et pur amour." Protected by this unearthly purity, Elvire can now talk about earthly as well as heavenly love without fear of corruption, and she does so with increasing complacency: "mes folles pensées . . . la faute que j'ai faite . . . les transports d'une passion condamnable . . . une personne que j'ai chérie tendrement [My mad thoughts . . . the sin I committed . . . the outbursts of a condemnable passion . . . a person whom I tenderly cherished]." As she rehearses her love for Dom Juan, her pace is quickened and intensified; earthly love is in danger of becoming confused with celestial: "Je vous ai aimé avec une tentresse extrême, rien au monde ne m'a été si cher que vous; j'ai oublié mon devoir pour vous, j'ai fait toutes choses pour vous. . . . Sauvez-vous, je vous prie, ou pour l'amour de vous, ou pour l'amour de *moi*. . . . Si ce n'est assez des larmes d'une personne que vous avez aimée, je vous en conjure par tous ce qui est le plus capable de vous toucher (italics added) [I loved you with the greatest tenderness, nothing in the world was dearer to me than you; for you I forsook my duty, for you I did all things. . . . Save yourself, I beg you, for the love of you, or for the love of me. . . . If the tears of a person you have loved are not enough, I pray you in the name of everything that is most capable of moving you]."

The speech thus ends with what, given Dom Juan's known opinions and state of mind, is a crashing ambiguity; Sganarelle perceives it, perceiving likewise that Dom Juan's perfidious silence has had no other objective than to let Elvire talk herself back into her original passion (whence Sganarelle's "Coeur de tigre!"—a stalking beast). Elvire, aghast, perceives it, and thinks only of escape: "Je m'en vais, après ce discours, et voilà tout ce que j'avais à vous dire [I am going, after these words, and that is all I had to say to you]." Dom Juan perceives it, and quietly moves for the checkmate: "Madame, il est tard, demeurez ici [Madame, it is late, stay here]." Elvire, frightened by him, but more by what she herself may do if she hesitates: "Non, Dom Juan, ne me retenez pas davantage [No, Dom Juan, don't keep me any longer]." Dom Juan moves once more: Elvire is now much troubled by the passion which his presence is inflaming in her; the tables have been turned completely; continued contact with him will destroy her resolution; she is in great haste to be away from him: "Non, vous dis-je, ne perdons point de temps en discours superflus. Laissez-moi *vite* aller, ne faites aucune instance pour me conduire, et songez seulement à profiter de mon avis (italics added) [No, I tell you, let us not waste time in superfluous words. Let me go quickly, make no move to lead me out, and think only of putting my advice to good use]." And she flees.[1]

From the moment that Elvire visualizes the eternal punishment threatening Dom Juan, the institutional vocabulary disappears from her language; what was impersonal becomes personal, zeal becomes passion,

---

[1] Only Jules Lemaître, as far as we know, has remarked that Elvire in this scene is still in love with Dom Juan: ". . . cette femme en deuil, amoureuse encore dans sa pénitence . . ." "Don Juan ou le Festin de Pierre" (13 Sept. 1886) in *Impressions de Théâtre*, Première série (Paris, n.d.), p. 67.

charity becomes love, angelic serenity turns into feminine agitation. Her passion originated in her betrayal of a religious form in favor of a social form; both forms having been torn away, ironically the passion remains, but now rendered criminal in her eyes. Having tried and failed to reconstitute a legitimacy for it, she has tried to renounce it and to seek refuge again in forms, first social, in crying vengeance, then religious, in deciding to become a nun. She has, unwittingly to be sure, but nonetheless voluntarily, returned to her passion, to dwell upon it with an almost catastrophically false sense of security. Refusing finally to choose passion instead of form, stripped of her faith in form's effectiveness, shatteringly aware of passion's continued intensity, her last recourse is the animal one of physical flight—a fruitless expedient, for she will carry her passion with her.

In this scene Elvire becomes for the first time a woman, tormented by the eternal woman's problem of having to express overwhelming emotion without transgressing strict conventional proprieties. This she succeeds in doing, enabling us to glimpse for a moment the passionate, wholly human beauty which is lacking from the noble gesticulations of the rest of her role. Elvire at this instant is still making gestures, but the abstract institutionalism behind them is now being forced desperately to combat the rich substance of a vibrant humanity. Tacitly, to be sure, hence the more dramatically, the woman has acknowledged and demonstrated her womanhood.

The world of Elvire is further dramatized by her brothers Carlos and Alonse. Like her, they subject themselves to the externally imposed sanctions of society and the cult. Carlos does so consciously, voluntarily; Alonse without thought or question. If we believe his language, Alonse is guided by the letter of the ideals he professes. Of his seven speeches, only two are noticeably personal, and one of these is the entrance speech in which he must explain his arrival. The other five are mostly in the third person; they are in the form of aphorisms occasioned, of course, by the specific situation, but equally applicable to any such: "Tous les services que nous rend une main ennemie ne sont d'aucun mérite pour engager notre âme. . . . Comme l'honneur est infiniment plus précieux que la vie, c'est ne devoir rien que d'être redevable de la vie à qui nous a ôté l'honneur. . . . Lorsque l'honneur est blessé mortellement, on ne doit point songer à garder aucunes mesures [All the favors done us by an enemy hand create no obligations for our souls. . . . Since honor is infinitely more precious than life, we have no debt for our lives to one who has taken away our honor. . . . When honor is mortally wounded, no restraints should stand in our way]," and so on.

But Carlos' resistance to such arguments finally forces Alonse to speak personally: "Quoi? vous prenez le parti de notre ennemi contre moi; et loin d'être saisi à son aspect des mêmes transports que je sens, vous faites voir pour lui des sentiments pleins de douceur [What? you take our enemy's part against me; and far from being transported as I am upon seeing him, you show feelings full of gentleness for him]?" It is here and in Carlos' reply that we see that Alonse, no doubt unknowingly, is using his aphorisms simply to justify the impulses of a brutal nature. "Ayons du cœur," says Carlos, "dont nous soyons les maîtres, une valeur . . . qui se porte aux choses par une pure délibération de notre raison, et non point par le mouvement d'une aveugle colère [Let us be the masters of our courage, let us have valour . . . which acts through the pure determination of our reason, and not through the impulse of blind anger]." Alonse, "feeling" himself "saisi de transports," accusing Carlos of yielding to "sentiments," thereby betrays himself. One does not yield to "sentiments" in the world Alonse professes; one's "transports" are dominated, at least, if they are not calculated, like those of Dom Juan in the wooing of Elvire. One's motivations are provided by reason, the principle of external authority, as Carlos is careful to assert in the language of Alonse, replacing this jargon, as he does so, in the theoretically proper relationship to its users from which Alonse has subverted it.

No one realizes more clearly than Carlos, however, the practical shortcomings of this theoretical propriety. Accepting it without rebellion, he nonetheless accepts it regretfully. Whatever the advantages of the "condition d'un gentilhomme," it does not necessarily procure the welfare of the individuals who share it; in this case its maintenance leads to much personal inconvenience and unhappiness—a fact immediately seized upon by Dom Juan, who says in effect that the gentleman whose duty to his honor makes him miserable can find consolation in the possibility of making others miserable also: a ridiculous state of affairs.

The heart of Carlos' complaint is the dependence of those elements essential to the realization of individual aspirations—property, peace of mind, and life itself—upon the surface aspects, the gestures, the conduct, however motivated, of others over whom the individual can exercise no control. In his opinions, therefore, Carlos is a potential Dom Juan, for he resents the regulation of his life by things external to it, the subjugation of the individual to the general, of the essential to the superficial, and the restriction of human aspirations to fit conventions which are artificial, abstract, and therefore inhuman. Where Dom Juan, however, tries to assert his humanity by defying conventions, Carlos attempts to humanize them. They in their turn tend to dehumanize him, forcing this noble and generous man to talk like a bookkeeper, to cast up his accounts in a picayune manner, in order to reconcile his common decency with the requirements of the conventions: "Je sais à quoi [notre honneur] nous oblige, et cette suspension d'un jour, que ma reconnaissance lui demande, ne fera qu'augmenter l'ardeur que j'ai de le satisfaire. Dom Juan, vous voyez que j'ai soin de vous rendre le bien que j'ai reçu de vous, et vous devez par là juger du reste, croire que je m'acquitte avec même chaleur de ce que je dois, et que je ne serai pas moins exact à vous payer l'injure que le bienfait (III. iv) [I know what our honor obliges us to do, and this delay of one day, which my gratitude asks in his favor, will do no more than increase my ardor to satisfy it. Dom Juan, you see that I am careful to return the favor you did for me, and from that you can judge the rest, and that I shall not be less rigorous in paying you back for your offense than for your good deed]."

This decency, expressed in conventional terms, has previously enabled Dom Juan, in a cynical burlesque of the same style, to render Carlos laughable in his solemnity. As Carlos, ignorant of Dom Juan's identity, is beginning an unfavorable description of the man he is seeking, Dom Juan interrupts to say that his honor does not permit him to hear evil spoken of this friend of his, continuing: "Il ne saurait se battre que je ne me batte aussi; main enfin j'en réponds comme de moi-même, et vous n'avez qu'à dire quand vous voulez qu'il paraisse [If he has to fight a duel, I shall have to fight it too; but in any case I answer for him as if he were myself, and you have only to say when you want him to appear]." Carlos exclaims against a "cruel destiny": "Faut-il que je vous doive la vie, et que Dom Juan soit de vos amis? (III. iii) [Can it be that I owe you my life, and that Dom Juan is one of your friends]?" In order to do his duty to his family, he must injure the man to whom he owes his life. He is caught between two obligations; one to that which is most personal, literally most vital, to him as an individual, the other to a traditional, impersonal code ultimately based upon, and ultimately expressible as, raw physical force. Dom Juan has rescued him by force, to be sure, but this use of force was motivated, in Carlos' eyes at any rate, by the opposite of force, which is here generosity. Carlos must recognize on the one hand a debt to an individual, illogical, human nobility, and on the other a duty to a codified, impersonal, inhuman nobility. It is a foregone conclusion that he will bow to the latter, fortunate enough if he can make the bookkeeper's compromise which emerges in III. iv.

Carlos' situation epitomizes the dilemma in which all the noble characters in this play find themselves. They are compelled to live according to a social and religious law which is external to them and merciless. Ironically, the law owes its force to their acceptance of it, and its force is such that he who opposes it loses his life, while those who obey it lose the essential human dignity that it is supposed to uphold.

For all but one of these latter seem to us ridiculous in this play, and the evidence leads us to conclude that Molière so intended them. Why else, for example, does he make Carlos, Alonse, Elvire, and Gusman speak the way they do? M. Arnavon, echoing nearly the whole critical tradition, deplores this language, attributing its use now to flagging "inspiration" and again to expedient deference to public taste. He finds, for instance, that it spoils III. iv, a scene "à maints égards cornélienne." [2]

---

[2] Jacques Arnavon, *Don Juan de Molière* (Copenhagen, 1947), p. 325. See also pp. 159, 182, note.

Neither he nor anyone else to our knowledge considers the possibility that the Cornelian situation and dialogue of III. iv verge upon caricature precisely because Molière is writing comedy. *Dom Juan* is a comedy not because it is in prose and contains scattered bits of farce, but because, as seventeenth century comedy should, it severely criticizes certain customs and usages by showing their effects to be ridiculous. III. iv exhibits the futility of Cornelian concepts and the absurdity of Cornelian language in the context of a flesh-and-blood society whose actual speech and conduct largely ignore the substance of the Cornelian tradition.

There is no doubt that at its origin the law which dominates the Cornelian hero was human, a valid expression of a human fact.[3] It is equally certain that in centuries of existence it has lost its human substance. The letter is preserved and obeyed; the living fact has altered so that the letter no longer expresses it. Hence Carlos bewails his "destiny"; his awareness of the separation of letter from substance is acute. Elvire, in anguished confusion, realizes it also. It remains for Dom Louis to spell out the dichotomy in his tirade of IV. iv, drawing together as he does so religious law and social law in one eloquent statement.

While Dom Louis represents the same sets of conventions as do Elvire and her brothers, he speaks a language for the most part different from theirs: the majestic, periodic *style élevé*. He has presumed to tamper with the will of Heaven, to set himself, by means of the formal activity of prayer, above his human lot. He has made prescribed gestures, which he recalls in almost his only lapse into the language of gesture: "J'ai souhaité un fils avec des ardeurs nompareilles [sic]; je l'ai demandé sans relâche avec des transports incroyables . . . en fatiguant le Ciel de mes voeux [I had hoped for a son with unequaled ardor; I asked for him ceaselessly, with unbelievable fervor . . . wearying Heaven by my wishes]." And the fatuity of his presumptuousness has been most forcefully demonstrated by the event: "Ce fils . . . est le chagrin et le supplice de cette vie même dont je croyais qu'il devait être la joie et la consolation [This son . . . is the chagrin and the torture of my life, the very life of which he was to be the joy and the consolation]." He has thus become aware of the painful futility of gesture without substance: his "souhaits" were "aveugles," his "demandes" were "inconsidérées," and he has suffered in consequence—justly so for having asserted his limited individuality against an infinite generality.

He suffers still, for Dom Juan's conduct is still forcing him to act as an individual, "à lasser les bontés du Souverain . . . [à épuiser] auprès de lui le mérite de mes services et le crédit de mes amis [wearying the Sovereign and his kindnesses . . . exhausting in his eyes the value of my services and the credit of my friends]." He knows that sooner or later

<hr />

[3] Rank at its origin appears to have been based on virtue and strength as well as birth. See, e.g., A. Furetière, *Dictionnaire universel,* art. "Gentilhomme."

his credit will be at an end, and he will be able to cease acting individually, to return under the sway of the general law. And he looks nostalgically back to the day when the law was formed to express the sum of individual, real merit, contrasting that day with the present, in which matter is neglected in favor of form and the ancestry of a Dom Juan can be used to cloak his crimes in impunity. "Ne rougissez-vous point de mériter si peu votre naissance? . . . Vous descendez en vain des aieux dont vous êtes né . . . tout ce qu'ils ont fait d'illustre ne vous donne aucun avantage; au contraire, l'éclat n'en rejaillit sur vous qu'à votre déshonneur. . . . Apprenez enfin qu'un gentilhomme qui vit mal est un monstre dans la nature, que la vertu est le premier titre de noblesse, que je regarde bien moins au nom qu'on signe qu'aux actions qu'on fait, et que je ferais plus d'état du fils d'un crocheteur qui serait honnête homme, que du fils d'un monarque qui vivrait comme vous [Do you not blush at being so unworthy of your birth? . . . It is to no purpose that you come from the ancestors you do . . . all their illustrious deeds give you no privileges; on the contrary, the brilliance of them reflect on you only to your dishonor. . . . Finally you must learn that a nobleman who lives wickedly is a monster in the midst of nature, that virtue is the first title to nobility, and that I should think more highly of a docker's son who was an *honnête homme* than of a monarch's son who lived as you do]."

Knowing that orthodoxy largely fails to express human reality, Dom Louis, like Alceste, bitterly deplores its lack of substance, but it does not occur to him, any more than it does to Alceste, to advocate the alteration or the elimination of the gesture to fit the fact. Both men, on the contrary, would alter the fact to fit the gesture. The disillusionment wrought in Dom Louis by Dom Juan convinces him, as Elvire has been convinced in Act I, that the fact of Dom Juan, at least, will not be altered. Like Elvire, Dom Louis threatens to break the *impasse* by punishing Dom Juan; once again the defender of orthodoxy is driven to rely finally for a sure agency of punishment rather upon himself than upon the institutions that he advocates. "Je saurai . . . prévenir sur toi le courroux du Ciel, et laver par ta punition la honte de t'avoir fait naître [I shall manage . . . to have my wrath fall upon you before that of Heaven, and by your punishment to cleanse my shame in having begot you]." He, not Heaven, will chastise his son, thus washing away his shame in the eyes of men.[4] Having castigated himself for wishing to be "plus avisé" than Heaven, he nonetheless places his ultimate confidence in himself;

---

[4] Dom Louis, like all the other characters except the Poor Man and Dom Juan, is very seriously concerned with the preservation of appearances. This preoccupation is a constant and obvious trait in Corneille's plays and generally in *précieux* writings. In addition to being virtuous, one must at all times appear scrupulously correct. Cf. on this point, Scudéry's Mandane with Chimène, Rodrigue, Sévère, Pauline, the Précieuses of Molière, Philaminte, and innumerable others.

and if for a moment (V. i) he is ready to see in Dom Juan's pretended conversion a most unexpected validation of institutional convention, he recognizes at the same moment that he is being worked upon by his paternal "tendresse," and in the midst of his incredulous joy he is careful not to take Dom Juan's stated wish for the deed. He will not rest his final conviction upon Dom Juan's words, but upon such actions as may subsequently conform to those words.

Dom Louis shows, in the suffering imposed upon him by the necessity of acting as an individual, and in the thesis that rank should be determined by merit, a desire to flee the present, or to banish it in order to make way for the past. He represents a moribund generation; and if Dom Juan is guilty of filial disrespect, he is also voicing the profoundest wish of every rising generation when he apostrophizes his father: "Eh! mourez le plus tôt que vous pourrez, c'est le mieux que vous puissiez faire. Il faut que chacun ait son tour, et j'enrage de voir des pères qui vivent autant que leurs fils (IV. v) [Eh! die as soon as you can, that is the best thing you can do. Everyone must have his turn, and it infuriates me to see fathers who live as long as their sons]."

Dom Louis' complaint is the opposite of that of Dom Carlos, for it is directed against the necessity of infringing upon form, whereas the individuality of Carlos would like to break the form in order the more truly to assert itself. The complaint of Elvire is less directly expressed, more primitive, more confused, more poignant. Her religious faith and her social faith are gone; she has nothing left but her passion and her personal will; and she uses her will to sacrifice the last possibility of acknowledging reality, of realizing her passion, to the articles of a faith in which she can no longer believe.

That the illusion of forms is not peculiar to the gentle class is shown in large measure by the second act. The same veneration of the letter of convention, the same failure of the letter truly to express the aspirations of the individuals involved, the same efforts by some to sacrifice convention to individuality, by others to sacrifice individuality to convention, these things appear in a brilliant succession of scenes. They are scenes which are customarily condescended to as the inevitable concessions to farce demanded of a comedian; they function nevertheless as details indispensable to the elaboration of the author's overall design. As in the rest of the play, the language of this act varies from role to role, and within a single role; it provides a wealth of indications to the speakers' characters and to the nature of their beliefs and intentions. . . .

M. Dimanche, like Pierrot and Sganarelle, vainly seeks refuge from his pusillanimity in the conventions. Charlotte and Mathurine are brought face to face with the emptiness of obligation. Dom Louis, knowing that present convention is not a valid expression of present reality, clings bitterly to the convention. Dom Carlos, less experienced, more idealistic, regretfully keeps faith with a code which tends, as he realizes, to annul his merit. Dom Alonse uses the same code to legitimize his brutality. Done Elvire seeks to escape from an almost overwhelming reality by embracing a convention which she knows to be an illusion. Each of these persons comes to acknowledge in his own way that he is compelled by something external to him to belie the truth that is in him.

Such is the effect of Dom Juan's corrosive presence upon his interlocutors; it burns away from the true metal of their individual characters the disfiguring incrustations imposed thereon from without. It strips them of the uniforms of the conventions they profess, revealing them naked to themselves and to us, in their strength and in their shame. Their dignity is for a moment no longer adulterated with subservience; their ignominy is no longer diluted with respectability. One after another, each comes to realize in the presence of Dom Juan the full truth of his own individuality.

What, then, is the Dom Juan who accomplishes this? He is first of all unorthodox. He breaks rules of behavior which are consecrated and venerated, laid down by institutions claiming divinity as their origin, and as their authority for ordering the actions of men. Whatever he may think of their origin, he knows that the institutions themselves are the sole guarantors of their divine authority. Like his father, he "regarde bien moins au nom qu'on signe qu'aux actions qu'on fait"; he knows from his own practice that if adherence to institutional gesture may curb activities decreed vicious, it is also used to disguise and hence to further such activities; he knows that if gesture may make manifest the intrinsic dignity of a man, it is also effective in concealing and vitiating that dignity. Dom Juan is completely impious where human institutions, religious, social, or scientific, are concerned.[5]

The claims of the institutional conventions are that they enable men the more fully to realize the aspirations of human beings by setting them apart from the beasts and making them aware of their domination of the rest of nature and of their responsibilities to one another and to divinity. It is to be noted that Dom Juan nowhere questions the theoretical validity of these claims. The ignominy of his fellow characters lies not in their fidelity to the conventions, but in the extent to which, bending their wills to confine, deform, and vitiate their dignity as individual men, they voluntarily enslave themselves to authorities of their own making.

Thus the great *scène du Pauvre* is the most important key to the play. The Poor Man has withdrawn from society, while retaining the courtesy born of society. He supplies his physical needs by means of alms, in

---

[5] He has been called an atheist for 300 years, but there is no evidence to support the epithet. He scoffs at doctrine and superstition, but he insists that his relationship with divinity concerns only divinity and himself (I. ii and III. ii) wherefore he will not discuss it (III. i). His belief in arithmetic is scarcely peculiar to atheism, and Sganarelle's evidence is neither discerning nor trustworthy.

return for which he prays Heaven for the welfare of the virtuous givers. He thus reconciles Heaven and earth: by submitting to the authority of the religious code he is able to satisfy the authority of the flesh. His words and actions spring undistorted from the depths of his being. He knows what he believes, and he speaks and acts in entire accordance with his belief. His language, while it is respectful and polite, is untainted with formulae. He is not the servant of the cult or of society; on the contrary, they serve him by giving form to his notion of life. He has complete integrity as an individual and he respects the integrity of other individuals. He does not allow Dom Juan to dominate him, nor does he, by remonstrance or other means, seek to dominate Dom Juan. He is the only character in the play who is completely at peace with himself, with the three institutional authorities, and with his fellow men. And Dom Juan, having repeatedly tried in vain to destroy his integrity, salutes him "pour l'amour de l'humanité," for love of the achievement of being admirably and wholly a man.

Reading the play with this scene in mind, we discover a coherent ideological unity in the character of Dom Juan. We find it misleading to conclude that Dom Juan is impious simply for the sake of impiety. Dom Juan is not a monomaniac, as Argan or M. Jourdain or Harpagon is said to be; he is not a *raisonneur,* libertine or otherwise, like Cléante or Philinte. His morality is indefensible in the practical terms of any civilized society; it seems to us inconceivable that Molière or anyone else would find it otherwise. Yet Dom Juan, like that other declared heretic of the following century, Rameau's Nephew, has a positive as well as a destructive function.

Dom Juan says in I. ii that "La beauté me ravit partout où je la trouve [beauty delights me wherever I find it]." He is speaking here of the beauty of women, to which it is his desire to render "les hommages et les tributs où la nature nous oblige [the homage and the tributes that nature forces us to]." For him, obviously, the beauty of a woman is solely physical, a beauty whose appearance can be justly appraised only if the woman is naked, stripped of all possible illusions lent by clothing and manner. He does not value the beauty of appearance for its own sake, however, but as a natural, material form, the domination of which is an activity peculiarly and essentially human. Dom Juan's intention with any woman is not to set her naked on a pedestal to be admired for the beauty of her form, but to take her to his bed so that he may master her as a lover. For him the only valid criterion of beauty is the functional excellence of the beautiful object. Thus he is curious to see the Commander's tomb (III. v), but the beauties of its execution only demonstrate to him the vain glory of its occupant and the modish incongruity of the statue's Roman costume merely provokes his laughter. Behind the objective beauty, behind the conventional trappings, he seeks always the individual person. And that person is indeed a human being only insofar as his will compels the forms and creatures of man and nature to serve him. The ideals represented by the conventions—aspiration to divinity, generosity, mastery of physical nature—are beautiful things because the pursuit of them requires that a man realize in action his potential superiority over the rest of nature. That superiority consists partly in his reason, his ability to create such ideals, and partly in his will, the faculty which enables him to act and to direct his activities toward a specific purpose despite adverse forces of any kind.

In short, for Dom Juan the excellence of humanity consists in a man's realization of his manhood by functioning fully as a man, not as an angel, not as a beast, not in passive potentiality, but in active fact. He must have the aspiration, the will, the knowledge, and the courage actively to prove himself superior to the rest of nature, as well as to whatever conventional opposition he may encounter. This is what the Poor Man does, and Dom Juan wishes to function in a like manner. The key to his character is in the assertion of his will, a point made by Sganarelle shortly after Dom Juan's first entrance (I. ii): "Assurément que vous avez raison, si vous le voulez. . . . Mais si vous ne le vouliez pas, ce serait peut-être une autre affaire [By all means you're right if you say you are. . . . But if you didn't say you were, that would be another matter]." In abducting Elvire, he has had to overcome not only her feminine modesty, but also the religious restrictions of a convent and probably the social restrictions of an engagement to marry elsewhere. In rejecting her, he rejects the demands of religious and social convention. The rescue of Carlos is joyfully undertaken against physically superior strength. In flouting his father, Dom Juan flouts filial obligation and physical protection. In keeping his engagement with the statue, he repudiates his own physical fears: "Allons voir, et montrons que rien ne me saurait ébranler (IV. viii) [Let us go and see, and let us show that nothing is capable of disturbing me]." In giving alms, he salutes the one person in the play whose will drives him against great odds to speak and act exactly as he believes, and who therefore exemplifies fully Dom Juan's conception of human excellence. Dom Juan tells us in so many words (I. ii) that his joy is not in success, but in the process of its achievement; that is, that accomplishment is less significant than function. From this point of view there is no inconsistency between his apparently vicious treatment of Elvire, the peasants, M. Dimanche, Dom Louis, and the rest, and his seeming generosity in giving alms and rescuing Carlos. All these actions are part and parcel of a single-minded striving to incarnate what he considers to be the excellence of humanity.

So, likewise, is his hypocrisy. Dom Juan follows a *carte du tendre* in wooing Elvire, and gives religious scruple as his pretext for rejecting her. He promises marriage to Mathurine and Charlotte. He states his belief to Sganarelle in terms of arithmetic, and uses arithmetical or economic arguments in attempting to corrupt the Poor Man. He explains his motive for rescuing Carlos in conventional social terms. His defiance of the statue is cast as a formal invitation. He gets rid of M. Dimanche by means of formality. He gets rid of his father and silences Elvire by a show of hospitality, insolent and cynical though it may be. His role in Act V, his persuasion of Dom Louis, his rendezvous with Carlos, are enacted in terms of religious convention. In some instances he makes it clear that he is using the conventions with his tongue in his cheek; in others he would have his interlocutor believe that he is taking them seriously. In all cases he adopts the conventions as a sort of protective coloring or camouflage when they would be an insuperable obstacle in any direct path to his objectives.

It is certainly justifiable to see in this play, as numerous critics have done, an account of the making of a hypocrite, the finished product being exhibited in *Tartuffe*. In *Dom Juan* it seems undeniable that the hero is driven to resolve finally upon hypocrisy as the only condition, given his particular society, in which he can realize his validity as an individual human being. It seems certain that Dom Juan does not have Molière's entire approval, but it seems even more certain that he does not have Molière's unqualified disapproval. Of all the characters in this comedy, only the Poor Man and Dom Juan are never ridiculous; their dignity remains intact from first to last.

We conclude that Dom Juan's reason for being is to oppose the dominance of the conventions, to lance and cauterize the ulcerous ignominy of the individual's subservience to monsters of his own making, as he forces Sganarelle to disgorge his lump of stolen food (IV. vii); to demonstrate the insubstantiality of appearances, as he passes his sword through the spectre (V. v). And the bitterest remark of all is the crushing of Dom Juan by the most monstrous insult to humanity in the theater of Molière: that orthodox, inhuman mockery of a man (a vainglorious and defeated man), a mere image wrought according to rule and fashion in cold, rigid, hard, dead stone. Not by accident, especially not for the sake of blind imitation of a nonsensical, if successful, title, is this play *Le Festin de Pierre*, the gala, or, we might say, the triumph, of stone.

A Comic *Dom Juan*

by H. Gaston Hall

A great deal has been written about the *Dom Juan* of Molière, but very little about its comedy, although it is now some ten years since Dr. W. G. Moore asked whether "this work of art [is] better and more fairly interpreted as a comedy or as a satire." [1] Elements of satire there undoubtedly are, as there are wit, *lazzi,* comic reversals, mistaken identity, and the other artful juxtapositions and contrasts which would be expected from so accomplished a master. Credulity, *libertinage,* cowardice, and hypocrisy come under its lash. The question is whether these are only comic elements in a play which essentially is not a comedy, whether, that is, as Michaut wrote of Act I, Molière has attempted occasionally to introduce a comic element,[2] or whether instead we have a play in which these elements of comedy are the natural expression of an angle of vision which is itself comic and not necessarily the less profound for being so. If *Dom Juan* is the latter, it is time to reconsider its structure in the hope that this will bring us nearer to its historical meaning.

Perhaps in the interest of clarity a few preliminary distinctions would not be out of place. Satire and comedy alike deal with the ridiculous side of things. But satire points up comic incongruities in order to discredit particular persons, ideas, or institutions (*"castigat ridendo mores"*), whereas comedy as I understand it presents us with situations which, however satirical, are also correlatives or images of the ridiculous side of

"A Comic *Dom Juan*" by H. Gaston Hall. From *Yale French Studies,* No. 23 (Summer 1959), 77-84. Reprinted here by permission of the author and *Yale French Studies.*

[1] W. G. Moore, *Molière, A New Criticism,* rev. ed., Oxford, 1953, p. 95. Dr. Moore has himself returned to the question in " 'Dom Juan' Reconsidered," *Mod. Lang. Review* LII, 4 (Oct. 1957), pp. 510-17, to which the reader is referred for acknowledgment to the many actors and scholars responsible for a new view of the play. It now seems clear enough that we need neither approach the play through external "rules" nor assume that a subject of known popularity with actors and audiences strictly represents its author's opinions. *La Table Ronde* devoted its entire issue of November 1957, to "Don Juan: thème de l'art universel," but with very little attention to the comic aspects of Molière's play. W. D. Howarth's *"Dom Juan* reconsidered" in *French Studies XII* (July 1958), 222-33, is an able defense of the text of the Amsterdam edition (1683) on which his own edition (Oxford, 1958) is based.

[2] G. Michaut, *Les Luttes de Molière,* Paris, 1925, p. 160.

human nature. It is doubtless because of this that it was common until recently to speak of Molière's "character studies," although it now seems more satisfactory to understand his plays as the artful arrangement of situations which produce comedy. Incongruous situations are selected, or else a situation is made incongruous by juxtaposition with another with which it is logically incompatible, as when upon the sudden reappearance of Dom Juan in II, iv, Sganarelle must reverse himself before the two peasant girls Mathurine and Charlotte ("My master is not at all the marrier of the human race . . ."). Of course, such a scene also teaches us something about the character of Sganarelle. Generally speaking, the more complex the character, the richer the comedy. We have more opportunities for contrast, and a certain resonance may be established.

Thus more of the comedian's art is apparent when we consider that the incongruity here is double, because Sganarelle has pretensions to morality and truthfulness. If then we also recall that here as throughout the play Dom Juan, who pretends to absolute independence, is dependent upon his limited but self-righteous valet, we are confronted with the complexities of the comic in this work. For incongruities exist on many planes: social, moral, political, and religious; and the various norms from which they are seen do not all appear to have had the same value in 1665 as they have today. In this scene, for example, where the norm has not significantly changed, it is easy to see the comic quality of Sganarelle's reversal: in hastily readjusting before his master the mask of his words, he unmasks before the audience something of his real character. The mask *shows* the man.

Here the comic is apparent. Yet when later on in the "scène du Pauvre" (III, ii) Sganarelle again lifts the mask on his real preoccupations ("Come on, swear a little; there's nothing wrong with it"), the comic is sometimes considered out of place. But is this not because our religious and especially our social standards have changed? "Le Pauvre" himself has indeed even been suggested as reflecting a norm, although others doubt that the norms which undergird this play can really be identified, in the absence of a formal *raisonneur,* with any particular characters as such. If we agree with Bergson that comedy results from rigidity rather than ugliness or evil ("plutôt raideur que laideur"),[3] we may see it here in the confrontation of two equally inhuman absolutes, one spiritual, the other material, in which each trips the other up: "le Pauvre" by the real though unavowed dependence on material support which Dom Juan mocks, Dom Juan by that vestige of spiritual life which is pride rather than what he calls "the love of humanity" in order not to mention God. The comic aspect of this meeting is redoubled by mutual incomprehension, and an accompaniment to the double "raideur" of the principal antagonists is developed as indicated above in the very flexibility of

[3] H. Bergson, *Le Rire,* 57 ed., Paris, 1941, p. 22.

Sganarelle. Surely then this is not merely an element of the legend retained, but a great obligatory scene from the point of view of its comic
treatment.

To show the comic coherence of the play as a whole, however, let us
first break a lance against anachronism. For clearly it is anachronism
which led Michaut, in his otherwise admirable study, to consider *Dom
Juan* contradictory in its very presuppositions (p. 149). For there seems
to be no true lack of coherence in the fact that we find "living reality"
captured in the famous peasant scenes in dialect in Act II side by side
with the "merveilleux" of the Statue. Surely these represent different
aspects, not of our "reality," but of reality to the seventeenth century.
One has only to read the proceedings in the trials of a few contemporary
witches (there was such testimony in the trial of Simon Morin and his
sect in 1663)[4] to discover that such figures as the "churlish monk" were
"realities" not only to the Sganarelles, but also to a large number of the
Dom Louis of 1665. As for miracles, who does not recall the miracle of
the Holy Thorn which occurred at Port-Royal March 24, 1656, between
Pascal's Fourth and Fifth *Provinciales?* It is of great interest, as Professor
Antoine Adam points out, that Molière restricts in his *Dom Juan* the
"merveilleux" of the legend.[5] That is in line with the main current of
ideas. But by no means does he eliminate it entirely. Significantly, while
the "merveilleux" is reduced, the supernatural which it represents
("Heaven") is not. The Statue in any case has the authority of legend,
together with the most elaborate literary preparation in this play from
the very first scene, in which Sganarelle anticipates "the wrath of
Heaven."

Let us then accept the assumptions of the play, as in *Macbeth* we
accept both the witches and the drunken porter, or in *Hamlet* both the
ghost and the gravediggers. Then we may see that in refusing to heed
the warnings of Sganarelle, of Dom Louis and of Done Elvire, as in
refusing to accept the *evidence* of the miracle wrought in the Statue,
Dom Juan is comic in exactly the same ways as Orgon when he refuses
to consider the evidence gathered against Tartuffe. "L'expérience a tort."

In this connection it does not seem particularly relevant that intellectually the role of Dom Juan is immensely stimulating. The success
of the legend, one of the rare myths of modern times, bears witness to
that. But Molière's Dom Juan does not "look forward to" the innumerable Don Juans that have followed, although most of these doubtless
look back to him. Like the legendary Don Juan, we all desire now to
enrich our lives by redoubling our experience—by "multiplying our ex-
istences," as Malraux wrote. For this Don Juan makes a convenient

[4] Fr. Ravaisson, ed., *Archives de la Bastille: Règne de Louis XIV (1661-1664)*, Paris,
1868, pp. 227-90.
[5] Antoine Adam, *Histoire de la littérature française au XVIIe siècle*, vol. III
("L'Apogée du siècle"), new ed., Paris, 1956, p. 327.

symbol, as in one way or another do Proteus and Prometheus, Ulysses and Faust. The myth of Don Juan, of an already astonishing complexity, seems capable of further inward and outward growth. Its hero has distinguished himself as an intrepid explorer in that modern region of life, or at least of literature, that modern abyss which is love. He is distinguished also in revolt. It is indeed difficult not to seize upon him as a hero struggling against all the contingencies of the human condition. None of this, however, is the real subject of Molière's play, a point that may be made with the greater conviction because Professor Adam has pointed out that here we do not even have "l'homme révolté" who figures in the earlier *Festin de Pierre* of Villiers (pp. 325-26). Molière's Dom Juan never summarizes like Villiers' the position which his actions imply: "I am my King, my Master, my Fate, and my Gods." [6]

Molière's *Dom Juan* is charged to be sure with social, political, and religious implications of the gravest consequence, which among contemporaries did not pass unnoticed and which are often (unduly?) stressed in performance today. Arnavon in particular emphasizes these when he presents the remonstrances of Dom Louis (IV, iv), attributing to Molière himself the bold ideas expressed by the angry old gentleman: nobility must be deserved, it is conditional upon merit and depends less upon birth than upon conduct.[7] But surely this is conventional moralizing. Whatever "sublime ventriloquism" the scene may contain, it is demonstrably subordinate to the comic.

For by comic I do not understand necessarily the humorous or funny. Progress toward isolating the comic is reported elsewhere in this issue of YFS and need not detain us here.[8] I would only recall that laughter in seventeenth century France was often harsh, cruel, or scandalous. Misfortune, deformity, ignorance, even insanity were often ridiculed. This applies especially to old age, for a stock character was "Géronte." One has only to dissociate one's feelings from the unfortunate in order to be amused by them. "Insensibility," suggests Bergson. Also, is it not just this attitude that the spectator is invited to adopt when he sees that the play which he is about to witness is a "comédie?" In the seventeenth century the word was of course ambiguous, but when to designate a *genre* it is used in preference to "comédie-héroïque," "tragicomédie" or "tragédie," surely it conveys some meaning, if only that the play is not designed to purge our emotions through pity and terror. Thus when Dom Juan wishes his father dead after hearing his reproaches (IV, v), no nausea need overcome us as it does Arnavon (p. 378). The corresponding

---

[6] For Dorimon and Villiers, see the critical editions by G. Gendarme de Bévotte, *Le Festin de Pierre avant Molière*, Paris (STFM), 1907. This verse (no. 342) is also quoted by Adam, p. 326.

[7] Jacques Arnavon, *Le Don Juan de Molière*, Copenhagen, 1947, p. 369.

[8] W. G. Moore, "French Aspects of the Comic," a Woodward Lecture in Yale University Jan. 8, 1959.

scene in Villiers ends in a farce in which Dom Juan actually beats his father (11. 353 ff.). The scene is no more nauseous than Géronte bagged and beaten in *Les Fourberies de Scapin* III, ii, but comic because it is an outrageous inversion of the "natural" order.

It is true that the play ends badly for Dom Juan. Yet however dire the event, it can scarcely move us unless its victim really has our sympathy. Nothing on the other hand seems so likely to lose a spectator's sympathy or to fix his attention instead on the comic incongruity of an unfortunate demise than the cocky self-assurance of a character, in the face of all evidence, that no such fate could possibly overtake him. There must have been something inherently comic about Dom Juan in the seventeenth century as an inversion of common sense: "And will we see a creature's pride today overthrow the order of nature?" asks Dom Juan's father of his son in Dorimon's *Festin de Pierre*. In such a case can we be certain that there was no complaisance in witnessing an impenitent end? The public burning of Morin two years earlier attracted a large crowd; and even though Morin actually repented, the gazetteer Loret reports the incident with satisfaction, finding only the heresy of Morin unattractive.[9]

Assuming then an attitude of insensibility, we do not need, like Pierrot, to effect a rescue of Dom Juan (II, i). We view the shipwreck of his life from the security of the shore, and if we think his *libertinage* absurdly incongruous with the laws of God or Nature (for to paraphrase a famous medievalist, nothing in the play is more natural than the supernatural) we need not be distressed. "Suave mari magno . . ." wrote a Latin poet whom Molière is said to have translated, Lucretius. The English Bible says: "Pride goeth before destruction, and an haughty spirit before a fall." Has this not its comic side? At the very least we may laugh at the final unmasking of Sganarelle's real preoccupation: "My wages!"

But in order to see how the comic and the supernatural are interwoven in this play, let us now return briefly to Act IV. The crux appears to be Dom Louis' famous expostulation, which ends as follows:

> Learn finally that a nobleman who lives wickedly is a monster in nature, that virtue is the first title to nobility, that I consider far less the name one signs than the actions one does, and that I should esteem more highly a porter who was an honest man than the son of a King who behaved like you.

To this tirade Dom Juan replies only: "Sir, if you were seated, you would be more at ease for speaking." Instead of seating himself, however, Dom Louis takes his leave, observing that his words have no effect on his son. To Michaut this is a "serious, indeed tragic" discourse, out of place beside the farcical scene which precedes it. In similar spirit,

[9] J. Loret, *La Muse historique*, ed. Ch.-L. Livet, Paris, 1878, vol. IV, p. 32, letter of Mar. 17, 1663.

Arnavon would let it interrupt the forward movement of the act, treating it extra-theatrically: "As Dom Juan does not listen and affects the most insolent indifference, one need not concern oneself with the situation."

A more humble criticism, however, might have sought the value of these words in their context. Danilo Romano indeed sees neither a political oration nor a "simple fiction of the mind," but a deeply human comic phenomenon transposed in this scene into an image of general validity. The two characters are in a comic situation because they speak and understand in two incompatible planes. A situation which in ordinary circumstances would be tragic here becomes exceedingly comic.[10] If this is in fact the case, we should be well on our way toward restoring coherence to the act.

What we have in Act IV is a series of "fâcheux" developed largely through the application of a single comic process into a comic insight of considerable scope. The first "fâcheux" is M. Dimanche, a creditor, whom Dom Juan resolves to pay with flattery ("it is good to pay them with something"), which he does in the third scene. Sganarelle, however, when faced by a similar claim toward the end of the scene, avoids payment by forcibly ejecting M. Dimanche. As so often in Molière, the man grotesquely apes the master, and the former's actions form a sort of gloss on the latter's words. The mask is lifted.

There is something very similar in the following scenes with Dom Louis and Done Elvire. In Dom Juan's reply to his father, for example, there is a comic adequacy which can only be expressed in terms of its inadequacy in the social situation. This is expressed almost perfectly by Argan in the first scene of Le Malade imaginaire: "Being civil is not everything, one must also be reasonable." For as in the preceding scene the comic lies in part precisely in the contrast between the apparent civility of Dom Juan's words and the real insolence of their irrelevance. Surely there is comic incongruity in this inversion, and it is repeated in the scene with Done Elvire (IV, vi), to whose exhortation Dom Juan replies lustfully: "Madam, it is late, remain here; you will be given the best accommodations possible." Furthermore, lest the implications be lost, they are spelled out by Sganarelle. For structurally perhaps the most significant device of this act is the commentary offered by the valet upon each of the important scenes. In the following reductio ad absurdum of Dom Juan's attitude toward his father do we not see that such an inversion of the natural order rather than the banal (though beautifully expressed) moralities of the old gentleman are the point? Sganarelle asks:

Has anyone ever seen anything so impertinent? A father come to castigate his son, and tell him to mend his ways, to remember his birth, to lead an honest life, and a hundred other stupidities of the same sort (IV, v).

[10] Danilo Romano, Essai sur le Comique de Molière, Berne, 1959, p. 42.

Even were there not a whole literature of sermons and plays in which the generations are at loggerheads we might understand that Sganarelle must be expressing the inverse of a widely shared assumption. The polarity of father and son is complete.

It is not only Dom Louis' words that have no effect on Dom Juan. After the departure of Done Elvire, Dom Juan remarks that in her resignation she again seemed physically attractive to him (IV, vii). It is hardly by accident that Sganarelle interprets, echoing Dom Louis' reply to his son's invitation to be seated: "That is to say, her words have had no effect on you." A common theme is replayed in variations.

The aspect of the comic common to the three scenes has been formulated by Bergson in the familiar observation: "Comic is any incident which draws our attention upon the physical nature of a person while his moral nature is in question" (p. 39). That is in fact exactly what Dom Juan and Sganarelle do in answer to the admonitions of three successive visitors, who are generally agreed to have a certain symbolic value as representing the unavowed obligations of Dom Juan toward his fellows. The last two indeed bring warning of supernatural punishment if those obligations are not soon recognized. Urgent messages are brought, and the gesture or remark of physical import in reply betrays incomprehension. Words spoken to communicate have no meaning, and no doubt is left that Dom Juan is impenitent before Heaven and Mankind.

The contrast between physical preoccupation and moral obligation, moreover, is reinforced throughout the act by the banquet. This theme, which is developed contrapuntally against the visits of the "fâcheux," is finally worked out in a full scene of its own (IV, vii) immediately before the entrance of the Statue. Sganarelle's short-lived tears for Elvire are forgotten as he grabs a mouthful of food and Dom Juan threatens to pierce the resulting "abscess" in his servant's cheek. The rhythmic alternance between comic incomprehension and farcical commentary, which reaches the intellectual limit of comedy in Dom Juan's refusal to heed Elvire, touches its physical limit here. The structure is bold, and as evidence that variety of rhythm rather than lapse of tone is what matters, one may recall again that in the *Festin de Pierre* of Villiers even the reproaches of Dom Louis end in a beating.

Then suddenly in the midst of the farce the Statue appears and speaks. We may ask again whether it is by accident that in its words the comic process of the preceding scenes is reversed, that here we move from the physical to the moral:

Dom Juan, to *Sganarelle*: Take this torch. *The Statue*: One needs no light when one is led by Heaven.

Or do these last words of the act in fact reply to the first, in which Dom Juan gives a "rational" explanation of the Statue's miraculous nod which ended Act III: ". . . it's a bagatelle, and we may have been deceived by an optical illusion . . ."? The Statue's answer seems to bind, by inverting a well-defined comic technique, the short progression of "fâcheux" representing "other people" or humanity in this act to the ampler ternary movement of the supernatural represented at the close of Acts III, IV, and V respectively by the progressive nod, invitation, and fatal hand clasp of the Statue.

We know that in other plays by Molière the inhuman schemes of Arnolphe in *L'École des Femmes,* Tartuffe, and Alceste are foiled by the very natural instinct of love or lust which none of them takes into account. Is it not the supernatural rather than the natural which in the play similarly foils Dom Juan, who is not only inhuman but also atheistic? At most only a vestige of humanity retained in his courage and pride prompts him to offer his hand to Heaven's avenger. Is there not something comic about a man borne off by a force in which he refused to believe? Sganarelle at least says at the close of the play that at his master's punishment "everyone is happy" except himself, and that is because he is defrauded of wages which he betrayed his principles to earn.

The Unreconstructed Heroes of Molière

by Robert J. Nelson

There are, as Bailly has said, no conversions in Molière.[1] To the end, Arnolphe remains a bigot, Harpagon a miser, Jourdain a parvenu, Argan a hypochondriac. Thus Molière remains true to a rule of comedy far more important than the conventions of time, place, and unity considered the hallmarks of classical dramaturgy: the rule of the unity of character. For conversion would take the spectator into affective and moral regions where the satiric purpose—laughter—might be compromised. A repentant Arnolphe, a disabused Jourdain, an enlightened Argan might satisfy our sense of the pathetic or the propitious, but only at the expense of our pleasure. In fact, to make us feel sorry for such characters at the end of the play or to make them share our superior view of their previous conduct would come dangerously close to identifying us with them in that previous conduct as well. In leaving these characters "unreconstructed" Molière earns our gratitude as well as our applause.

Yet, this "non-conversion" disturbs us in three of his greatest comedies: *Le Tartuffe*, in which the hypocrite remains a hypocrite; *Dom Juan,* in which the "sinner" refuses to repent; *Le Misanthrope,* in which the hater of men hates them more at the end of the play than at the beginning. Holding a similar place in the Molière canon to *All's Well, Troilus and Cressida,* and *Measure for Measure* in the Shakespeare canon, these plays might be described as Molière's "bitter comedies." In them, as Borgerhoff has observed, Molière has reversed his usual dramaturgy, unsettling the categories into which we have cast his work: triumph of the golden mean, the importance of common sense, the essentially bourgeois outlook, etc.[2] Usually, the "hero" (in the purely structural sense

"The Unreconstructed Heroes of Molière" by Robert J. Nelson. From the *Tulane Drama Review*, IV, 3 (Spring 1960), 14-37. Copyright © 1960 by the *Tulane Drama Review*. Reprinted by permission of the author and the *Tulane Drama Review*.

[1] "Mais,—et c'est un trait important du génie de Molière,—s'il récompense le jeunesse ou la vertu, et si, par là même, il châtie le vice,—jamais il ne nous le montre corrigé. Il n'y a pas de conversions dans son théâtre, et c'est peut-être là qu'il est le plus vrai." Auguste Bailly, *L'École classique française* (Paris, n.d.), p. 53.

[2] *The Freedom of French Classicism* (Princeton, 1950), pp. 149-160.

of the major role) is a monomaniac, a person lacking what Ramon Fernandez has called "la vision double"[3] or the capacity for what I have described in an earlier essay as "the deliberate multiplication of the self."[4] In a Molière play, the "others" have this capacity: the Agnèses. the Toinettes, the Scapins who use it to check the effects of the principal character's monomania. "The true hero of a comedy," I wrote in that essay, "is, in fact, the 'others' and their view ought more appropriately be compared with that of the tragic hero in any discussion of the tragic and the comic. . . . The comic 'others' are ready to assume a mask, they are willing to play a double game. The central figure (an Argan, an Harpagon) simply cannot play such a game, for he does not know of its possibility. Ironically, the tragic hero yearns for the singleness of vision of the comic figure, for whom appearance and reality coincide. However, if the tragic figure and the comic 'others' are alike in their doubleness of vision, they differ in the very essence of that vision: where the tragic hero sees discrepancy and even duplicity, the comic 'others' see combination and complementarity: of the social and the natural, of the logical and the illogical, of the conditioned and the instinctive, of the material and the spiritual."[5] Through the use of mask or ruse the "others" usually get the upper hand over the monomaniacal figure. However, in *Le Tartuffe* the unscrupulous Tartuffe also possesses the usually commendable "double vision." Indeed, short of the King's intervention, his wiles prove more effective than those of the "others" (Elmire, Dorine). In *Dom Juan,* throughout much of the play, the relationship between the "hero" and the "others" is turned completely inside out: aware of the doubleness of vision of the "others," Dom Juan asserts the moral superiority of his single vision and, in spite of a complex departure from it himself, succeeds in imposing it upon the spectator if not upon the "others." Finally, in *Le Misanthrope* as in *Dom Juan,* the monomaniac, though fully aware of doubleness, tries to impose his single vision upon the double vision of the "others." However, unlike Dom Juan, Alceste does not find ultimate victory in the very face of defeat.

These three plays are marked by a questioning and at times aggressive outlook and their dates suggest that the outlook was an enduring one: *Le Tartuffe* (in its first version during the festivities at Versailles) dates from May 1664; *Dom Juan* from February 1665; *Le Misanthrope* from June 1666. Only *L'Amour médecin* (September 1665) interrupts this mood, a fact to which I shall return. Whatever causes account for this mood (professional bitterness at the prudish criticism of *L'École*

---

[3] *La Vie de Molière* (Paris, 1929), p. 136. Fernandez defines the concept in slightly different terms, pp. 74-77.

[4] *Play Within a Play: The Dramatist's Conception of His Art: Shakespeare to Anouilh* (New Haven, 1958), p. 69.

[5] Nelson, p. 74.

des femmes; personal unhappiness because of marriage difficulties, etc.) the outlook itself, the patent reversal of dramaturgy and the chronology of the plays suggest that at this stage of his career Molière sees in a different light the relationship between appearance and reality, the theme which Lionel Trilling has described as the essential theme of all literature.[6] I should now like to look at Molière's "review" of this theme in some detail, in order to assess its meaning for Molière's art in particular and for comic theory in general.

I. *Le Tartuffe*

Though Molière has divided the limelight between the Impostor and his victim, the play can still be inserted into the typical formula of Molière dramaturgy: the monomaniac (Orgon) is the butt of the satire and the entire action is organized around the effort to break down his fanatical devotion to Tartuffe. The play thus resembles the very last, *Le Malade imaginaire*, with Tartuffe corresponding to the doctors (and possibly Béline), Orgon to Argan, Elmire to Béralde, Dorine to Toinette, etc. Yet, certain aspects of *Le Tartuffe* make it very untypical: the monomaniac is finally disabused—Orgon sees the light about Tartuffe as Argan does not about the doctors; the "others" are saved not by their own wit but by "chance." At first glance, of course, the "chance intervention" of the king need not be seen as untypical: chance also frustrates Arnolphe on the verge of triumph in *L'École des femmes*. Yet, the nature of "chance" in the two plays is profoundly different. In *L'École*, though Enrique's return has been "dramatically" prepared for in Horace's (casual!) reference to his father's expected return (I. iv), the timing of the return could not be more fortuitous. It is conceivable within the terms of the situation that the return be too late—with Agnès wed to Arnolphe. But in *Le Tartuffe* the king's intervention is not really a matter of chance. However dramatically surprising it may appear at this time, it was bound to occur in time to frustrate Tartuffe's ultimate designs. For, the king has been wise to Tartuffe for a long time:

> Ce monarque, en un mot, a vers vous détesté
> Sa lâche ingratitude et sa déloyauté:
> Et ne m'a jusqu'ici soumis à sa conduite
> Que pour voir l'impudence aller jusques au bout
> Et vous faire par lui faire raison de tout.
>
>   (V. vii)[7]

[6] *The Liberal Imagination* (New York, 1950), p. 207.

[7] Molière, *Oeuvres*, ed. Eugène Despois et Paul Mesnard (Paris, 1873-1900), 13 vols. *Le Tartuffe ou l'Imposteur* appears in vol. IV, *Dom Juan ou le Festin de Pierre* and *Le Misanthrope* in vol. V.

[This monarch, in a word, has loathed his cowardly lack of gratitude to you and his treason; and has asked me to accompany him to this house only to witness how far impudence could go and have him make amends for everything he did.]

Like God in the work of Flaubert, the king has been "partout dans l'oeuvre, mais nulle part visible." The appearance of the *exempt* "just in time" is not the mere convention (a *deus ex machina*) it appears to be; the king—through the *exempt*—is a key character and his intervention is not a "convenient" way out of the dilemma but the only way out of it.

Now, this interpretation of the king's role would seem to support those Molière scholars who have maintained against Michaut that a supposed three-act version of the play without the king's saving role did not exist—at most, the three acts of May 1664 were either only the first three acts of the five-act version or simply a compression of the present five acts.[8] Yet, as Michaut has insisted almost in vain, there is nothing incompatible between a three-act version without the king's saving role and the play as we now have it. We need not be shocked that Molière might have written *Le Tartuffe* first of all without a "happy ending," with Tartuffe in full command of the situation, master of Orgon and his possessions. In this case one is not so much shocked by the hypocrisy of Tartuffe as by the gullibility of Orgon. Michaut's brilliant thesis has been rejected by leading Molière scholars for reasons which tell more about the prevailing climate of Molière criticism than they do about the climate in which the play was written. Thus, seventy-five years ago, Mesnard and Despois in their monumental edition of Molière summarized and fixed that didactic approach to the play which characterizes most of the criticism surrounding it. They believed that Molière had envisaged the king's intervention from the very beginning of the play, holding it to the very end in order to show "la fausse dévotion en train de devenir maîtresse de la société avec une entière sécurité d'insolence, si la plus haute des puissances tutélaires ne l'arrêtait pas[9] [false devotion starting to dominate society with completely self-assured insolence, if the highest protective power did not stop it]." The plural "puissances tutélaires" is revealing, casting as it does the absolute power of the king in the anonymous functions of modern theories of government, robbing the act of its personal providential character and of its status as a tribute to Molière's patron, Louis XIV. Again, Lancaster, while accepting the possible existence of a completed three-act version, includes

[8] See G. Michaut, *Les Luttes de Molière* (Paris, 1925). For a review of theories on the first version see Henry Carrington Lancaster, *A History of French Dramatic Literature in the Seventeenth Century: Part Three—The Period of Molière* (Baltimore, 1936), II, 620-623.

[9] Molière, *Oeuvres*, IV, 276.

the intervention of the king in both versions on the grounds that comedy demands a "happy ending"—a requirement called for also by Mornet (who differs from Lancaster, however, in rejecting the existence of a completed three-act version on purely historical grounds).[10] Finally, the most recent and the most scrupulous of those scholars who have studied the problem, John Cairncross, has rejected Michaut's thesis of a triumphant Tartuffe, although he has reconstructed his own three-act version terminating with the exposure of Tartuffe at the end of the present Act IV. "The *Urtartuffe*, was, it will be remembered, described as a 'comédie fort divertissante.' It could not therefore conceivably have terminated . . . on such a sombre note as the ruin of an entire family owing to the donation or even (if it is admitted that the donation was only added in 1667) on the expulsion of Damis from home and the seduction of Elmire. It is worth stressing the consistency with which in seventeenth century France virtue is always rewarded and vice punished on the stage. Nor is it likely that Molière should have gone out of his way to weaken his hand in dealing with the dévots by so obviously running counter to the accepted convention." [11] One senses behind these and similar objections the didactic view of Molière as a judge handing out rewards and punishments in his "lecture plays." (There is, too, perhaps an unconscious fear of facing up to the fundamentally tragic bases of satire, a notion to which I shall return here.) Evidently, if we accept the widespread view of Molière as a social satirist with a bourgeois outlook, it is difficult to conceive of him writing such a "vicious" play as a *Le Tartuffe* without the rescue of Orgon by "tutelary" intervention of some kind.

However, certain critics have discovered in the great comedian not a bourgeois but an aristocratic poet in whom cruelty toward the Prud'-hommes is a marked trait. Such a poet could write a *Tartuffe* showing

---

[10] *History: Part Three*, II, 622.

[11] It is impossible within this short article to reply in detail to Cairncross's intricate argument. However, it might be noted that the "donation" is not so arbitrarily inserted as the critic would have us believe. If the reference to it in IV. i does indeed smack of "patchwork," that in III. vii, to borrow Cairncross's criterion, flows quite naturally out of the situation. That the versification in III. vii "may not be of the strongest" is not only debatable—it is irrelevant. As for Cairncross's reconstruction of the end of the play, there is as much reason to believe that Tartuffe is triumphant at the end of IV as that he is not: what greater way to underscore his villainy than to show him casting Orgon out of his own house even after he has been "unmasked" in the act of seducing Elmire. Again, it is true that Michaut weakens his argument by insisting on Elmire's penchant for Tartuffe, but Cairncross himself follows Michaut in seeing greed rather than lechery as the hypocrite's principal motive. Finally, Cairncross fails to grasp the esthetic significance of the festival atmosphere in which the first *Le Tartuffe* was played. Whether triumphant at the end of III as Michaut conjectured or at the end of IV, as I conjecture modifying Cairncross, the sting is taken out of Tartuffe's triumph by the king's laughter. See John Cairncross, *New Light on Molière: Tartuffe; Élomire hypocondre* (Paris, 1956).

the impostor triumphant at the end; such a *Tartuffe* would make negatively the same point that the present version makes positively: the king
is as powerful in the moral realm as in the physical. In laughing at
Orgon, helpless at the hands of Tartuffe, the king in no way approves
of the unscrupulous Tartuffe. On such an occasion the king can enjoy
undiluted the pleasure of laughing at that figure who almost everywhere
in the work of Molière, according to Bénichou, "est médiocre ou ridicule": the bourgeois.[12] Louis XIV did not want to laugh at false devotion
(Tartuffe) but at blind devotion (Orgon). Neither Molière nor the king
had any doubts about the evil of false devotion, but in a version destined
expressly for the king's pleasure there was no need to spell out the obvious.[13] Thus, as Michaut has conjectured, in the first version Tartuffe
probably remained in the margin and the ridiculous Orgon held the spot-
light. A dangerous procedure undoubtedly, for there was no protagonist
on-stage—a fact which provoked the wrath of Molière's enemies, the
dévots, and a fact which might have led Molière to take the royal protagonist out of the audience and to put him into the play itself when he
decided to rewrite it.

Nevertheless, until the "ur-*Tartuffe*" is found (or another reliable
document on the contents of the 1664 performance), Michaut's thesis
must be treated for what it is: a brilliant but debatable conjecture. Yet,
whether we regard the scene of the *exempt* as tacked on to an earlier version or as part of the play in all of its versions, we must acknowledge that
it strikes an unusual, though not necessarily unpleasant, note in the play.
In contrast to the satirical realism of the preceding scenes, it is lyrical in
effect. The speech of the *exempt* is less a reproach to Tartuffe than a
eulogy of the Roi-Soleil. The king is a "Prince . . . dont les yeux se font
jour dans les coeurs"; the king "donne aux gens de bien une gloire im-
mortelle"; with this king "le mérite . . . ne perd rien, / Et que mieux
que du mal il se souvient du bien (V. vii) [Prince . . . whose eyes see
through the hearts of men; . . . 'gives good people immortal glory': . . .
'merit . . . is always rewarded, and he remembers good better than
evil]." The tone of the speech is affirmative, expansive, exultant; if this
king is a *deus ex machina* the emphasis is upon the divinity and not the
vehicle. And it is upon the divinity of the king himself: nowhere in this
speech of forty verses do we hear the king speak in that role traditionally
associated with the Catholic Monarchs of the *ancien régime*: Defender of
the Faith. Nor is the divinity of the god-king Christian in any sense:
Louis's divine faculties of omniscience (the emphasis in the speech on

---

[12] See Paul Bénichou, *Les Morales du grand siècle* (Paris, 1948). Bénichou does not
discuss the content of the first version, but his general theses support Michaut's conception.

[13] There is even a tradition that Louis XIV persuaded Molière to write *Le Tartuffe,*
but this has been generally discounted by Molière scholars. See Francis Baumal,
Tartuffe et ses avatars (Paris, 1925), p. 200.

metaphors of vision-intelligence) and Justice (his reward to Orgon for services rendered and his judgment upon Tartuffe) are not tempered by the specifically Christian attribute of the godhead: Mercy. The king rescues Orgon not out of merciful understanding of his weakness in supporting the Fronde, but on balance: his service outweighs his misdeeds. In short, the king who appears in these verses looks less to the royal saint whose name Louis continued than to the splendid figure of the pagan divinity who was to be the hero of Molière's most emphatic tribute to his royal patron, the Jupiter of *Amphitryon*. However briefly, the denouement of *Le Tartuffe* is marked by the euphoria which pervades the whole of *Amphitryon* and the so-called court plays in general.

Given the essentially lyrical character of the intervention, then, is it surprising that for a number of critics the denouement destroys the realistic focus of the rest of the play? Even if we maintain that the intervention is the only solution for the moral anarchy of "Tartuffism," we cannot help but note that the tone of the denouement does not fuse with the rest of the play. Molière has used a dramatic form inappropriate to his inattention to flatter the king. To recall Baudelaire's division of the Molière canon, the dramatist has used the mode of the "comique significatif" to create an example of the "comique grotesque." [14] Or, more precisely, he has juxtaposed the two modes. One cannot sing the praises of anyone with mordant satire; satire is by definition negative and to sing of glories some other form is required. Earlier in 1664 Molière had begun to work in such a form with *Le Mariage forcé*, his first *comédie-ballet*. Possibly, with the first version of *Le Tartuffe*, he counted on the context of *Les Plaisirs de l'île enchantée*, which included his second *comédie-ballet* as well (*La Princesse d'Élide*), to dilute the negativism of the satire (just as he counted on the "dilution" of the bitterly satirical *George Dandin* in the context of *Le Grand Divertissement royal de Versailles* in 1668). Be that as it may, in the final version of *Le Tartuffe* he has tried with the scene of the *exempt* to "take back" the negativism of the satire— and failed. The "significatif" and the "grotesque" did not fuse and would not until much later with *Le Bourgeois gentilhomme* and *Le Malade imaginaire*.

II. *Dom Juan, ou le Festin de Pierre*

As the quarrel of *L'École des femmes* has already taught us, Molière is not one to back down in a close fight. So, in *Dom Juan*, he gives a fuller, more affirmative expression of the ideals only negatively implied in most of *Le Tartuffe* and brought out briefly in the final scenes of that play. The

[14] In the essay "De l'essence du rire," *Oeuvres complètes*, ed. Y. G. Le Dantec (Paris, 1951), pp. 712-714.

statement is astonishing only if we persist with generations of unsym-
pathetic critics in taking the Dom Juan of the first part of the fifth act as
the same character we see earlier in the play or if we see in the denouement Molière's own punishment of the legendary lover. For Dom Juan
adopts hypocrisy in the fifth act only temporarily and in clear contrast
with his open behavior in the first four acts, where he gives himself only
for what he is. In fact, as James Doolittle has shown in a character-by-
character analysis of the play, it is just this honesty which sets Dom Juan
in such violent conflict with the "others" of this play.[15] But, one objects,
perhaps Dom Juan is honest with Sganarelle and Dimanche and Dom
Louis—but what about his behavior with Elvire and the peasant girls? Yet,
can we really judge these "deceptions" on the same ethical grounds as the
deceptions of Tartuffe? We have only to compare Dom Juan's courtship
of the peasant girls with the nervous, sly courtship of Elmire by Tartuffe
to sense immediately a profound difference between the two "hypocrites."
With Dom Juan, "hypocrisy" is not a matter of ethics but of esthetics: he
is a hypocrite only in the etymological sense of the word: an actor. The
lies of courtship are only conventions of his role in the game of love. The
Charlottes and even the Elvires are well aware of this. However, like many
an actor in this game, they forget or want to forget that the first and most
important rule of the game is that it must not be taken seriously. Unlike
Tartuffe, Dom Juan seeks no victims in his "conquests"—only fellow
actors. Thus, if the other "actors" take the game too seriously, they have
only themselves to blame. That Charlotte and Mathurine should get
burned in this game does not affect us too deeply, for, as even the most
antipathetic critics have admitted, we identify with the appealing Dom
Juan even in disapproving of him. However, the nobility of Elvire's
worldly station and her dignified airs make her defeat in the game of love
seem especially pathetic. Yet, this "grande dame" is less honest with
herself than the relatively simple peasant girls and so deserves our sympathy even less. In reproaching Dom Juan she blames him not for infidelity—she knows the rules of the game too well for that—but, as Doolittle
says, "for his seeming inability to hide it . . . for his silence . . . for his
failure to cloak his action in a set of conventional phrases." [16] For, the
game being over, Dom Juan in all honesty makes the clear distinction
between appearance and reality which the occasion calls for. Indeed, if
his conduct in the courtship of the peasant girls is any clue, even in courtship Dom Juan makes the more subtle but no less clear distinction between appearance and reality which the occasion calls for; we assume,
then, that he acted in the same way in his courtship of Elvire, which we

[15] "The Humanity of Molière's *Dom Juan,*" *PMLA,* LXVIII (1953), 509-534. This
is the most penetrating study of the play to date. However, I cannot agree with
Doolittle that the work has a "perfect consistency and cohesion of characters, ideas,
events and style" (p. 510).
[16] Doolittle, p. 531.

do not actually see in the play. Being pure conventions, the deceptions of courtship do not really obscure the courtier's objective of sensual satisfaction; rather, they "sublimate" animal drives, translate them into human terms. Not that I would minimize the importance of physical possession for this "grand seigneur." Dom Juan is no Marivaux prince wryly delighting in the playing of the game of love for its own sake; his sense of reality is too great to allow that. Nevertheless, Dom Juan is not Lady Chatterley's lover either and to miss the conventionality of his courtships is to miss his humanity.

No matter how much we may ultimately justify the amorous aspects of Dom Juan's behavior in terms of the rest of the action and whatever the emphasis in the legend, criticism of the play has made too much of Dom Juan's "attachments." Actually, much of the action is concerned not with Dom Juan's supposedly unscrupulous wooing but with the shortcomings of the "others" of this play: Sganarelle, who blandly justifies selling phony medicine to gullible peasants on the sole authority of appearances, the doctor's robes he buys (III. i); Dom Louis, who presumptuously identifies his own with God's purposes; Alonse, whose brutish loyalty to the code of honor makes a mockery of that code as it is more sympathetically represented in his brother, Carlos; etc. These self-deceivers remind us by contrast of Dom Juan's chief virtue: his refusal to deceive himself, his intention to give himself on every occasion only for what he is. Nor is this virtue simply moral in character—*vertu*; it is also *virtu*, the manliness of a brave man, as is clearly evident in Dom Juan's rescue of Carlos and in his courage before threats made by the highest as well as the lowliest of powers: the Statue and Pierrot (who are, by the way, linked etymologically as well in the very sub-title of the play: *Le Festin de Pierre*).[17]

Thus Dom Juan is the most authentic of Molière's heroes, a *généreux* in the Cornelian mold who refuses to accept any compromise of his ideal of self-assertion. This affiliation with Corneille inevitably calls to mind Poulaille's thesis, so let me say immediately that I am in no way subscribing to the preposterous notion that Corneille really wrote Molière's plays in whole or in part.[18] Nevertheless, Poulaille, like Bénichou more responsibly, has sensed a kinship between the two writers, one that I feel I should explore in some detail before going on with my assessment of *Dom Juan's* place in the entire Molière canon.

Remembering the parodistic rehearsal of various Cornelian dramas in *L'Impromptu de Versailles,* we tend to read Molière comedy as the very evacuation of "Cornelianism"—nothing, we feel, could be further from its supposed posturings. Yet, both as producer and dramatist, Molière had quite sincerely turned at an earlier stage of his career to the Cornelian mold. Fernandez reminds us that Molière had been formed intellectually

---

[17] As a "stone" Pierrot is only a diminutive, a mere pebble, and so no real challenge to Dom Juan. Also, see Doolittle, pp. 532-533.
[18] Henri Poulaille, *Corneille sous le masque de Molière* (Paris, 1957).

and artistically in the "age of Corneille" and that a tragedy of Corneille accompanied each of the new comedies Molière presented upon arriving in Paris.[19] And most critics agree that this preoccupation with Corneille gives a decidedly Cornelian stamp to Molière's only attempt at a "serious" play: *Dom Garcie de Navarre, ou le Prince jaloux* (first presented in February 1661, although generally believed to have been written much earlier). It should be said, however, that most of these critics feel that the Cornelianism is incomplete or misdirected: the heroine, Elvire, is Cornelian; the hero, Dom Garcie, is not. Fixing an interpretation of the hero which has obtained throughout the history of the play's criticism, Rigal, writing fifty years ago, objected that Dom Garcie's jealousy, unlike that of Othello and Alceste, is unmotivated.[20] Lancaster, following Michaut, regards Dom Garcie as "un maniaque de jalousie," [21] while Fernandez, in the most pointed criticism of the play to date, regards him as an "intrus dans un monde dont il est indigne, ou comme un enfant gâté pour lequel on est trop bon[22] [intruder in a world of which he is unworthy, or like a spoiled child with whom one is too lenient]." Dom Garcie doesn't belong in the same world as Elvire because "d'après les canons cornéliens la jalousie est un crime contre l'amour: elle ravale l'objet aimé et l'amant lui-même, elle donne le pas à l'animal sur l'homme; surtout elle rompt tout rapport entre l'amour et les hauts principes de l'idéal humain[23] [according to the canons of Corneille, jealousy is a crime against love: it lowers the beloved object and the lover himself, it gives the animal precedence over man; mostly, it breaks off all relations between love and the high principles of the human ideal]." The subject, indeed, seems more Racinian than Cornelian, so that Rigal and others perhaps do a disservice to Molière in asking him to justify the hero's behavior: in Dom Garcie, ever ready to accuse his mistress of infidelity, we could read an instance of the Racinian character's tendency to find in reality the confirmation of his own inmost desires—whether it is there or not. In short, intelligence at the service of will or desire. Thus, Léon Emery has been led to describe Dom Gracie as 'un document à illustrer le passage du style cornélien au style racinien de la tragédie. Plus de complications romanesques en dehors des postulats conventionnels que tout le monde connaît; plus de tirades qui se déroulent avec pompe ou qui jaillissent comme des épées nues[24] [a document to illustrate the transition from the Cornelian style of tragedy to the Racinian. No more novel-like complications outside the conventional postulates well known to all; no more long speeches that unfold with great pomposity or that flash like naked swords]."

[19] Ramon Fernandez, *La Vie de Molière* (Paris, 1929), p. 87.
[20] Eugene Rigal, *Molière* (Paris, 1908), I, 130 ff.
[21] Lancaster, *History: Part Three*, II, 539.
[22] Fernandez, p. 89.
[23] Fernandez, pp. 88-89.
[24] Léon Emery, *Molière: du métier à la pensée* (Lyon, n.d.), p. 32.

Yet, in Dom Garcie himself, we are with neither Corneille nor Racine; Molière's attitude toward his hero is very much his own. Though nowhere so subtle as in the great plays, Molière's dramaturgy is familiar enough here. Following W. G. Moore's brilliant analysis of *Le Misanthrope*, we might say that in *Dom Garcie de Navarre*, too, "the successive scenes do not so much narrate events as expose an attitude and a relationship." [25] However, the early play lacks the poetic subtlety and the dramatic complexity (the "suffusion" as Moore speaks of it) of the later one: Molière concentrates too exclusively on a single dramatic device for "illuminating" the central aspect of character (jealousy) which is his subject in the play. Each act is like a little play in itself, but we get the same little play over and over: Elvire assures Dom Garcie that she loves him; he comes upon something (a letter [used twice]; the presence of a "rival," etc.) which feeds his jealousy; she finally disabuses him. There is some forward motion at the ending of certain acts as a secondary character (the Iago-like Dom Lope) or the report of some new circumstance feeds the hero's jealousy, but instead of carrying us along in an ascending dramatic movement, the successive acts remain at the same expository level of dramatic interest. The "surprise ending" is a happy enough one, but rather than being a denouement (in the strictest sense) to the problem of the play, it seems more designed simply to bring the repetitive action to an abrupt halt. Dom Garcie's jealousy never issues in a tragic insight into himself, a recognition of his "tragic flaw." Indeed, his "flaw" is without such universal significance; rather, like the obsessions of Molière's other monomaniacs, it is peculiar, beyond the human as it were. The mechanical, repetitive dramaturgy of the play suggests a quizzical, tentative attitude on the part of Molière in the face of this peculiarity, as if his desire to remain "serious" prevented him from taking the obvious comic attitude which the hero's obsession calls for. Circumstance, not the wiles of the "others" of this play, provides the temporary resolution of the conflict of the play: Dom Sylve, the supposed triumphant rival for Elvire's love, turns out to be her brother, Dom Alphonse. I say "temporary," for here as well, Bailly's "rule of non-conversion" holds true: even this latest circumstance, Dom Garcie admits, finds him "tombé de nouveau dans ces traitres soupçons" and Elvire accepts him "jaloux ou non jaloux."

Given Dom Garcie's character, then, we might see in the play the proof of Molière's "intentional" criticism of Corneille in *L'Impromptu*. Yet, this would be to forget the presence of a truly Cornelian character in the play: his mistress. "Elvire," writes Fernandez, "est une héroïne de Corneille, une cousine de Pauline, un peu à la mode de Bretagne. Toujours, dit-elle, notre coeur est en notre pouvoir, et s'il montre parfois quelque faiblesse, la raison doit être maîtresse de tous nos sens[26] [Elvire . . . is a

---

[25] W. G. Moore, *Molière, A New Criticism* (Oxford, 1949), pp. 82-83.
[26] Fernandez, p. 88.

Cornelian heroine, a cousin of Pauline, actually a first cousin once re-
moved. At all times, she says, we are master of our heart, and although it
sometimes shows a little weakness, reason should control all our senses]."
It is true that even Elvire's _générosité_ is inevitably compromised in the
love she bears Dom Garcie, for, unlike her Cornelian counterparts, she
cannot really be said to find in her lover a perfect reflection of herself.
Nevertheless, as Baumal has argued, her pity is dictated to her by her reason—she recognizes that Dom Garcie's vice is "incurable et fatal"—and
her reason thereby teaches her that she cannot deny her lover the "estime"
she otherwise owes him.[27] Her love as seen in this gesture is not of the
heedless, self-destructive kind in Racine's _Andromaque,_ for example, but
recalls rather Auguste's patronizing and self-congratulatory clemency in
Corneille's _Cinna._ Though she is indeed touched by her lover's incurable
malady, Elvire accepts him because "on doit quelque indulgence / Aux
défauts où du Ciel fait pencher l'influence (V. vi) [we must have some
indulgence for the failings provoked by Heaven's influence]." One owes
such indulgence to the victim himself, of course, but, more fundamentally, one owes it to oneself. Elvire's love is narcissistic.

Molière's serious imitation of Corneille in the character of Elvire
should make us wary of that tradition which pits Molière against Corneille almost as automatically as it does Racine. To link Molière and
Racine in this way against Corneille is to misconstrue both Molière
comedy and Corneille "tragedy." Actually, with his unlimited confidence
in man Corneille is the least tragic of writers. As for Molière, once we
begin to see that not the limiting motions of satire but the expansive
notions of what we can only call the "pure comic" are the real essence of
his work, then we can begin to see his true relation to Corneille. Both the
comedian and the so-called tragedian have an optimistic view of "man's
fate." There is, to be sure, a crucial difference between the two: Corneille's
optimism is cerebral and is expressed as an unrestrained voluntarism;
Molière's is visceral and is grounded in a confident naturalism. In Cartesian terms, if the will follows the intelligence (_entendement_) so closely as
to be identified with it in Corneille, in Molière the will follows the appetitive so closely as to be identified with it. (I am speaking of this relationship in "others," of course. Also just as the will is passional in Corneille, so the appetitive is intelligent in Molière—witness the naturally
wily Agnès and the numerous shrewd peasant types.) There is, in sum, in

[27] Francis Baumal, _Molière, auteur précieux_ (Paris, n.d.), pp. 116-117. To the extent
that Elvire's pity is part of her _générosité_ this virtue is more Cartesian than Cornelian
(see the _Passions de l'âme,_ Articles 185 and 187 in Descartes, _Oeuvres,_ ed. André
Bridoux, Paris: Bibliothèque de la Pléiade, 1952). Pity is not an aspect of Cornelian
générosité, as can be seen most dramatically in Corneille's "hero-villains" (Cléopâtre
of _Rodogune,_ for example). Yet, Elvire's Cornelian pride of station and her sense of
the image she gives to the world are far from the impersonal and self-effacing character
of the Cartesian _généreux._

the two writers a difference in both the psychical functions and in the ends to which man should direct those functions, but in each there is no doubt that man has it within his power to direct those functions to whatever ends he chooses. The difference from the truly tragic sense of human limitation in Racine could not be greater.

And so the failure of *Dom Garcie* is not due to a contradiction between two radically different views of the human condition. True, the play is fractured in conception, but it is fractured in terms familiar to us already in *Le Tartuffe*: Molière has tried to fuse not the tragic and the comic but two modes of the comic—the heroic and the satiric. As with all Molière plays, the hero's obsession (here, jealousy) is not symbolic of irrational, destructive forces which really govern "la condition humaine." Rather, that obsession is peculiar and special—fantastical, as Béralde might put it—and we can accommodate ourselves to it. What makes Dom Garcie exceptional in the Molière canon is that the means of accommodation are not the familiar ones of ruse and wile and justified duplicity, carefully articulated throughout the entire play. Accommodation is possible, rather, because of a frankly "noble" conception of the heroine's character. And, most significantly for my purposes here, that "nobility" is undoubtedly Cornelian.

In light of Molière's demonstrated sympathy for Corneille then, we might take a very different view of the parodistic rehearsals from Corneille's plays in *l'Impromptu*: it is more the director aiming his satire at the acting style of his rivals than it is the dramatist aiming his barbs at the writer whom he had so frankly imitated in his own career. Further, in light of that imitation, Bénichou's interpretation of *Dom Juan* is given an especially Cornelian force: that play, the critic believes, is based "sur la conception d'un héros souverain, dont les désirs se prétendent au-dessus du blâme et de la contrainte[28] [on the conception of a sovereign hero, who claims that his desires are above blame or restraints]." Of course, *générosité* in *Dom Juan* is far more concrete in its expression than it was in Elvire and certainly more so than in any Cornelian hero (although, even in the case of the latter, the tendency to abstraction and introversion has been vastly exaggerated). Nevertheless, the *données* of characterization are the same: self-assertion and self-definition in action.

Yet, this authentic Cornelian hero becomes a hypocrite. Dom Juan is a Molière character who, at a certain point, undergoes a conversion. Bailly's term becomes richly ironic in this play: from an anti-religious outlook Dom Juan pretends to convert to a religious one. Now, from a strictly religious point of view, Bailly's "rule of non-conversion" is sustained, of course: Dom Juan only pretends to be converted. Nevertheless, the rule of Molière comedy is broken: in the very act of pretending to be converted to religion Dom Juan no longer gives himself for what he is; he

[28] *Les Morales,* p. 167.

converts to hypocrisy not in the etymological sense of "play-acting" but in the acquired moral sense of "lying." He ceases to be *généreux*.

Now, it is for this derogation from the purely human ideal of *générosité* and not from the Christian ideal of sincere self-abnegation that Dom Juan is to be reproached as a hypocrite. Christian doctrine has too readily regarded hypocrisy as a vice having particular reference to its system of values. This is understandable: of all vices, hypocrisy is the most fundamentally destructive of any system of sanctions, but especially one of invisible sanctions. The sinner who admits to wrongdoing acknowledges the validity of the moral code according to which he is reprimanded. But a hypocrite rejects radically the whole system of values and sanctions which pretends to reprimand him. Doctrinally speaking, what we might call the true hypocrite does not believe in an ultimate day of judgment and he is incapable of feeling remorse based on a fear of hell, the threat of damnation which is the Christian moralist's ultimate weapon. At most, this weapon can hope to reach only those sinners who might be described as unsystematic or half-hearted hypocrites: the gamblers of the Christian faith who count on weekly confession or deathbed repentance or God's inscrutable mercy to "insure" the risks they run. Such "hypocrites" are unworthy of the name, for, in the very act of hoping to get by the sanctions, they admit their existence. But the only sanctions which a true hypocrite recognizes are of a more practical nature: threats to his physical safety or of an exposure which will make it impossible to continue to practice his duplicity. Since, theoretically, the final proof of exposure depends on the hypocrite himself, on his decision to drop his pose, it is impossible to "catch" a true hypocrite. Indeed, the true hypocrite will turn every attempt at exposure by others to his own advantage. Thus, Tartuffe's attempt to pass himself off as the self-sacrificing instrument of the very power which arrests him reveals the frightening moral anarchy to which a thoroughgoing hypocrisy leads.

"N'aurons-nous donc pas de règle [Will we then have no rule]?" The poignancy of Pascal's question is felt even by that thinker whom we usually pit against him: Descartes. The very founder of modern rationalism required a Guarantor of the truth of his first principles. Like Pascal, though by a different route, he found his Guarantor of moral as well as epistemological truth in God.[29] And Molière, does he too find his Guarantor of Truth in God? One wonders. We may speculate endlessly about the extent to which his conventional deferences to religion (for example, the baptism of his children or the remarks of the first and second Placets to *Le Tartuffe*) reflect a genuine piety. As for the plays, at most they suggest a secularist separation of the things of this world from those of the next and, at worst, from the religious viewpoint, an exclusively human

---

[29] For further discussion of the "God-Guarantor" in these two thinkers see my "Descartes and Pascal: A Study of Likenesses," *PMLA*, LXIX (1954), 542-565.

solution to the moral dilemmas they pose. Thus, in *Le Tartuffe,* the king is Molière's answer to the poignant question of Pascal: he and not God is the Guarantor of Truth. Lest it be objected that, in good monarchical theory, the king is only God's surrogate on earth, I would point once again to the decidedly non-Christian tone of the *exempt*'s speech. In the resplendent image of the king, who restores order and truth to the anarchical situation created by Tartuffe, man, Molière tells us, is his own Guarantor of Truth.

This anthropocentrism, which emerges only in the denouement of *Le Tartuffe,* is the guiding theme of *Dom Juan.* Dom Juan's humanism harks back to the ancient pagan and aristocratic ideal of man as self-sufficient and self-determining. This ideal, which Christianity tried in vain to assimilate, persisted in the ideals of feudalism which were still felt in the seventeenth century. For practical reasons it was unnecessary and for moral reasons unthinkable to the holders of this ideal to use hypocrisy to achieve their ends: practically, their power was subject to almost no checks, since, being aristocrats, they were to be found at the top of the social and political structure; morally, they could not tolerate the thought that any situation could require the *concealed* expression of their power. Obviously, the dynamics of such an outlook are ultimately destructive of the outlook itself: at some point, one aristocrat's self-assertion will run counter to another's. Both theoretically and practically, only one aristocrat can hope to attain to the purest embodiment of the ideal: absolute monarchy. Even this expression of the ideal has proved historically untenable: the self-assertion of the absolute monarch has run counter to the combined assertions of the other elements of society and been frustrated by revolution. But the historical and the political ramifications of the ideal need not concern us here. More to the present point is the moral basis of the ideal: the injunction to an absolute identification between appearance and reality, between intention and deed. In pretending to convert to religion, Dom Juan breaks this injunction. This constitutes his real hypocrisy and his real conversion.

Why does Molière have Dom Juan convert to hypocrisy? Did he wish to appease his religious enemies by "exposing" the legendary scourge of Christian morality? In the Dom Juan who scolds Sganarelle at the beginning of the fourth act, Michaut sees the signs of a bad conscience—as if Dom Juan were anxiously trying to deny to himself the truth of the Christian view.[30] Yet, these transports might as easily be explained as revealing the impatience and exasperation which finally attains a Dom Juan forced to live in the world of the Sganarelles and the Dimanches. It is difficult to be—or to remain—Dom Juan in such a world. In Dom Juan's irritability we get a glimmering of that other Molière hero who finds himself in a world too confining for his noble ideals: Alceste, the

[30] *Les Luttes,* p. 165.

généreux become *atrabilaire*. In fact, one lesson of Dom Juan's hypocrisy seems to be that the only way in which he can fulfill the law of his being —the overriding drive to self-definition in action—is through hypocrisy. Yet, the context of his hypocrisy suggests that there is a higher lesson to be learned from it. For it is a curious hypocrisy which exposes itself even before it is practiced: Dom Juan announces his intention to be a hypocrite to Sganarelle. His servant (and we the audience) thus becomes his witness that the hypocrisy is not "for real." Rather, we learn that it is only a tool to show the "others" the futility and inhumanity of their reliance upon a system of invisible sanctions. In attacking the "dévots" against whom it was presumably aimed, *Dom Juan* attacks the very idea of religion and the social ideas which flow from the Christian religion in particular: the notion of man's nature as fallen from a "state of grace" and the reliance upon sanctions outside of man to regulate his "fallen" nature. Dom Juan's adoption of hypocrisy is a frightening pendant to the king's crushing of it in *Le Tartuffe*. In the latter, the highest example of humanity guaranteed truth and restored order; in Dom Juan, the highest example of humanity abandons truth and disrupts the true order which only he has represented in the play to this point. And Dom Juan is *obviously* the highest example of humanity: in him appearance and reality coincide not only with respect to moral intention and deed, but in moral nature and physical appearance. Dom Juan's handsomeness not only explains his appeal to the ladies—it defines his inner reality: truth and beauty are one. Thus, if the highest example of humanity shall adopt hypocrisy, who shall be the guarantor of truth? If Dom Juan, the enemy of illusion and self-deception in the first four acts, shall hypocritically claim to speak in God's name, who can really be said to speak in God's name? If we cannot trust to the natural appearances of integrity, how can we trust to *artificial* evidences: a priest's robes, for example? Sganarelle's donning of doctor's robes to sell patent medicines gives special point to this question. This is the lesson of Dom Juan's hypocrisy in the larger context in which it occurs.

Nevertheless, we cannot deny that this larger context is itself compromised by Dom Juan's hypocrisy. "I hope you have not been leading a double life," Cecily says to Algernon in Oscar Wilde's *The Importance of Being Earnest,* "pretending to be wicked and being really good all the time. That would be hypocrisy (Act II)." [31] In Dom Juan's compromised *générosité* we see that the only way in which humanity can affirm its self-sufficiency is in an act of pretended dependence; the only way in which man can affirm himself is through an act of pretended self-denial. Dom Juan's good intentions in some larger context notwithstanding, the appearance which Dom Juan gives to the world belies the reality; unlike the Dom Juan of the first part of the play, the one who speaks as a

---

[31] *The Plays of Oscar Wilde* (New York: The Modern Library, n.d.).

Christian convert to Dom Carlos in V. iii does not give himself for what he is. At least in the Christian world, Dom Juan's hypocrisy tells us, there are limits to the power of *générosité,* cases in which it can express itself only by denying itself. This cruel perception borders on the tragic. Yet, the denouement of the play robs this tragic paradox of its force. In refusing to repent for his false conversion both before the specter and the statue, Dom Juan actually repents or "re-converts" to the ideals we saw him uphold in the first part of the play. In "testing" the specter, which Michaut sees as a symbol of Divine Grace,[32] Dom Juan clearly resists God in his most mysterious and supposedly irresistible form. As for the statue, there is a sublime simplicity in Dom Juan's "La voilà" as he gives it his hand. In light of this gesture it is difficult to accept W. G. Moore's view of Dom Juan as "a man who despises humanity, who sets himself apart and above the rest and is thus bound, being human, to fail." [33] Suicide and damnation are the means by which Dom Juan defines the superiority of his purely human ideals over the Christian ideals represented by the specter in their most appealing forms and by the statue in their most terrifying forms. In best Cornelian fashion, Dom Juan uses death as an instrument of self-assertion. In this test with the highest power, the *généreux* proves himself without limits, transcending tragedy not through resignation but through affirmation.

But what of Dom Juan's last words before falling into the abyss?— "O Ciel! que sens-je? Un feu invisible me brûle, je n'en puis plus, et tout mon corps devient un brasier ardent. Ah (V. vi) [O Heaven! what do I feel? An invisible fire burns me, I can stand it no longer, and my whole body is becoming a hot blazing mass. Ah]!" Do they not acknowledge a "tragic illumination" of his "failure?" Possibly, although they do no more than acknowledge the failure and express no particular attitude toward it. Merely recording a physical event, this "illumination" contains no repentance: at most, Dom Juan admits a limitation ("je n'en puis plus") without in any way disowning what he has been able to do up to this point. Indeed, in this purely objective recognition of the supernatural we can see a reproach directed not at Dom Juan, but at the supernatural for using brute force to overwhelm an adversary who has proved its equal in the spiritual realm.[34]

We can understand, then, that in spite of the orthodoxy of the denouement, the *dévots* did not like *Dom Juan* any more than they did *Le Tartuffe.* The manner of Dom Juan's death belies the orthodoxy of the damnation itself. In the language of one of its Jansenist critics, the play

---

[32] *Les Luttes,* p. 182.
[33] "*Dom Juan* Reconsidered," *MLR,* LII (1957), 514.
[34] ". . . the bitterest remark of all is the crushing of Dom Juan by the most monstrous insult to humanity in the theater of Molière: that orthodox, inhuman mockery of a man (a vainglorious and defeated man), a mere image wrought according to rule and fashion in cold, rigid, hard, dead stone." Doolittle, p. 532.

offended "ce qu'il y a de plus saint et de plus sacré dans la religion[35] [everything that is most sacred and holy in religion]." It reaffirmed the "orgueil des grands" against which Bossuet and the Jansenists in particular directed their anathemas: it depicted man as self-sufficient, able to get along without God in order to achieve his fullest dignity as a man. Nevertheless, this heroism is defended with a disturbing aggressiveness. In spite of the good intentions behind it, Dom Juan's hypocrisy strikes a jarring, unpleasant note in the play. Furthermore, the satiric butts of Dom Juan's aggressive *générosité* share the limelight as much as he: like Alceste in the next play, Molière uses this hero as a dramatic lever to force the "others" in all their ridiculousness into our view. Thus, *Dom Juan* shows a lack of fusion similar to that in *Le Tartuffe,* though obviously not so pronounced as in that play. Here Molière has done more than juxtapose two modes of comedy, but, to borrow a metaphor from chemistry, the combination is as yet only a mixture. It will not be a compound until he suffuses it with the poetry of his *comédies-ballets.*

III. *Le Misanthrope*

If Tartuffe is the only hypocrite in a world of innocents, Alceste is the only innocent in a world of hypocrites. In describing the most controversial of Molière's characters as "innocent" I am not implying that he is naïve nor in stressing his uniqueness do I mean to forget Philinte and Eliante. Like Dom Juan, Alceste knows only too well the duplicity of human behavior. He himself compromises his integrity in his behavior with the writer of the sonnet and with Célimène. Nevertheless, to the contrary of the "others" of this play, at the moment of ultimate decisions he upholds the ideal of absolute integrity; his deeds then match his intentions. In his readiness to pay the supreme price "selon les lois constitutives de l'univers de la pièce" [36] Alceste differs from Philinte and Eliante. The latter are but relatively innocent, set apart by the "virtue" of their tolerance from the rigid Alceste, cast very much in their relationship to him as Le Pauvre to Dom Juan.

Isolated from the "others" of this play, Alceste is a kind of Dom Juan *raté,* one seen in the distorting mirror of "la vie mondaine," one who salvages nothing from his defeat at the end of the play. The implicit lessons of *Le Tartuffe* and *Dom Juan,* obscured in the triumphant accents of the final scenes, become explicit in the final scenes of *Le Misanthrope.* The absence of a Guarantor has been remarked and Alceste does not banish himself to his "désert" with the *éclat* of Dom Juan sublimely prof-

---

[35] Quoted by the editor in Molière, *Oeuvres complètes,* ed. Maurice Rat (Paris: Bibliothèque de la Pléiade, 1956), I, 893, n.1.
[36] A concept I borrow from Lucien Goldmann, *Jean Racine: dramaturge* (Paris, 1956), p. 13.

fering his hand to his destroyer. The anarchy of hypocrisy has reached man not in his relations with the invisible but in his relations with his fellow man. In *Le Misanthrope* Molière questions the root idea of society: the good faith of its members upon which the social contract is based. The denouement offers us two symbols of the most somber significance: Célimène telling us that society is committed to doubleness, to a discrepancy between appearance and reality, between intention and deed; Alceste telling us that the correspondence of intention and deed is possible only in a social void.

Alceste's *désert* is, of course, only metaphorical. "On le dit . . . d'un homme qui, aimant la solitude, a fait bâtir quelque jolie maison hors des grands chemins et éloignée du commerce du monde, pour s'y retirer[37] [It is used . . . for a man who, loving solitude, had some pretty house built away from the highways and far from the business of the world, in which to withdraw]." Yet, given Alceste's quasi-religious fervor, the term re-acquires some of its literal meaning, evoking for us those early Christian saints who monastically retreated to the desert in their search for purity. In announcing his intention Alceste is only making explicit what we assume about the other great monomaniacs of Molière comedy: they too go to a desert at the end of the play. Not that the denouement of *Le Misanthrope* simply repeats the lessons of the other plays. We should remember that Alceste willingly banishes himself to his desert; the Harpagons and the Arnolphes are banished unwillingly. Or more precisely, unwittingly. In fact, they have been living psychologically in a desert from the very beginning of the play: the desert of their particular obsessions. Monomania prevents them from effectively participating in society, the arena of compromise, self-criticism, and, to a certain degree, self-sacrifice. What makes Alceste unique among these monomaniacs is his awareness of the compromise upon which society is based. Thus, his self-exile constitutes a powerful doubt as to the value of self-sacrifice for the sake of society. For the first time the self is posited as an equal and possibly superior value to society. Alceste represents that bifurcation of the personality into public and private selves which characterizes man in society and which creates the tensions of "civilization and its discontents." As the demands of society become greater, molding the self to acceptable "norms," the self is forced into its own recesses, into its own "désert."

Of course, in the ideal world of the *généreux,* Alceste would have no problems—were he not so single-minded, paradoxically enough, in his *générosité.* For, in spite of a basic similarity, Alceste differs from Dom Juan in one essential aspect: he is incapable of that esthetic hypocrisy which justifies, from a moral point of view, Dom Juan's behavior toward women. If Alceste is right in his condemnation of many of the forms of

---

[37] A. Furetière, *Dictionnaire universel* (edition of 1690), quoted by Gaston Cayrou, *Le Français classique* (Paris, 1948), p. 260.

society, he is wrong in his failure to recognize the value of the esthetic in the domain of love. There, his integrity dehumanizes him and renders him ridiculous. Does this mean that Célimène's behavior is implicitly justified? Hardly, for her estheticism is only an opposite extreme to Alceste's integrity. She is an artificial character: Half Dom Juan, half Tartuffe. Like the former she plays a role, but like the latter she plays the role everywhere. In Dom Juan, the esthetics of courtship led to sensual satisfaction; in Célimène they are subverted to the purely social: satisfaction is frustrated in order that the game might go on. Her sociability exacts as high a price as Alceste's sincerity. Her "tartuffism" is not thoroughgoing, of course: she accepts exposure, admits to wrongdoing. But in the very admission she remains unconverted: looking forward to the spirit of Marivaux comedy, she believes that everything can be arranged after the damage is done in the simple admission that her intentions were not after all vicious, that it was all only a kind of game—a cruel one, to be sure, but a game.

Le Misanthrope ends in a moral stalemate. It is a comedy without a happy ending, a tragedy without a tragic illumination. Both Célimène and Alceste are presented to us with strong reservations; each is the object of Molière's satire. The play is, in fact, Molière's supreme achievement in the satiric mode. In this mode he invites us to laugh at man's foibles, to delight in the depiction of man's obsessions and pretensions and so to rise above such "vices" in ourselves. Now, it is in this self-protective laughter that we usually locate the essence of Molière's "comic view of life." Yet, it is debatable whether the definition of comedy as self-protective or dissociative laughter is a valid one—at least in contradistinction to tragedy. Satire points up the discrepancy between ideals and performance, between reality and appearance; it emphasizes man's limitations. Indeed, to the extent that in the "non-conversion" of the comic figure a given limitation is shown to be ineradicable, Molière's satirical comedy repeats the lesson of tragedy without offering the paradoxical victory of tragedy: in the very act of perceiving the limitation which is inherent in the scheme of things (fate) man transcends his limitation.

Seen in this perspective, the happy endings of the satiric plays are "smoke screens" to cover up the negative, depressing view of the unreconstructed comic figure who has just been taught a lesson whose point he cannot see. In the euphoria of Horace's union with Agnès, for example, we lose sight of the fact that Arnolphe has been left "holding the bag," we are spared the uncomfortable reminder of his humanity. Traditionally, criticism has tried to escape this bitter lesson by locating the real lesson of the play somewhere in between convention and obsession—in the moderateness of the Chrysaldes and the Philintes. Thus, with Philinte's marriage to Eliante, *Le Misanthrope* seems a typical Molière play, one teaching a familiar lesson: society, the marriage of different wills and temperaments, depends on a spirit of compromise. But is it not indeed a watered-down euphoria which this marriage creates? Eliante, we remember, takes Philinte as a sort of consolation prize. Moreover, far from seeing Molière's position in Philinte's moderation, we might see in it only a dramatic foil which casts the extremes on either side of it in a stronger light. Even so, whether dramatic principle or lesson of the play, this moderation accepts the basically tragic notion of man as a limited creature, ultimately frustrated in his fondest ambitions and his highest aspirations.

Indeed, a professional psychiatrist, Ludwig Jekels, has seen in the climate of comedy the same preoccupation with Oedipal guilt which we have become accustomed to find in tragedy. He reads the ascension of the young in comedy as a "doing away with the father" so that the son can fulfill his wish to take the father's place sexually. In such a reading, the son is the true monomaniac, but he transfers his monomaniacal love rivalry and its attendant guilt feeling onto the father figure. "This withdrawal of the super-ego and its meaning in the ego are all in complete conformity with the phenomenon of mania . . . In each we find the ego, which has liberated itself from the tyrant, uninhibitedly venturing its humor, wit and every sort of comic manifestation in a very ecstasy of freedom." [38] Frankly admitting the Bergsonian echoes of his theory, Jekels says that "comedy represents an esthetic correlate of mania." [39] Yet, such a theory of comedy fails to account for those comedies in which the father figure remains dominant, or in which the pattern of relationships cannot be fitted into the Oedipal scheme. By its very premises, of course, the psychoanalytical interpretation must regard the former types as tragedies and the latter type as nonexistent. Thus, Jekels reads into *Le Tartuffe* a disguised Oedipal relationship: Tartuffe is the son who displaces his guilt onto Orgon. Yet, what would Jekels make of *Dom Juan,* where the "mania" is not displaced but is steadily defended by the son-figure? Indeed, the whole point of *Dom Juan* in Freudian terms is that the son refuses to accept as blameworthy his desire to replace the father and, as I have shown, successfully defies both father figures of the play (his biological father and the statue). Or to take a Molière play in which the father figure remains dominant, in *Amphitryon* we might read the pattern of relationships between father and son figures in two ways, but in each the father-figure remains dominant: (1) Jupiter, without being a clear rival of his "son" Mercure, keeps the latter in his place—a pattern repeated in the Amphitryon-Sosie relationship; or in a truer Freudian parallel (2) Jupiter and Mercure play father figures to Amphitryon and Sosie respectively, displacing their "sons" in the love intrigues of the play. Yet these

---

[38] "On the Psychology of Comedy," *Tulane Drama Review*, II, No. 3 (May 1958), 60.
[39] Jekels, p. 61. The comments on Bergson appear on pp. 58-59.

plays, like the Oedipal comedies Jekel cites, also end in a "very ecstasy of freedom." Obviously, comedy in which this is true is an "esthetic correlate" of something different from mania.

Thus, we can define Molière's "comic view of life" in the Jekelian sense only by dismissing that part of his work in which a different sense of the comic prevails. This is in the so-called "court work," the series of *comédies-ballets* which makes up nearly one-half the canon, but which has been treated as "minor" by the main current of Molière criticism since the early nineteenth century. Essentially liberal-bourgeois in ethos, this criticism has found it difficult to assimilate these poetic plays, created to please Molière's royal patron, into its portrait of the "scourge" of the *ancien régime,* the unmasker of social hypocrisy in a class-structured society, the enemy of all absolutisms in the very heyday of absolutism. Yet, however convenient, the division of the canon into major and minor, satire and poetry, is ill-founded. The entire canon expresses a single, consistent "comic view of life." Like the first *Le Tartuffe,* the satiric plays reflect an aristocratic bias negatively. This negative bias reached its peak in *Le Tartuffe, Dom Juan,* and *Le Misanthrope,* in the period of approximately one year between the first version of *Le Tartuffe* (May 1664) and the completion of *Dom Juan* (February 1665). For, as Jasinski has shown, in conception *Le Misanthrope* belongs between those two plays, Molière having completed the first act before writing *Dom Juan*.[40] All three bitter comedies are enclosed between two *comédies-ballets: La Princesse d'Élide* of May 1664 and *L'Amour médecin* of September 1665.[41] *Le Misanthrope,* with its unhappy ending, is "negative" only in the sense that the positive faith on which it is based is implicit. The absence of a Guarantor of truth in the play does not mean that one does not exist: he is in the audience in the person of Molière's royal patron. Or was to have been, the play having been first shown to the "town" due to the unforeseen departure of the king and much of the court just before the scheduled premiere. Like the plays which immediately surround it, the play was written with the court in mind, Molière actually having read it before its production to members of the court and accepting minor revisions. Rousseau notwithstanding, the stalemate with which the play ends is thus no more of a tragic defeat for man than was the triumph of the hypocrite at the end of the three-act *Le Tartuffe.* In the negativism of this great satiric play we see only the underside of Molière's "comic view of life."

However, the dates show that even while bringing the mode of "le significatif" to perfection, Molière has been experimenting with "le grotesque." The revision of *Le Tartuffe* actually dates from the period of

[40] *Molière et le Misanthrope* (Paris, 1951), p. 47-48.

[41] Jasinski finds *L'Amour médecin* (September 1665) "assez grave et amère sous la fantaisie savoureuse" (*Molière et le Misanthrope,* p. 48). To the extent that this is true, this *comédie-ballet* may be said to show the influence of the satiric mode of *Le Misanthrope* which Molière continues to work on "entre temps" (Jasinski, p. 48).

the *comédies-ballets,* a fact reflected in the imperfect fusion of the two modes in the play. You cannot move toward the "grotesque," you must start from it; it must inform—literally: give form—to the entire work. Of the fifteen plays written after *Le Misanthrope* (including *Psyché*) ten are *comédies-ballets* as against three out of fifteen in the period preceding. The first *Le Tartuffe* and *Le Misanthrope* are the only directly satirical plays between *L'Impromptu de Versailles* (October 1663) and *George Dandin* (July 1668), itself contained in a festival atmosphere like the first *Le Tartuffe.* Remembering that the very combination of modes makes *Dom Juan* problematic, only *Le Médecin malgré lui* (August 1666) in this period comes close to *Le Misanthrope* in the directness of its satire. Yet, like the later *Fourberies de Scapin,* the satire of this comedy is edulcorated by the emphasis upon the instrument of comedy, the wily Sganarelle, rather than the butt, Géronte, and by its ballet-like treatment of physical action as the rhythmic vehicle of meaning. The comedy in these plays is not satire, a species of tragedy; it is pure.

"Pure comedy" shows man not as a creature of limitations but of possibilities. In the "naturalism" of plays like *L'Amour médecin* and *Le Malade imaginaire* we find the moral bases for this confident outlook. In a play like *Amphitryon* the physiological bases of this naturalism become explicit. In celebrating the sexual conquests of Jupiter, Molière is doing more than justifying the love affairs of his royal patron. Such a subject provides the perfect symbolism for affirming a comic belief in life's possibilities, even as death provides a perfect symbolism for recognizing life's limitations. Comic belief rather than comic relief lies behind the laughter of such a play. For all its value, Bergson's theory of laughter cannot explain the comedy of *Amphitryon,* where laughter expresses not a release from forces which threaten to mechanize life but a release of forces which give life. In sexual release there is undoubtedly a sense of physiological relief, but we should be wary of reading into it an analogue of the superior laughter which is the essence of satiric comedy. In the latter, the "life" which is in danger of being mechanized is the artificial, man-made life of society, just as the threats to its functioning are artificial: hypocrisy, pretense, obsession, etc. "Society," to paraphrase the Marxists, "contains the roots of its own destruction." So it is not surprising that Jekels should find that the true psychological climate of satiric comedy is anxiety. However, to the very contrary of the man-made tensions on which satiric comedy is based, true comedy is based on the natural tensions of the sexual act, those from which we can always expect a happy release. For orgasmic release is predictable and inevitable and, most importantly, fruitful. It will go on and because of it life will go on. The psychological climate of true comedy is thus the very opposite of that of satiric comedy: confident rather than anxious, optimistic rather than pessimistic. This is the real meaning of Molière's naturalism, an affirmation of rather than an accommodation to the "facts of life."

This affirmation of nature in its most basic function—self-perpetuation —is heard even in the satiric comedies. Significantly, it is usually a marriage between young people which the socially derived obsession of the central figure threatens: Arnolphe's fear of cuckoldry leads him to raise Agnès in a "social hothouse" where she will be unable to succumb to the court of "jeunes galants" like Horace; the "femmes savantes" would put the library in the bedroom; etc. But nature inevitably overcomes obsession and, seen in this light, the "conventional marriage" at the end is not a smoke screen to conceal the monomaniac's defeat but itself expresses the "pure comic." Our very sympathy for the "others" of satiric comedy lies in their desire to restore the "law of nature," as they abet the young people in their wiles against the monomaniac. The "happy ending" of these comedies is possible only because the natural has been "given its head." Agnès in *L'École des femmes* is a wonderful example of this naturalism: her wiles are defensible because they serve natural purpose, while Arnolphe's are blameworthy because they would frustrate nature. Nevertheless, naturalism is less important in the satiric plays than its opposite: the oversocialization of the central figure. And in certain "oversocialized" figures we see that even the comic instrument of natural wile can be subverted to unnatural ends: Tartuffe and Célimène are the real anti-heroes of Molière comedy, not Dom Juan and Alceste. The subversion of natural wile must be undone and truth of "natural law" guaranteed by a more worthy exemplar of humanity.

Molière's naturalism need not be construed as a classical anticipation of the Lawrentian mystique of sex. Sensualism is not an end in itself. Even in Dom Juan, the legendary lover, Molière stresses the ethical significance of the hero's behavior: the drive toward self-satisfaction, the exaltation of self-reliance, the autonomy of the human. In *Amphitryon* the emphasis upon the ethical becomes even more pronounced. Jupiter's "treacherous love affair" is justified on the grounds that from it will be born humanity's greatest hero, Hercules. This legendary exemplar of man at his best is a worthy son of the Olympian creature in whom Molière is said to have portrayed the noblest man of his age, Louis XIV. In the blinding image of this Roi-Soleil of classical mythology we are reminded of a Pascalian truth without a Pascalian pathos: the order of the "grands" is distinct from the other social orders and the laws of the latter cannot be made to apply to the former. Inevitably, Jupiter's "intervention" into the inferior social order of Amphitryon and Alcmène must be condemned by the laws of that order. But, the king's "self-exposure as a 'hypocrite'" reveals that a higher ethical purpose has been at work. Jupiter's sensual self-indulgence has really been more than that. Amphitryon's body, the physical sign of his humanity, has not been a mere plaything of the gods; it has been their instrument. In the divine purpose (the half-man, half-god Hercules) appearance (Amphitryon) and reality (Jupiter) coincide. Hercules, man at his best, thus stands in stark contrast to Tartuffe, man at his worst; the eulogy of man which we hear only at the end of *Le Tartuffe* informs the entire conception of *Amphitryon*. Against the unconverted monomania of the Arnolphes and the Harpagons, against the thoroughgoing hypocrisy of the Tartuffes of Molière's world we must place the unconverted integrity of the king-figures, who guarantee the truth of the natural order. In its most glorious exemplars, mankind knows no limitations.

We cannot dismiss *Amphitryon* as an opportunistic compliment to Louis XIV nor discount the role of the King in *Le Tartuffe* as a meaningless convention. Molière's king-figures (including Dom Juan) remind us that in both the "significatif" and in the "grotesque" his comedy is pivoted on an axis of faith in man. In its very lack of fusion the definitive version of *Le Tartuffe* arrests the "development" of that faith like a film suddenly brought out of the "dark room" in the midst of processing. For in the truly comic *comédies-ballets* which make up the bulk of his work after *Le Tartuffe* of 1664 Molière is not reversing himself; he is only printing the "positives" from the "negatives" he took earlier in his career. This relation of the "court" to the "town" plays, of pure comedy to satiric comedy, gives special meaning to Bailly's observation that there are no conversions in Molière.

From Alceste to Scapin

by Alfred Simon

I. The Opponent

In the years 1665-1666, any new work by Molière necessarily appeared to be a manifesto and a provocation, even L'Amour médecin, a comedy-ballet that continued the attack initiated by Dom Juan against medical practice. The elementary chronology that places Dom Juan at the center of this polemical tangle, Tartuffe at the beginning, and Le Misanthrope at the end is admissible if one remembers that the Impostor comes to life in 1669, and that Alceste preoccupies Molière as of 1664.

The testimony of his contemporaries as to possible relationships between Molière's life and his works has often been systematically denied. There are those, on the contrary, who thought they detected in his biography the pulsebeat of a man personally involved in his writings. "The highly praised Misanthrope, limited to itself, would not be the masterpiece it is after three hundred years if it were not fed by a reservoir of personal pain, and if we were not constantly aware of this." (François Mauriac)

There is considerable distance between the mania for attributing the syndromes of neurasthenia in Alceste to Molière, and the simple fact of recognizing a personal echo in Le Misanthrope. One is reluctant to hear in Molière's theater the throbbing of a confession, or to recognize the hand of the chronicler. And yet Lagrange, a friend and collaborator of Molière, was not afraid—alluding to Le Misanthrope—of stating that Molière "made fun of his own family affairs in many places in which reference is made to events in his private life," while Donneau de Visé maintains that he "attacked the mores of the period."

THE FACE

To interest the public in the mythical face of the actor is an opportunity denied to the mere histrion, be he as brilliant as Kean. "Insofar as laughter is the singular gift of man," the comic supersedes the subject of the comedy, unless one agrees—as suggested in *La Lettre sur L'Imposteur*—"to look at everything that goes on in the world as the various scenes in the great comedy enacted on earth by men." Since the actor often plays his role for his own glory, the duet between the comedian and the laughing spectator distorts the character—the original center of interest— who is then forgotten. There is less risk of this when the character, the actor, and the creator merge into one.

The public comes to laugh and it is by laughing that it attributes comic significance to the behavior of the actor. In the same way that individuals, once gathered together to become the "audience," are willing to respect the conventions because of which (in a given period and environment) hilarity is unleashed through encounter with a certain type of situation, so the poet relies on a repertory of traditional gags, from the grossest to the subtlest.

However, the most expressive medium for comedy is the face of the man disfigured by the actor. The actor then dissolves in his resemblance to unreal figures and, if the character seems to crystallize, he feels as exalted as a truly great clown on a night when the laughter of the crowd empties him of himself. The creator then tries to recapture himself. A prisoner of the theater for life, he places his destiny in it and seeks in it his salvation.

The destinies of Molière and Chaplin follow parallel lines. Both are victims of their times. Neither one is really loved by the public (which still watches over the "fragile" happiness of the aging Chaplin). And *Limelight* goes as far as *Le Misanthrope* in exposing the man to the judgment of the audience.

THE FÂCHEUX

Le Misanthrope is the culmination of the two themes that run constantly through Molière's theater: the *fâcheux* and the mask. The subject is the frustrated dialogue. The *fâcheux* prevent or interrupt Alceste's confrontation with Célimène:

> Il semble que le sort, quelque soin que je prenne,
> Ait juré d'empêcher que je vous entretienne.

[It would seem that no matter what I do, fate has sworn to keep me from talking to you.]

In a society where love relations are assumed to conform to their public image, the workings of chance dissipate precious solitude. Célimène's
salon is a place of encounter, like the street corner where Éraste waits
for Orphise.[1] In Molière's first comedy-ballet, the *fâcheux* appear one
after the other, display their foolishness, and are only guilty of making
another *fâcheux* miss the passing of the awaited lady. But the smoke of
comedy was already rising:

> Sous quel astre, bon Dieu, faut-il que je sois né,
> Pour être de fâcheux toujours assassiné!
> Il semble que partout le sort me les adresse.

[My God, under what star could I have been born, to be always murdered
by nuisances! It would seem that, everywhere, fate directs them to me.]

Is the situation in *Le Misanthrope* much different? In what way is
Alceste anything more than a little marquis, a bit less insignificant, a
bit more disagreeable than the others? What is he doing in this setting
in which his presence is a useless paradox and a futile provocation?

Molière made a lordly figure of this character, who is closest to him.
But Alceste has in him the same complicity—though purer and more
demanding—that had already united Molière with Chrysale and Sganarelle. He fashions him more painstakingly and creates between him and
the audience that very rare sympathy that brings the spectator closer
to the character. Alceste's misfortunes multiply to a tempo of burlesque
that mocks his seriousness. Over this provocation of mischance his impatience explodes. The vanity of the writer, the pretentiousness of the
two marquises, the gossip of the prude, and even the sagacity of the
friend, all spite his plans and undermine the situation which they burden
with the threat of absurdity. Alceste is vulnerable. The pettiness of his
woes is what unsettles him most of all. His inability to remain impassive
and unconcerned is the root of his trouble.

> Mes yeux sont trop blessés et la cour et la ville
> Ne m'offre rien qu'objets à m'échauffer la bile.

[My eyes are too offended, and both the court and the town show me
nothing but objects that excite my bile.]

The irritation of a thousand annoying details aggravates the two
"chagrins" of his life, which has become no more than one vast misunderstanding. His lawsuit and his love affair are the two poles of

---

[1] In *Les Fâcheux*. (*Trans. note*)

Alceste's misanthropy. Molière allows uncertainty to float over this nasty affair, and his silence on this subject appears to be reticence. Through allusions, we understand that Alceste is involved in some literary activity, that his opponent in the lawsuit is a bigot supported by the *Cabale*,[2] and that he is made out to be the author of a *livre abominable*,[3] an offense serious enough to hang him. In short, Alceste's very civil status is imperiled by this lawsuit, whose purpose and origin are undisclosed. We can well understand his irascibility, paralyzed as he is by an affair (as serious and as complicated as the litigation over *Tartuffe*) which activates a mechanism of anonymous powers and which alludes to Molière through reference to the *Livre abominable*.

In the first comedy-ballet dedicated to them, the *fâcheux* are no more than bores. In *Le Misanthrope* they are responsible for more serious problems. They immobilize Alceste in an impasse, prevent him, in his litigation and his love affair, from attaining an aim that we suspect can be identified with Molière's own. We also suspect that Molière suffers from the same trouble as Alceste. He transforms into pathetic circumstances the insignificant little obstacles he cannot overcome. And so, although admiring Philinte's lucid acceptance of reality, Alceste sees in him one more *fâcheux*. And since every *fâcheux*, hardened in his foolishness, becomes an enemy of Alceste, we see him at odds with all the great eccentrics—Tartuffe, Harpagon, Jourdain—who invaded Molière's theater after the defeat of the man with the green ribbons.[4]

CÉLIMÈNE

The mask goes all the way back to the origin of the theater. In the old tradition of farce, it superimposed itself on docile faces in order to animate elementary types. A face that sees and speaks through the eyes and mouth of another, the mask was at that time symbolic of all comic interpretation. Molière gradually reserved it for certain poetic rituals— the intervention of Mascarille characters and charlatan doctors—punctuated by fantasies of music and dance. Once the separation between the theater and reality was consolidated, a subtler travesty concealed the human face, and Molière was simultaneously confronted with the masks of his plays and his enemies in disguise. While the characters of comedy assume the dimensions of social types, the individuals in society play the roles of the characters. In both cases, however extreme the adaptation, the suppleness of the face and the rigidity of the mask allow for some

[2] *La Cabale des Dévots*: allusion to a conspiracy of bigots who had *Tartuffe* banned and who were enemies of Molière during the better part of his lifetime. (*Trans. note*)

[3] *Livre abominable* was the term applied to one of the books under attack by the *Cabale* and attributed to Molière. (*Trans. note*)

[4] Alceste. (*Trans. note*)

degree of movement between the individual and the character. The whole creation is crowned by an enormous edifice of make-up, the wig: "Ils avont des cheveux qui ne tenont point à leur tête[5] [They have hair that isn't attached to their heads]," says Pierrot, having witnessed the man without a face.

Le Misanthrope is a carnival of these faces detached from souls. If Molière had not borne the brunt of their malice, he would not have tried so hard to destroy them all (even the subtler face of a Philinte) in order to arrive at the soul and vitality of Célimène. Alceste's panic in front of the constantly multiplying *fâcheux* is counterbalanced by Célimène's terror of isolation. "La solitude effraye une âme de vingt ans [Solitude terrifies the soul at twenty]." Is she wrong in bringing her age to bear on the question? Is she that "brilliant insect that destroys a man's life" (François Mauriac), or rather a woman bound by the official code that makes coquettishness a prelude to prudery?

> Il est une saison pour la galanterie
> Il en est une aussi propre à la pruderie.

[There is an age for love, and another for prudishness.]

There comes a time when the coquette gives up the inebriating game of playing all roles at once in exchange for one role alone, that of Arsinoé, unless she has the opportunity of taking life seriously by knowing the love of Alceste. Célimène provides the key to the masquerade. Boredom and bewilderment are the confirmation of her inner vacuity. But her sincerity cannot be questioned. She is exactly what she appears to be. Her only aim in life is amusement. She is devoid of fatuousness and has no illusions. The only one to fall into her trap is someone who willingly covers his eyes and plays blindman's buff. Like Dom Juan, she is provocative (but she only challenges male vanity), and like him, she is a faceless being, therefore maskless. Then Alceste comes along. In order to defend herself, Célimène places between them the cohort of *fâcheux*.

LE MISANTHROPE

On one occasion—in a remarkable scene in the fourth act in which the amorous torment enacted is no longer mere pretense, but a bitter dialogue in which Molière and Armande confront one another under the guise of the characters—Célimène would have been redeemed through

---

[5] In *Dom Juan. (Trans. note)*

Alceste's humanity if the *fâcheux* had not reappeared in the person of Dubois, thus reviving Alceste's obsession of the lawsuit. On another occasion, Célimène, humiliated and abandoned, expects Alceste's judgment, which represents the seriousness of the situation. They finally part without having revealed the secret they might have shared.

If Alceste were not his own mask, *Le Misanthrope* would not be a comedy, and silence would weigh more heavily. The comic is an element essential to the sympathy inspired by the characters. Alceste's sincerity is masked by illness. He is physically incapable of tolerating the slightest travesty of truth. His suffering must indeed have gone beyond all limits for him to propose to Célimène:

> Efforcez-vous ici de paraître fidèle
> Et je m'efforcerai, moi, de vous croire telle.

[Try to appear faithful, and I will try to believe that you are.]

Alceste no longer believes in the face because it is a grimace, distrusts the act because it is a trap, disbelieves language because it is a lie. He initiates a suit against appearances, against the senses that betray the soul, against social life that degrades individual differences through its imposition of cowardly servility. It is only too evident that he should later reject the very usages on which civilization is based. Contrary to the classical ideal of the "honnête homme" which dissembles the individual, he demands the right to reveal himself. The heart and the soul are also part of man:

> Je veux qu'on soit sincère et qu'en homme d'honneur
> On ne lâche aucun mot qui ne parte du coeur.
> . . .
> Je veux que l'on soit homme et qu'en toute rencontre
> Le fond de notre coeur dans nos discours se montre.
> . . .
> Je veux voir jusqu'au bout quel sera votre coeur.

[I want people to be sincere and, as men of honor, not to say a word that doesn't come from the heart. . . .
I want us to be men and, on every occasion, to show the bottom of our hearts in all that we say. . . .
I want to see, by going all the way, how your heart will react.]

"One does not see into the heart." One must nevertheless make an affective choice, knowing that every man is unique.

"I want to be set apart." Literally, misanthropy is the reverse of phi-lanthropy—the cult of anonymity, of generality, of irresponsibility.

"A friend to humanity is of no concern to me." Only friendship and esteem among individuals can build relations among men. The concern with appearances has falsified everything. Alceste can neither accept this deterioration, which Philinte does, nor can he fight it. In spite of his outbursts, he submits to it and enjoys his role of victim. This is his weakness. It poorly disguises a need to love and be loved, which reduces his final decision to a solution of despair. The pursuit of friendship, the desire to be left alone and the fear of solitude, and the presence of im-minent danger, all of this weaves through the play (friend, betrayal, and grimace are the most frequently used words in his vocabulary) and pro-vide a gauge for Alceste's sensitivity—this man betrayed on all sides and crushed by injustice. Conforming in these aspects to the typical Molière character, Alceste does not succeed in fulfilling his condition of responsi-ble manhood. He withdraws into the pouting attitude of a child, which is both moving and embarrassing. Far from discovering the retreat of a mature man in his desert, he will remain in his "dark little corner with his black mood."

THE IMPASSE

Alceste's protestations may appear theoretical and inconsequential. He reprimands his age for its mores without questioning the root of the evil. His nobility of heart does not lead him to any commitment. It would seem that Molière, afraid that Alceste would carry him even farther than Tartuffe and Dom Juan, retreats. After giving contemporary significance to plots that the Italian theater had treated as inoffensive farces, he holds back a character that threatens to become compromising. In a statement to the world, the play condemns the age by reducing the hero to failure and retreat.

Alceste does no more than withdraw from a game whose rules he rejects. He does not tell all, but his reticence is striking enough to reveal, behind the façade of comedy, a decisive trial whose verdict has not been handed down. The case of *Le Misanthrope* remains forever open. Be-neath the charges made by the comedy, graver issues are discernible.

A popular author maintained in a discussion with Louis Jouvet that the scene of the poor man in *Dom Juan* "is left hanging. There was a chance for a marvelous development at that point and at many others as well. Instead it is botched." La Bruyère found Tartuffe too sketchy and so corrected him in the character of Onuphre. Onuphre is subtle but less dangerous than Tartuffe. And we are fully aware of what our playwrights can do with the possibilities suggested in Molière.

When Alceste replies to Oronte's sonnet, which the audience doubtless found charming, with the imitation of a popular song, one sees in his vehemence the protest of the author against the vilification of art by those who, in the name of their high birth, pride themselves on being able to "judge without knowledge and discourse on everything." The court replaced the salon. Molière reserved the premières of his plays for the court. He even found it present on the stage of his theater, showing off and disrupting the performance. On its caprices, its intrigues, depended the fate of a work in which the essence of the poet is identified with the theater and with the destiny of the actors, his comrades in arms. The marquises are no longer the inoffensive puppets that appear in *L'Impromptu*. Acaste and Clitandre, in their complacency, have something rotten and sinister about them. Clitandre, in particular, is a little scoundrel adept in maneuvering through the network of intrigue that allows him to make and break reputations, to win or lose lawsuits:

> Mon Dieu, de ses pareils la bienveillance importe
> . . .
> Ils ne sauraient servir mais ils peuvent vous nuire
> Et jamais quelqu'appui qu'on puisse avoir ailleurs
> On ne doit se brouiller avec ces grands brailleurs.

[Oh well, it is important to be in the good graces of him and his equals. . . . They can be of no help, but they can very well do you harm, and despite any support one may have from elsewhere, never must one have trouble with those big bawlers.]

When he censures all men, Alceste limits humanity to that which surrounds him—the court and its courtiers. What is involved here is not morality but satire that irresistibly leans toward social criticism. Alceste indicts the caste of those in power, the particular regime whose intrigues, frauds, even denunciations are its activating ingredients. He does not spare the reigning power. Bigots and lawyers are attacked as accomplices. Alceste loses his case, but the rascality of his adversary, which includes such means as slander, is officially approved:

> Lui? de semblables tours il ne craint pas l'éclat.
> Il a permission d'être franc scélérat
> Et, loin qu'à son crédit nuise son aventure,
> On l'en verra demain en meilleure posture.

[He? He has no fear of scandal from that kind of trick. He has permission to be an out and out scoundrel, and this affair, far from injuring his prestige, will put him in an even better position tomorrow.]

This is the other face of the famous line: "Nous vivons sous un prince ennemi de la fraude." [6] In this play set among the high nobility there is no mention of the king. The only trait that suggests him is the bragging young fop "loved by the fair sex and in the good graces of the master."

Let us respect this silence, noting only that it hangs as heavily as a threat. Molière is in the king's favor, but in the Tartuffe affair he learns how fragile a thing this is, and soon after sees it volatilize, capricious and haughty. "Kings like nothing better than instant obedience . . . A thing is good only so long as they desire it." [7] Molière alone, in this France that Colbert organized as though it were a royal spectacle, was able to create an art both courtly and popular. Molière's audience was equally balanced—on one side the king, on the other the people. Is he lucid enough to penetrate the sordid truth of the reign, or blind enough to be distracted by the singular favor he enjoys?

Can Molière—a preacher who defends his priesthood, a traditional clown who nurtures a more or less feigned madness, an artist, an artisan, and a servant—move from moral satire to political opposition? The very principle of absolute monarchy makes this leap unlikely, and clandestine hatred, as yet incapable of reaching the king, can only attack Colbert, the principal culprit in this vilification of the nobility and in the subordination of the artist.

In Molière's theater, *Le Misanthrope* is both a peak and a dead end. Out of this accepted impotence, this distortion that prevents Alceste from going on to political opposition out of fear of betraying the theater, emerges the singular beauty of the play. One can imagine a Molière who might have been the accusing and prophetic witness of his age, who might have put an end to the facile homilies on the meeting of art and monarchy. Such a Molière can be seen in *Tartuffe* and *Dom Juan*. But in *Le Misanthrope* he goes further. He gives Alceste a mandate and commands him to divulge his message obliquely:

Je ne dis pas cela, mais enfin lui disais-je. . . .[8]

[That is not what I'm saying, but anyway, to him I was saying. . . .]

---

[6] In *Tartuffe*. (*Trans. note*)

[7] In *L'Impromptu de Versailles*. (*Trans. note*)

[8] A recent Spanish film, *The Death of a Cyclist,* illustrates fairly well this kind of indirect criticism. A disgruntled film-maker succeeded in avoiding official censorship by camouflaging under a sentimental drama and a satire of mores, acceptable to the orthodoxy of the regime, a highly subversive social criticism that may fool the domestic spectator, but not the foreign public (or posterity).

He uses against his times the same guiles as Alceste against Oronte. Then silence and retreat ensue.

> Je n'ai point sur ma langue un assez grand empire.
> De ce que je dirais, je ne répondrais pas
> Et je me jetterais cent choses sur les bras.

[I do not have enough control over my tongue. I could not account for what I would say, and I would give myself hundreds of difficulties.]

The force that propels Molière is so violent that although he makes a lover of his misanthrope in order to tame him, recaptures for him the rhetoric of "ardor" and "love's bonds," and borrows his strongest accents from verses written five years earlier for an indifferent play,[9] he ends by running head on into unmitigated impudence. Alceste and Célimène . . . Molière can never again transmute in them his own torment. Alceste's rupture with society and the century, his retreat into the desert (that some people have taken to be Port-Royal), are for Molière a signal to retire to another desert.

II. *The Providential Scapinade*

Alceste's withdrawal and Molière's resignation are the victories of comedy—a victory at the price of a defeat. A political comedy that recorded the moment when the reign received its mortal wound—easy enough to camouflage for a little while longer—might have corresponded to the political tragedy outlined by Corneille. But politics are considered incompatible with art, especially when they challenge the established order. What audacities beyond *Le Misanthrope* could have been possible without the intervention of censorship, or without confusing the public through too much obscurity? After *Tartuffe* and *Dom Juan,* the comedy of Alceste took hold without clamor or opposition because it has already reached an extreme. The experience of many centuries was needed before the public could see *Le Misanthrope* as something more than a masterpiece of social observation and psychology of the individual. Molière explored the frontiers of the theater and subjected it to an unnatural experience. He won, but with no hope of return. This was a salutary and heroic act, but one that he had to forget lest he join Alceste in a solitude closer to exile.

Molière, traditional wandering minstrel, then finds his true place within the framework of the great reign. Classical doctrine subjects any

[9] *Dom Garcie de Navarre.* (*Trans. notes*)

enterprise to the perspective of royal glory. Political measures, technical achievements, artistic creations, all are obliged to emanate from the genius of one being—not god or man, but the king. When Molière arrives in Paris, the personal reign is about to begin. When he dies, the heavings of an interminable agony are starting. For fifteen years the entire nation basked in the rays of the Roi-Soleil. The few pamphlets that attack Colbert are not to be mistaken for a denial of this unanimity. All the deteriorating agents are present, but the rays are so blinding no one notices them. Colbert imposes his own absolute order on reality, complex and contradictory though it is. The image left to posterity of an oppressively majestic domain in which everything is dedicated to intelligence and pride, and nothing to tenderness, is a price worth paying for the subjugation of the nobility, the blinding of the people, the intimidation of the outside world. Admiration is obligatory. Nothing has any value except through the king's favor. Neither personal initiative nor dissension is tolerated. Art is official. The pomp of monarchy is the uniform of art.

Molière, among the first, experiences the difficulties involved. At the same time as the festivities in Vaux and the *Plaisirs de l'île enchantée* delight this accomplished master of ceremonies, *Tartuffe* shows him how to lose royal patronage, and *Le Misanthrope* is a prelude to silence and buffoonery. Acrobat that he is, he will perform on other tightropes. Servant and friend, but irreverent courtier (see his admirable *Remerciement au Roy*), he seizes on the extraordinary opportunity offered to him by the king. He will consider the court and the pit as the normal components of his audience, and Versailles as the testing ground for the "Comédiens du Roy." Since the king and France are one, in creating a royal theater he will give the age its first popular theater. He will make the heroics of the aged Corneille look superannuated forever. In this light, his fight with Racine seems almost providential.

MACHINES

Architecture, rites: apotheosis explodes amid the geometric perspectives, the trajectories of water, stone, fire, and flora, amid the perfect curves and lines that are immobilized in time by the avenues, the façades, the fountains, and activated in space by nocturnal festivities. In order to introduce without scandal the cult of the Roi-Soleil into the ancient realm consecrated to the religion of the true God, a team of sculptors, painters, and poets chose a mythology previously cleansed of any dangerous paganism, a bloodless allegory, a menagerie of domesticated gods willing to pay all the cavalcades and indignities in exchange for the caresses of lovely ladies and the precious verses of poets. The greens descend steplike from the formal gardens toward the round terrace and the square pools. All the paraphernalia for the festivity is ready. The magicians—Lenôtre, the gardener, and Vigarani, the machinist—set up their walls of greenery, their movable groves of cypress and orange trees, hang the Gobelins tapestries, string hundreds of crystal chandeliers, and "from the end of an avenue comes the whole theater, composed of infinite characters who appear imperceptibly and enter dancing in front of the theater" (Madame de Lafayette). The spectacle is everywhere. The gods turn into princes, the princes into actors. And the actors, mounted on exotic animals or emerging from terrifying machines, carry baskets of fruit so real one would think it artificial. The ladies of the court are ready to sink their lovely teeth into it as one tears into one's vanquished rivals. It is an age of metamorphoses in which the burning debris of Alcina's palace flames in the night winds, and Armande-Venus rises from a shell to pay a compliment to the king. Vaux, Fontainebleau, Chambord, the Louvre, and finally Versailles: allée du Roy, allée de Saturne.

Before long the stage is as grandiose as the reign and its prestige. Along with music by Lulli and choreography by Beauchamp, Molière dramatizes the comedy of royal love affairs and diplomatic intrigues. Through similar irreverence, the libertine and subversive gods justify the king's escapades by ridiculing Amphitryon, and the Sublime Porte adds its grotesqueness to the madness of the *bourgeois gentilhomme* in whom—so whispers the *vox populi*—one is to recognize Colbert. At the same time that he acquires considerable freedom, Molière conceives of untried possibilities for the theater.

Out of the wings, the flies, the squeaking pulleys, the networks of ropes, the tension of weights and counterweights, emerges Scapin, master of ceremonies and manipulator of schemes. A word begins to resound in all quarters: industry, which simultaneously suggests mechanical production and ingenuity of the mind, recalling the machine at Marly,[10] the mechanized sets designed by Torelli, and the knaveries of Scapin. Molière discovers the resources of the "spectacle à machine," to which he adds the final touches when he transforms the Palais Royal in 1671.

As a result of preparing, for the bourgeois' amazement, those endlessly repeated miracles of *trompe l'oeil* and fireworks, the theater will eventually be debilitated by the machine and linear perspective. For the time being, they are excellent auxiliaries to marvelous theatricality. Furthermore, everyone plays an open game. Open at the beginning of the performance and closed at the end, the curtain is accomplice to no trickery. Open scene changes are obligatory, and the machines, far from disguising their technical workings, glory in them.

[10] A famous hydraulic machine installed at the castle in Marly-le-Roi, which brought water to Versailles from underground streams. (*Trans. note*)

Molière, the comic genius, provides his theater with the enrichments of the symphony, the dance, the machine. In the light of these spectacles, often constructed from the poorest available material—pastoral and courtly gallantries—the traditional dissertations on Molière's philosophy appear ridiculous. He delegates his buffoonery to the energies of the musician and the dancer whom he surveys in a supporting role from beneath his clown's mask: Moron in *La Princesse d'Élide* or Clitidas in *Les Amants magnifiques*. He creates masterpieces: *George Dandin, Monsieur de Pourceaugnac, Le Bourgeois gentilhomme, Le Malade imaginaire*. And he goes even further in his projects. Music, dance, machines on the one hand, Tartuffe, Dom Juan, Alceste, on the other, meet with Scapin in this setting that is simultaneously the scene of festivities and a crossroads of encounters, which achieves a compromise between the legendary cities built by Italian decorators of the Renaissance and the ancient fair ground. Scapin has become the orchestra, the dancers, the supreme mechanic: the *ingénieur*. Two steps from the completion of his destiny, Molière offers up his Proteus-valet in homage to the *commedia dell'arte*. With a gaiety enlivened by time-honored gags, Molière appears on this Neapolitan scene as fresh as a water color, as abstract as a blueprint, as open to the breezes as a circus tent. There he meets his twin and his witness in the company of pranksters—Harlequin and Charlie Chaplin.

A descendant of the family of *zanni*, and one of the most obscure, although his twin, Brighella, provided Harlequin with a worthy partner, Scapin waited for Molière to form him. Molière shoulders Scapin's sack, which Boileau speaks of with pedantic contempt. Once the tests are passed and the gags eliminated, he marvels that these two factors should have refined Scapin's body and soul so effectively that his capers and grimaces have an elegance and an ease unknown to Mascarille.

Les Fourberies de Scapin are related to the misfortunes of Sophie, the vicissitudes of Candide, and the tribulations of Charlie Chaplin. In some cases the character undergoes a metamorphosis, in others it is the adventure that deviates. In no case does the hero evolve during the action. Immobilized under his mask, his uniform, and his name, he proceeds by jumps, he exists in intermittences. When he is no longer part of the action, he fades into hibernation or day-dreaming. His domain is hazard, and chance meeting is his fortune. He seeks to recapture himself in his contact with adventure, which is to say with the theater. Vagrancy or a Neapolitan climate are favorable to him. "That day," the chronicle states, "the Tramp [Charlie Chaplin] wandered through the streets of the City." It is precisely during one of these ideal vacations that Octave meets Scapin at the beginning of *Les Fourberies*. He is not, however, a marionette like the others. Let us put aside Harlequin and Charlie Chaplin, those epic adventurers, those vagabonds of the infinite, and look at the passers-by, Mascarille and Sganarelle. They have neither the ubiquity, the density, or the authority of the first two. There is a Mascarille cycle and a Sganarelle cycle. In Scapin's case Molière buries him in an avalanche of gags. He goes wild over this character, he takes him apart, and in the end whisks him out of sight, this jeering facsimile of a corpse on a burlesque stretcher. There is no Scapin cycle; there is only *Les Fourberies.*

On *Les Fourberies de Scapin*

by *Jacques Copeau*

"Molière did not slow down until his last day. . . ." These words from a text by Louis Moland take on a very special sonority with relation to *Les Fourberies* and to the date 1671. Molière's spirit never seemed more lively. And, in effect, his last day was approaching. He was to die two years later.

"The proximity of Italian actors," said Moland, "kept him on the alert, made him always revert to quick action. It would not have taken much for the crowd to prefer to him the mimes and the tumblers with whom he shared the theater of the Palais Royal. . . ."

Which influence is the healthiest for a writer of comedies? That of intellectual snobbery which, in urging him to be subtle, leads him to the strange and sometimes to the absurd? That of a social or would-be social élite which, in lavishing its favors upon him, keeps him rigidly to one manner? Or that of the crowd which, in order to understand, asks that he simplify, even that he somewhat coarsen, the detail and gain in energy what he loses in finesse? Let us not underestimate Molière's tendency to feel and to show himself a "friend of the people." Those people of good stock have for three centuries responded to his friendship.

We know that he liked and associated with the *mimes* and the *tumblers,* that he studied them and thoroughly understood them, that he perfectly discerned in them the extraordinary gift of life which we can in no way imagine, having never seen them on stage, that he drew every possible lesson from their theater, and got his first élan from them. But what we find astonishing is that he never disdained them, even after he had long surpassed them, that he agreed to stay with them on a footing of emulation until the end of his career. And far from diminishing his value, those returns to straightforward playing toned him up and rejuvenated him. Molière was forty-nine years old. His need was not to

seek perfection in all that is "agreeable and subtle." Judging from the
five or six masterpieces behind him, there is no doubt that he carried off
the prize of his art. I believe he was anxious, if not to become dazzled—
which would have been natural—then at least to seize every opportunity
to give new bloom to his gaiety, new timbre and new bite to his lines,
so that on stage he would feel the firmness of his bearing, the agility of
his step and of his leaps. An emulator and an equal of the purest of the
ancients, the author of *Le Misanthrope* and *Tartuffe,* a perfect observer
of manners and characters, he remained haunted—and this is his singular
merit—by a comic poetry of which truth was merely a prop, and whose
fantasy—or indeed, paroxysm—was to strike, by its élan, hidden po-
tentialities and to force man, body and soul, into extreme postures.

Molière was not ashamed of Tabarin, who for him was a source of
life. He gave style to Tabarin. Molière's taste for things primitive and
alive kept him from ever falling into the literary. When he imitated a
work of culture, such as *Phormio,* he knew that he had to look at it from
some distance, and thus recover range, ease, and freedom. He exposed
the subject matter of Terence to the impetuous scenic current of Flaminio
Scala, which stirred it up, unbridled it, and made it breathe freely.
Molière's genius was to illuminate everything. He arranged, condensed,
simplified. In his hands themes took on scope, constructions were tight-
ened and made more dynamic, dialogues became articulate, figures
gained in stature. Boileau said that they grimace. That was because they
are never seen full-face or in repose but in evolution and in perspective,
deformed by the movement that carries them along. The comedy *Les
Fourberies* is a race, a chase: what the English call horse play, implying
brutality and animal strength. In it one finds more of the scintillation
and glitter of young, ardent, bounding, intractable, almost savage gaiety,
than actually comic aspects—at least in the main character. Louis Moland
very rightly emphasized that savagery in such Renaissance comedies as
Giordano Bruno's *Il Candelaio.* It is also in Scapin, that habitual of-
fender and corrupter of youth, that direct descendant of Brighella,
masked in black and dressed in white, "the most infamous scoundrel
that exists," himself descended from Ruzzante's Slavero, who said, in *La
Pionvana*: "As for me, nothing is too much trouble. I am used to quarrels. I must have the two young girls, and if killing one man is not
enough, I'll kill two. . . ."

Molière did soften, in the words of his Scapin, the coarseness of the
slave of antiquity and the violence of the ruffian from Italy. The "crafty
artisan of machinations and intrigues" becomes a character of great
French style. No less gifted in cunning and cowardice than the traditional *zanni,* he heightens his instinctive baseness with a kind of bravura
which seems to parody the intellectual pride of a Dom Juan. Like the
hero of *Le Festin de Pierre,* he theorizes about his own character: he

means to justify his pernicious force, and the consciousness of his real superiorities is expressed with a touch of lyricism:

> . . . la tranquilité en amour est un calme désagréable; un bonheur tout uni nous devient ennuyeux; il faut du haut et du bas dans la vie; et les difficultés qui se mêlent aux choses réveillent les ardeurs, augmentent les plaisirs . . . Je me plais à tenter des entreprises hasardeuses . . . et je hais ces coeurs pusillanimes qui, pour trop prévoir les suites des choses, n'osent rien entreprendre . . . (Act III, scene 2.)

> . . . tranquillity in love is a disagreeable kind of peace; happiness, when it's altogether smooth, becomes boring to us; life must have its ups and downs; and the difficulties mixed up in things awaken our ardor and increase our pleasure . . . I like to undertake risky adventures . . . and I hate timorous hearts, which, foreseeing too much the results of things, recoil from any undertaking. . . .

Les Fourberies de Scapin was performed at the Palais Royal on Sunday, May 24, 1671. It is said that Molière, as a good head of a troupe, wanted his public to remain patient during the rehearsals of *Psyché*, which were about to begin, and that, with an easy play, was preparing a recourse for the possible failure of his big mechanical spectacle before a Parisian public. But it was *Psyché* that had the success. The eighteen performances of *Les Fourberies* did not bring in big receipts. The play was not even given at the Court during Molière's lifetime. And it was not until after his death that it would seem to have gained a popularity in the city that has continued up to the present. From 1673 to 1715 it was performed one hundred and ninety-seven times.

On the occasion of a revival in 1736, the *Mercure* informs us that the actors Dangeville and Dubreuil, who then played Géronte and Argante, *performed with masks*. The article adds as a note: "It is the only play left in the theater in which the use of masks has been retained." The commentary in the edition "Les Grands Écrivains," from which I quote the above note, shows astonishment, but does not contest the idea. It goes so far as to wonder, on the strength of that authority, whether Gui Patin was right when, with a shrug of the shoulders, he discarded the tradition of masked doctors in *L'Amour médecin*. We have said elsewhere, with regard to that comedy, how plausible the tradition seemed to us. It is dismissed on the strange conviction that former stage practices show an almost barbaric naïveté, and that our modern devices prevail over their predecessors as unquestionable "progress" in technique. Nothing is less certain. It is perhaps the contrary that is true. Writers, scholars, and critics condemn the mask as an expressionless instrument. With great assurance, they reproach it with having immobile features. *That is because they have never seen it act.*

A masked actor has far more power than an actor whose face is exposed. The mask lives. It has its own style and its own sublime language. It was not out of ignorance or whimsey that the great Italians of the *Commedia* went back to it, and once they went back to it, giving it up would have meant giving up their very characters. And who but a wretched actor would have behaved like that Busoni—a traitor to his art, I am certain—who, when at his Paris début in the role of Pinnochio he was asked by the audience in the very second scene to lift his mask, is said to have been cowardly enough to take it off. . . . But this is not the place to settle that dispute. Be that as it may, if one grants that Argante and Géronte were played masked, why not grant that all the characters in *Les Fourberies* were also? In 1752 the Chevalier de Mouhy, in his *Tablettes dramatiques,* wrote: "The former use of masks is still retained in this play." I personally have no difficulty in imagining Molière, after his experience with *L'Amour médecin,* taking up the wager to fit out his *Fourberies* completely *à l'Italienne.* Consequently, I can better understand the reluctance of the Court, the early resistance of the public, and Boileau's ill humor.

Boileau got angry. What he remembered from that spectacle were images that had shocked him. We recall the eight lines in *L'Art poétique* which end in a reproach full of affectionate commiseration:

> Dans ce sac ridicule ou Scapin s'enveloppe
> Je ne reconnais pas l'auteur du *Misanthrope.*

[In that ridiculous sack in which Scapin wraps himself, I do not recognize the author of *Le Misanthrope.*]

"That sack" of Tabarinesque farces and Straparola's *Pleasant Nights,* that sack in which Molière was already enveloping *Gorgibus* in 1661, that sack which joins Falstaff's basket in the storehouse of eternal theatrical props—that sack has given rise to conjectures. For Boileau's line is ambiguous. It is not Scapin but Géronte who is clothed in the sack. Many have therefore wanted to correct "s'enveloppe" to "l'enveloppe." But "the author of *Le Misanthrope*" did not play the part of Géronte. He played that of Scapin. And Boileau's line thus remains obscure. M. Paul Mesnard has suggested an ingenious interpretation. In a note in his edition, he writes:

The ragged *zanni* of Callot, in the dance in which he so admirably grasped their violent gesticulating, are shaking round themselves strange fragments of material; but when they stopped their frenzied movements, they could loosen those fragments enough to make a kind of sack showing almost nothing of the shape of their bodies. Seeing *Scappino's* roomy costume, one might get the idea, if one wanted to make a fine distinction, that it *could* possibly be the ridiculous covering in which Boileau, more or less metaphorically, accused Scapin, and the poet who played the part, of having rigged themselves out to the shame of their art.

The hypothesis is tempting. It fits in with Boileau's expression: "s'enveloppe," and brings us back to the vision of a completely Italian staging of *Les Fourberies,* including the costumes and masks. However, M. Mesnard adds:

> But to all appearances, never did Molière's costume even vaguely recall those early Italian types and thus suggest such a comparison with them; it was most certainly to the prop of the Tabarinesque stage, to the real sack used by Scapin for what is probably the most celebrated of his *fourberies,* that Boileau meant to allude.

And, for that matter, it would have been strange if Boileau had not been apprehensive about being misunderstood in speaking of a sack other than the one clearly used in the comedy. One should therefore have to grant that it has an indirect and metaphorical meaning, and believe, with M. Mesnard, that the character Boileau saw disappear in the sack "was not the actor Molière but *the author of Le Misanthrope,* thus falling from the height of his genius."

But there is a far simpler explanation, and one, it would seem to me, that answers everything. It came to me in the most natural way while I was directing *Les Fourberies* for the first time, in 1917. At the beginning of the third act, Scapin is preparing his revenge on Géronte: "J'ai dans la tête certaine petite vengeance, dont je vais goûter le plaisir [I have a little revenge in mind, and I shall take pleasure in it]." He knows the nature of that revenge. He had worked it out beforehand. He already has his sack. The sack is an attribute of farce, just like the bat . . . Géronte approaches. Scapin says to the young people: "Allez, je vous irai bientôt rejoindre. Il ne sera dit qu'impunément on m'ait mis en état de me trahir moi-même, et de découvrir des secrets qu'il était bon qu'on ne sût pas [Leave, I shall soon join you. No one will ever say that anyone, with impunity, has made me give myself away and made me reveal secrets that should not have been known]." As he says that, he is preparing to attack Géronte. What does he do with the sack? *He puts it on.* He makes it into some strange piece of apparel. One would no longer take it for a sack. He will then soon unwind it before Géronte, saying: "Voici une affaire que je me suis trouvée fort à propos pour vous sauver [Here's something that I found, which is just what we need to save you]." This seems to me, for lack of a better explanation, the secret of *ce sac ridicule où Scapin s'enveloppe.*

On *L'Avare*

by Charles Dullin

On what can we rely to assure a performance [of *L'Avare*] that is both alive and faithful? On that unique and unassailable piece of evidence: the work itself. Now if we consider not merely its outer aspect, but strive to see it from the inside, in all its dramatic reality, we realize that the reproaches it incurs come from the fact that most of the time *it is not the play that is performed* but rather *a series of sketches on greed.*

The plot and all the characters are sacrificed to *that of Harpagon.* Didn't I once see, at the Théâtre Français, the play begin with Harpagon's entrance: "Hors d'ici tout à l'heure et qu'on ne réplique pas [Get right out of here, and don't answer back]." Why should people be surprised at not understanding a thing about the conventional romanesque denouement, peculiar to the period in which Molière wrote his play, when they have not seen the charming and equally romanesque scenes that open the play? A lack of balance and an aridity are created which lead to abstraction and monotony. To fill in the gaps, one is reduced to inventing such unwarranted stage effects as that of the candles: Harpagon, during the scene with the constable in Act V, blows out one of the two lighted candles on the table. Maître Jacques relights it; Harpagon again puts it out. Maître Jacques relights it; Harpagon blows it out and puts it in the pocket of his breeches, a part of it protruding. Maître Jacques relights the candle in Harpagon's pocket. Harpagon moves, feels the flame of the candle, puts it out, and pushes the candle down in his pocket.

Here tradition (for it appears that this stage effect belongs to tradition) no longer simply miscarries, it becomes stupid to the point of leading us to wonder whether that tradition is any more than a mere idiosyncrasy passed down from father to son which, instead of serving truth, distorts it, instead of bringing us nearer to it, removes us from it even further.

"On *L'Avare*." From the "Collection 'Mises en scène'" edition of *L'Avare*, mise en scène et commentaires de Charles Dullin. Copyright 1946 by Editions du Seuil, Paris. Translated and reprinted by permission of the publisher. The pages printed here, and translated by June Guicharnaud, are from the Introduction.

If we try quite simply to perform the play, we shall sense, from the very beginning, a bracing element, inherited from Plautus, at the heart of which the action develops. Indeed, we cannot concern ourselves with *L'Avare* without recalling the work of Plautus and its influence on Molière's comedy; for, to my mind, here the question is more one of influence than of actual imitation. Whatever the importance of Molière's borrowings, there is—even more than the situations or the gags—a very definite inspiration that comes from the general tone, the environment—in a word, the spirit—of Plautus' work. The situations that Molière took from Larivey's *Les Esprits,* Boisrobert's *La Belle Plaideuse,* and Ariosto's *I Suppositi* are of value only as transformed by Molière's genius. They have no inner extension in the work itself.

Plautus' climate imposes a certain realism (and realism is never to be confused with naturalism); it leads to familiar relations among characters of the most diverse milieus; it will make us flee abstraction, at the price of coarsening certain details and preferring a little naïveté to too much literary thinking. If we put ourselves back into that climate, we shall more clearly understand characters like Frosine and Maître Jacques —Frosine, because she is the classic procuress, the woman of intrigue, in all Plautus' comedies, as well as a sister to Fernando de Rojas' Celestina; Maître Jacques . . . because in Moliére's comedy he is a hand-down from Latin manners, a kind of freedman, a disguised factotum. The very presence of the garden in which Harpagon has buried his *cassette* recalls the rooster that gave the unhappy Euclio such anxiety by scratching the earth with its claws at the very spot where his crock full of gold was buried.

It is that pleasing fragrance of the Latin atmosphere which remains to us in the transposition made by Molière, situating the action in a Parisian bourgeois home, with a family and a certain style of living. Molière probably knew that typical bourgeois, Harpagon, and perhaps saw something of him. For Molière, who owed so much to the observation of men and life, he who Despréaux called "le Contemplateur" and who in *La Critique de l'École des femmes* himself says: "Lorsque vous peignez les hommes, il faut peindre d'après nature; on veut que ces portraits ressemblent, et vous n'avez rien fait, si vous n'y faites reconnaître les gens de votre siècle [When you portray men, you must paint them according to nature; people want those portraits to be faithful, and you have done nothing if you have not made the men of your century recognizable]," Molière certainly never intended to portray an abstract character. That Latin milieu of *Aulularia,* thanks to Molière's very alive genius, mysteriously increases the impression of power and life which comes through in *L'Avare.* Harpagon is thus inseparable from the milieu in which he lives. If he lives in it *alone,* it is his own fault, and his isolation, which could be tragic, becomes comic precisely because of that heterogeneous milieu and the circumstances and intrigues woven around him.

On the other hand, what violates, as it were, Harpagon's greed and outdoes it? The spirit of intrigue put into the service of love and justice. If one takes away the intrigues, what will be able to combat the vice? Nothing; it remains the victor, which is immoral and contrary to the objective put forth by the comedy.

Performing the play is the one and only tradition in which I believe. . . .

I mentioned elsewhere the importance I attached to the play's plot. I need not recount the play here, but I should like to draw attention to what is generally made to vanish: *the love interest or sub-plot.*

Valère, a young Neopolitan, separated from his family following the same type of social turmoil we are witnessing today, saved Élise from drowning. He falls in love with her and, driven by his passion, takes a job as a steward in the home of the girl's father, Harpagon. Once he has the job, he can keep it only by constantly playing a part.

The young Élise, who aspires to escape from the suffocating atmosphere in which she lives, is sensitive to the adventure's fantasy, and if her natural shyness and modesty do not permit her to exteriorize her passion in the play's opening conversation with Valère, she gives in to it with touching grace in the following scene with her brother Cléante. Cléante loves Mariane with the fire and generosity of his age. Mariane, marked by that feminine ambiguity in which grace does not exclude a certain latent duplicity, moves between father and son, seduced by the son's charm and quite rightly terrified by the fate that threatens her if she agrees to marry Harpagon.

It is against this background of love and intrigue that we shall see a projection of that hideous vice—greed—torment the selfish bourgeois. Harpagon stands out as black against a luminous background of youth and freshness.

If we skip the adventures of the five acts of the play and get to that denouement which almost all textbooks call slapdash, artificial, and out of place, we realize that its romanesque quality is perfectly suited to the beginning. Anselme, the *deus ex machina,* a kind of Neopolitan Puss in Boots, has really no need of being anything but what he is: a pleasant marionette. Played with the heaviness and solemnity that is now fashionably considered the tradition, the end seems long and boring; played with spirit and lightness, it provokes laughter; and that is certainly what Molière would have wished. But in any case, it is essential that it properly resolve the plot prepared at the beginning. . . .

Harpagon. I have perhaps played the part of this character too often to give a sufficiently objective interpretation. Obviously, I see him—as well as feel him—from an actor's point of view. . . .

I emphasized the danger of making the play into a series of sketches for Harpagon. The only way to avoid that is always to keep to the truth in his relations with the other characters, never to ask the question whether he should be dramatic at such and such a moment or comic at another. If one plays out the situations, one will quickly realize that the audience reacts exactly in the way intended by the author. But the role is long and painful; the actor must deal carefully with a progression to which it is very difficult to adhere, because from the very beginning the character is tense, irascible, always on the lookout. It is in the variety of his reactions, in their aggressiveness, often for futile motives, in the subtle variations of sanctimoniousness, naïve trickery, grotesque vanity, cynical egotism, and traits of sordid greed, at the moment chosen by the author, that one must find the nuances, the respiration of the text, and the gasping of passion. Harpagon must almost always have one ear strained toward the garden, while he lends the other to the person with whom he is conversing. He must be perpetually divided between anxiety about what is happening in the garden and the interest he takes in his partner. At the same time, all his feelings of selfishness toward his children, of distrust and callousness against his servants, of gullibility with Valère and Frosine, and his attitude as Mariane's grotesque suitor must be played and spoken distinctly, with the actor wholly expressing himself in each case.

Harpagon often lowers himself to acting a part before the person with whom he is speaking—as, for example, in Act IV, when he makes Cléante admit his love for Mariane. Such frequent pieces of hypocrisy need to be played both in an *exaggerated* way and yet with enough wit and finesse to remain within living truth: this is perhaps the most difficult part of the role.

Such intentionally extravagant details as: "Montre-moi tes mains. —Les voilà. —Les autres. [Show me your hands. —There they are. —Now, the others]." must, in their very exaggeration, remain natural. It is obvious that Harpagon is often deranged by passion. He sees double! It is almost comic pathology! As when he turns against himself in his well-known monologue and, believing that he is catching a thief, grasps his own hand. The actor must avoid treating all such *lazzi* casually and conventionally.

As for the monologue, it is a question of the actor's temperament. Here, Harpagon is sincere: the excess of his despair, the sinister pretence when he acts out his own death, his harangue to the spectators—in such cases, the more sincere he is, the more laughter he will provoke. But to avoid the monologue's degenerating into a piece of bravura, it must not be understood or played separately but, on the contrary, should be connected—by the rhythm and by maintaining the intensity of passion—to the scenes which open Act V. Harpagon's despair begins with his first shouts of "Au voleur!" and he does not calm down until his *cassette* is returned to him. I am indicating a moment that is difficult to play during the time that the explanations of "recognition" last in Act V. As long as I tried to fill that ending with stage effects, in better taste than that of the candles, but artificial all the same, I felt a void and so did the audience; the day I met the situation with the character's inner passion, I was no longer uncomfortable, and I noticed that all the other actors were also at their ease.

The Doctor's Curse

by J. D. Hubert

I. *The Theme of Obedience*

In *Le Malade [imaginaire]*, Molière gives a new twist to a theme which had played a dominant part in *Les Femmes savantes*: that of command and obedience. In Argan's specialized universe, only the hierarchy of medicine and disease really matters. Physicians have discretionary powers, and the patient must obey them without murmur. For that reason, Purgon feels entitled to curse the apparently rebellious Argan and anathematize him by abandoning him to the weakness of his constitution in the same manner that the Church might abandon heretics to the corruption of human nature.

Within the hierarchy of medicine, Monsieur Fleurant takes orders from Purgon. When Argan attempts to put off for a while his enema because of Béralde's intervention, Monsieur Fleurant protests: "De quoi vous mêlez-vous de vous opposer aux ordonnances de la médecine, et d'empêcher Monsieur de prendre mon clystère? Vous êtes bien plaisant d'avoir cette hardiesse-là! (III, 4) [By what right are you interfering with medicine's prescriptions, and keeping this gentleman from taking the enema I prepared? How absurd of you to make so bold as that!]." The term *ordonnances*, which generally signifies a medical prescription, subtly takes on its original meaning, that of a government or a church decree, for the apothecary does not refer to the "ordonnances de Monsieur Purgon" or "du médecin," but to those of a more august power: "de la médecine." He may, for that reason, accuse Béralde of *hardiesse*.

Béralde's answer is masterful: "Allez, Monsieur, on voit bien que vous n'avez pas accoutumé de parler à des visages [Well, well, Sir, it's clear that you are not accustomed to speaking to faces]." Fleurant must then appeal to higher authority—to Monsieur Purgon. The latter, sensing the danger of rebellion, rushes over and repeatedly accuses his patient of disobedience before uttering his final curse: "Voilà une hardiesse bien grande, une étrange rébellion d'un malade contre son médecin. . . . Un attentat énorme contre la médecine. . . . Un crime de lèse-Faculté, qui ne se peut assez punir. . . . Puisque vous vous êtes soustrait de l'obeissance que l'on doit à son médecin. . . . Puisque vous vous êtes déclaré rebelle aux remèdes que je vous ordonnais" (III, 5) [That is being very bold indeed, a strange revolt, that of a patient against his doctor. . . . An enormous offence against medicine. . . . A crime of *lèse-Faculté* which cannot be punished enough. . . . Since you shirked the obedience that one owes to one's doctor. . . . Since you openly rebelled against the remedy I prescribed]." Purgon's attitude shows that Molière meant by *ordonnance* much more than a medical prescription, for the mad physician really believes that Argan's disobedience deserves the direst punishment, as though his patient had committed a crime against the king or against religion.

Argan apparently believes that the mortal sin of disobedience has put his life in jeopardy. Béralde implies as much when he tells him: "Il semble, à vous entendre, que Monsieur Purgon tienne dans ses mains le filet de vos jours, et que, d'autorité suprême, il vous l'allonge et vous le raccourcisse comme il lui plaît. Songez que les principes de votre vie sont en vous-même . . . (III, 6) [It would seem, upon hearing you, that Monsieur Purgon holds the thread of your life in his hands, and that, with supreme authority, he lengthens it and shortens it at will. Remember that the principle of your life is within yourself . . .]." But our hypochondriac cannot help believing everything that his doctor has told him: "Il dit que je deviendrai incurable avant qu'il soit quatre jours [He says that in less than four days I shall be incurable]." Argan does indeed attribute to Purgon absolute power over life and death as though he actually held sway over destiny itself which, like Fleurant and like his patients, must obey his least command. Béralde's surprising statement: "Songez que les principes de votre vie sont en vous-même" appears to transcend the realm of medicine and to deny all externalized occult powers that men, including priests as well as physicians, invoke for bodily and spiritual salvation. And taken out of context, it could serve as an epigraph to almost any work of Jean-Paul Sartre! Béralde's wisdom has hardly any effect on his brother: "Voyez-vous? j'ai sur le cœur toutes ces maladies-là que je ne connois point, ces . . . (III, 7) [You see, I have on my mind all those illnesses I know nothing about, those . . .]." In other words, Argan fears the unknown, fears those mysterious forces that his disobedience has unleashed.

The hierarchical aspects of medicine reappear in the burlesque masquerade which ends the comedy:

> Totus mundus, currens ad nostros remedios,
> Nos regardat sicut Deos;
> Et nostris ordonnanciis
> Principes et reges soumissos videtis.

Although physicians may impress a minority of their patients by their power, although rulers submit to their prescriptions, they tend throughout the play to behave in a most obedient manner. Purgon, as we have seen, slavishly follows the rules of his profession; and Thomas Diafoirus, like his father, does not dare depart from the teachings of the ancients. Moreover, young Thomas requires his father's permission for everything he does, even outside the realm of medicine. After having recited his lengthy compliment to Argan, he asks Diafoirus senior, as though he were speaking to a schoolmaster: "Cela a-t-il bien été, mon père? (II, 5) [Did all go well, Father?]." And when he meets Angélique, he asks his father whether or not he should kiss her hand. Finally, when he gets mixed up in his compliment to Béline, Monsieur Diafoirus orders him: "Thomas, réservez cela pour une autre fois (II, 6) [Thomas, leave that for another time]." May we then say that physicians, because of their submissive attitude to dogma, their complete lack of skepticism, their authoritarianism, tend to suggest the behavior of priests and monks?

As a foil to this type of subservience, Molière has introduced the filial obedience of Angélique to Argan. Angélique, who somehow believes that her father intends to marry her to her beloved Cléante, carefully emphasizes her submissiveness: "Je dois faire, mon père, tout ce qu'il vous plaira de m'ordonner (I, 5) [It is my duty, Father, to do everything you should like to command]," and "C'est à moi, mon père, de suivre aveuglément toutes vos volontés [I am obliged, Father, to follow blindly your every will]." But when it transpires that Thomas Diafoirus, and not Cléante, is the intended bridegroom, Toinette questions Argan's authority in the matter and, despite her low rank in the household, speaks as though she had as much power as Argan. She tells the father that this ludicrous marriage will never happen because Angélique will never give her consent. The scene reaches a climax in the following exchange: "Argan: 'Je lui commande absolument de se préparer à prendre le mari que je dis.' Toinette: 'Et moi, je lui défends absolument d'en rien faire.' [Argan: 'I order her absolutely to prepare herself for taking the husband I say.' Toinette: 'And I, I forbid her absolutely to do anything of the kind']." Their quarrel ends with the hypochondriac running after the servant and ordering his daughter to help him catch her: "Si tu ne me l'arrêtes, je te donnerai ma malédiction [If you don't stop her for me, my curses upon you]." Toinette, in her retort, usurps the role of father: "Et moi, je la déshériterai, si elle vous obéit [And I, I shall disinherit her if she obeys you]." Her behavior differs from that of Dorine in *Tartuffe,* for instead of rebelling against her master, she simply assumes his authority and his prerogatives. Whereas Dorine had been content to play the part of Mariane, who did not dare oppose her father's will, Toinette reduces the whole idea of authority to absurdity. Moreover, this usurpation of power makes Argan behave like an enraged but perfectly healthy and vigorous human being. It may, for this reason, correspond dramatically to the usurpation of authority which characterizes the *corps des médecins.* This correspondence or parallelism is much more obvious later in the play when Toinette actually "creates" the part of a famous physician, so drastic in his prescriptions that even Argan voices some timid objections: "Me couper un bras, et me crever un œil, afin que l'autre se porte mieux? J'aime bien mieux qu'il ne se porte pas si bien. La belle opération, de me rendre borgne et manchot! (III, 10) [Cut off one of my arms and put out one of my eyes, so that the other will feel better? I prefer that it doesn't feel too well. A fine operation, making me one-eyed and one-armed]." By their very absurdity, Toinette's drastic remedies emphasize the perils of contemporary medicine. She actually reasons about disease in much the same manner as Monsieur Purgon or Diafoirus, father and son. Her prescription may contain, however, an allusion to religion: "Si ta main est pour toi une occasion de chute, coupe-la: mieux vaut pour toi entrer manchot dans la vie, que de t'en aller, ayant deux mains, dans la géhenne, dans le feu inextinguible . . . Et si ton œil est pour toi une occasion de chute, arrache-le: mieux vaut pour toi entrer borgne dans le royaume de Dieu (Marc, IX, 43-47) ["And if thy hand offend thee, cut it off: it is better for thee to enter into life maimed, than having two hands to go into hell, into the fire that never shall be quenched . . . And if thine eye offend thee, pluck it out: it is better for thee to enter into the kingdom of God with one eye."] Could Molière be alluding to the symbolic denial and amputation of the human spirit, which appears so scandalous to a *libertin,* and even to a humanist? Perhaps Toinette's gruesome joke coincides fortuitously with a passage in the New Testament; but there are so many suggestive retorts in the play that we cannot entirely ignore the irreligious implications of Toinette's drastic cure. After all, the Christian denial of the body and of nature may, from a certain point of view, render man, as Argan says, "borgne et manchot."

The idea of hierarchy leads, in the course of the comedy, to several ludicrous situations based on Argan's belief in a close connection between his physician's *ordonnance* and his eventual cure. This aspect of the play particularly impressed Madame de Sévigné, who even quotes passages which Molière or at least his editor did not retain. She does, however, refer directly to a well-known passage concerning the exercises which Purgon has prescribed for his patient: "Monsieur Purgon m'a dit de me promener le matin dans ma chambre, douze allées et douze venues;

mais j'ai oublié à lui demander si c'est en long, ou en large (II, 2)
[Monsieur Purgon told me to walk back and forth in my room in the
morning, twelve times back, and twelve times forth; but I forgot to ask
him if it was lengthwise, or broadwise]." Argan's attitude strikes us by its
absurd rigidity—by the idea that the organism closely depends upon the
exact number of steps that Argan will take in his daily constitutional.
Earlier in the play, the same Argan had established a numerical relationship between the amount of treatment he had undergone and the state
of his unhealth: "Si bien donc que de ce mois j'ai pris une, deux, trois,
quatre, cinq, six, sept et huit médecines; et un, deux, trois, quatre, cinq,
six, sept, huit, neuf, dix, onze et douze lavements; et l'autre mois il y
avoit douze médecines, et vingt lavements. Je ne m'étonne pas si je ne me
porte pas si bien ce mois-ci que l'autre. Je le dirai à Monsieur Purgon,
afin qu'il mette ordre à cela (I, 1) [Therefore, this month, I took one, two,
three, four, five, six, seven, eight medicines, and one, two, three, four,
five, six, seven, eight, nine, ten, eleven, twelve enemas; and last month,
there were twelve medicines and twenty enemas. I am not at all surprised
that I am not in as good health this month as I was last month. I shall
tell this to Monsieur Purgon, so that he'll set it all to rights]." The use
of figures throughout this scene is rich in comic effects, for it brings out
the idea of rigidity, all the more so because it attaches to these exact
quantities of medication a very precise price tag. The main result of all
this medication is the depletion of Argan's purse, a fact which makes the
other type of causal relation—the supposed rapport between medication
and health—all the more preposterous. Monsieur Diafoirus, no less than
Argan, insists on the numerical aspect of remedies. When the hypochondriac asks him: "Monsieur, combien est-ce qu'il faut mettre de grains
de sel dans un œuf [Sir, how many grains of salt must one put in an
egg?]." he receives this strange answer: "Six, huit, dix, par les nombres
pairs; comme dans les médicaments, par les nombres impairs (II, 6) [Six,
eight, ten, using even numbers; just as in drugs, you use uneven num-
bers]." This reply shows that Argan derives his superstitious reliance on
exact figures from the doctors themselves, and that he has merely exaggerated a normal tendency of the profession.

We may wonder why Molière has attached so much importance to
these numbers. Was he concerned only with the hilarious reaction of his
public or did he have another axe to grind? Moreover, the author insists
also on Argan's ritualistic punctuality in taking his various medicines and
in relieving himself. By combining this ludicrous punctuality with the
idea of quantitative precision we obtain a bizarre type of causalty, tanta-
mount to the complete denial of nature. Medicine has finally transformed Argan into a strange, biological mechanism, quite devoid of
human qualities, as Béline's outspoken funeral oration over his supposed
dead body shows. Argan, with his pharmaceutical mathematics, has meta-
morphosed himself into a gut: "Un homme incommode à tout le monde,

malpropre, dégoûtant, sans cesse un lavement ou une médecine dans le ventre . . . (III, 12) [A man who is unpleasant to everyone, unclean, disgusting, always an enema or a medicine in his belly . . .]." It would seem that Molière has satirized the tendency of physicians to introduce a rigid, mathematical type of reasoning into natural processes; but he may also be poking fun at certain religious practices and beliefs. Mathematics plays a not unessential part in the system of indulgences: such and such a prayer, such and such a pious gesture will pay for a specific number of days, months, or years in purgatory, either for oneself or for other sufferers.[1]

II. *Pleasure and the Imagination*

The term *plaisir* provides one of the metaphorical keys to the comedy. The idea of pleasure or diversion provides, for instance, a transition between the play itself and the second *intermède,* of which Argan is a spectator. He apparently does not have anything to do with the first, and he of course plays the main part in the third and last. And this transition does more than serve as a connecting link between two disparate parts of the play, leading from the actual comedy to the diversion and then back again: "Ce sont des Egyptiens, vêtus en Mores, qui font des danses mêlées de chansons, où je suis sûr que vous prendrez plaisir; et cela vaudra bien une ordonnance de Monsieur Purgon. Allons (II, 9) [They are Gypsies, dressed as Moors, who both dance and sing, and who I am certain will please you; and that will surely be worth a prescription from Monsieur Purgon. Let's go]." At the beginning of the third act, Béralde continues his comparison between medicine and entertainment: "Eh bien! mon frère, qu'en dites vous? cela ne vaut-il pas bien une prise de casse?" Toinette adds, sarcastically: "Hon, de bonne casse est bonne" (III, 1). But why should Molière compare entertainment to a mild form of purgation? Actually, the dramatist had all along injected into the medical aspects of the play the idea of pleasure, and the double transition between the second and third acts serves to make the blending of medicine and pleasure more explicit. This strange analogy appears for the first time in Monsieur Fleurant's bill, couched in insinuating language, which Argan is reading out loud when the curtain rises. The latter is pleased by the style but revolted by the prices: "Ah! Monsieur Fleurant, tout doux s'il vous plaît; si vous en usez comme cela, on ne voudra plus être malade [Ah! Monsieur Fleurant, gently please; if you go on like that, we won't want to be sick anymore]." This excellent joke implies that Argan regards disease as a sort of hobby, as though he could take it or leave it!

[1] James Joyce, in his *A Portrait of the Artist as a Young Man,* dwells on the spiritual mathematics of indulgences, and with as much humor as Molière. Cf. pp. 170 ff. in Modern Library Edition.

The theme of pleasure reappears in the very next scene in the course of Argan's quarrel with Toinette. The latter exclaims: "Si vous avez le plaisir de quereller, il faut bien, que de mon côté, j'aye le plaisir de pleurer: chacun le sien, ce n'est pas trop. Ha! [If you can have the pleasure of quarreling, then I for my part must have the pleasure of crying; everyone to his taste, that's fair enough. Ha!]." Most people would consider quarreling as scarcely more pleasurable than sickness. And later in the same scene, Toinette actually connects pleasure with medicine: "Ce Monsieur Fleurant-là et ce Monsieur Purgon s'égayent bien sur votre corps [That Monsieur Fleurant and this Monsieur Purgon have a lot of fun with your body]." Admittedly, the word *s'égayer* means, according to Littré, *se donner carrière*—to display activity; nonetheless, it definitely evokes its primary meaning of having fun or even of making fun, which implies that the doctor and his soft-spoken apothecary derive enjoyment as well as money from their tender treatment of Argan's complacent body.

Still later in the play, Cléante, after having listened to Thomas Diafoirus' second display of eloquence, establishes a clearer and more ironical connection between disease and enjoyment: "Que Monsieur fait merveilles, et que s'il est aussi bon médecin qu'il est bon orateur, il y aura plaisir à être de ses malades (II, 5) [What wonders Monsieur does, and if he is as good a doctor as he is an orator, it would be a pleasure to be one of his patients]." It remains, however, for our fledgling physician to bring out the inherent absurdity of this connection: "Avec la permission aussi de Monsieur, je vous invite à venir voir l'un de ces jours, pour vous divertir, la dissection d'une femme, sur quoi je dois raisonner [Again, with Monsieur's permission, I invite you to come and see, one of these days, to amuse yourself, the dissection of a woman, about which I have to hold forth]." And Toinette takes advantage of this remark to cross all the t's and dot all the i's: "Le divertissement sera agréable. Il y en a qui donnent la comédie à leurs maîtresses; mais donner une dissection est quelque chose de plus galant [The entertainment will be pleasant. There are those who offer a comedy to their mistresses; but to offer a dissection is something even more gallant]." It is then Cléante's turn to entertain the company. He produces a pastoral scene in music in which he explains his love and his intentions to Angélique. Argan, who appears to have seen through Cléante's little stratagem, is not amused: "Les sottises ne divertissent point [Silliness is never entertaining]." More than anything else, he enjoys his illness: "Ah! que d'affaires! je n'ai pas seulement le loisir de songer à ma maladie (II, 8) [Ah! so many things! I haven't even the time to think about my illness]." He sees his imaginary disease as a sort of pastime, which lesser activities tend to interrupt. It will take the final entertainment, where Argan becomes a doctor, to conciliate these antithetical types of pleasure.

It is of course outlandish to combine disease, even imaginary disease, with songs and dances. Molière may have enjoyed the absurdity of this combination. Nonetheless, the pleasure involved has, to say the least, a dubious quality, because Molière, who chose to play the part of Argan, states within the comedy that he is seriously ill: ". . . il n'a justement de la force que pour porter son mal (III, 3) [. . . he has just enough strength to bear his own illness]." Molière has put these words concerning his illness in the mouth of the wise Béralde, entrusting, on the contrary, Argan with the cruelest remarks about himself: ". . . quand il sera malade, je le laisserois mourir sans secours [. . . the day he gets sick, I should let him die without help]," and: "Crève, crève! cela t'apprendra une autre fois à te jouer à la Faculté (III, 3) [Die, die! that will teach you in the future not to mock the Doctors]." The author has made the scene highly paradoxical from a dramatic point of view; and Béralde, in defending Molière against Molière himself (Argan), puts the audience in a piquant situation, partly pleasurable and partly disturbing. Argan is both Molière and not Molière; both a malingerer and a sick man; both a madman who enjoys his imaginary illness and a sufferer who, with barely enough strength to support his disease, has done his utmost to entertain the audience. Molière had used a similar trick, though in a less unnerving manner, in his *Misanthrope*, where Philinte meanly compares Alceste (played by Molière) to the Sganarelle of *L'École des maris*. In *Le Malade imaginaire*, however, it is more than a clever device, not only because of the constant equivocation between pleasure and medicine, but because the idea of impersonation plays a fairly important part in the comedy. Toinette, as we have seen, had impersonated a famous physician who happens to look just like her—just as Argan happens to look exactly like Molière. But then, why should Molière want to make fun of theatrical illusion by destroying it at the very moment when he seems to be creating it?

Strange as this statement may appear, we can find something *wrong* with almost every action, situation, and character in the play. Argan is both terribly ill and perfectly healthy; disease brings both suffering and pleasure; the notary, instead of limiting his activities to legal matters, mentions lawyers who fail to understand what he calls *détours de la conscience* (I, 7) or, in other words, casuistry: Monsieur Purgon speaks more like a theologian than a doctor; Cléante and Angélique discuss their love in terms of entertainment. . . . A willful distortion of one kind or another marks practically every event in the play.

There is something rather puzzling, comic in a breathtaking sort of way, in the scene where the hypochondriac feigns death. His little daughter, Louison, had put on a similar performance earlier in the play in order to avoid a whipping. She had even succeeded in frightening her not too intelligent father. Argan's mimicry of death allows him to discover the truth, not about himself, but about his mercenary wife. Illusion will also play an important part in the burlesque travesty that ends the comedy: it will arrange everything, particularly the marriage between Cléante and Angélique. But in every illusion, whether or not it acts as a catalyst of truth, reality must enter the picture. The separation between the real and the illusory, at least on the stage, should never become too sharp. Molière, for this reason, makes his hypochondriac say: "N'y a-t-il pas quelque danger à contrefaire le mort? (III, 11) [Isn't it somewhat dangerous to sham death?]." After all, his imaginary death might suddenly become as real as his imaginary disease! And we should not forget in this particular instance that Molière, then a dying man, took it upon himself to impersonate a corpse. Contemporaries of the author dwelled at length on this morbid paradox.[2] Death thus emerges as a spectacle and, temporarily, steals the show from Argan's imaginary disease. Toinette, dressed in a doctor's habit, had introduced herself to Argan as an admirer, as a fan: "Vous ne trouverez pas mauvais, s'il vous plaît, la curiosité que j'ai eue de voir un illustre malade comme vous êtes; et votre réputation, qui s'étend partout, peut excuser la liberté que j'ai prise (III, 10) [Please don't be offended by my curiosity in wanting to see such an illustrious patient; and your renown, which has spread everywhere, may be considered an excuse for the liberty I have taken]." Toinette addresses herself to Argan as though he were a celebrity, a fascinating spectacle worthy of a long trip. In this joke, the author attempts to combine illness with spectacle, suffering with entertainment. Toinette's admiration suggests that Argan has actually transformed himself into an "illustre malade"—illustrious in the sense that an actor can make himself famous. Her words take on an additional meaning if we consider that she addresses them to Molière—to Élomire Hypocondre—rather than to a character in the play.

Theater as metaphor appears almost everywhere. Cléante's courting of Angélique takes the form of a performance, or at least of a rehearsal. Moreover, Angélique had met Cléante at a play, where one of the spectators had persecuted her with his insults. Béralde puts on a show for the

---

[2] See the many epitaphs concerning Molière's death, published in various *recueils*, for instance in the *Mélange de pièces fugitives tirées du cabinet de Monsieur de Saint-Evremont* (Utrecht: François Galma, 1697), which accompanied an edition of the *Voyage de Messieurs de Bachaumont et de La Chapelle*. Here is a fairly typical one:

> Cy gît un qu'on dit être mort,
> Je ne sçays s'il l'est, ou s'il dort,
> Sa Maladie Imaginaire,
> Ne peut pas l'avoir fait mourir,
> C'est un tour qu'il joüe à plaisir,
> Car il aimoit à contrefaire,
> Quoy qu'il en soit, cy gît Molière;
> Comme il étoit grand Comedien
>   Pour un mort imaginaire,
> S'il le fait, il le fait bien (p. 134).

Here lies one who is said to be dead. I don't know whether he is or whether he is sleeping. His Imaginary Illness could not have killed him. It's a trick he is playing for fun, for he liked to sham. Anyway, here lies Molière; since he was a great Actor, if he acts the part of an imaginary corpse, he does it very well.

benefit of his brother who, in turn, performs a part in order to discover Béline's and Angélique's true feelings. And the whole thing ends with a burlesque ceremony put on by a troupe of actors. Dissection itself becomes a spectacle performed no doubt in an *amphithéâtre*. Everywhere we turn, we witness a triumph of the theater, particularly over sickness and death. Living and dying become gigantic systems of make-believe in a world that has become meaningless. As Béralde claims, the veils are too thick, and only the present requires our attention. Only entertainment really counts, for, as Béralde puts it, ". . . chacun à ses périls et fortune, peut croire tout ce qu'il lui plaît (III, 3) [. . . everyone, at his own risk, is free to believe anything he wants]."

EPILOGUE

Poquelin and Chaplin

by Jacques Audiberti

It was in the theater that [Molière] earned his living and his death. He earned them fairly. Never was he untrue to himself. Never did he deceive us, never.

Similarly, a young clown from London, with a troupe of mimes, traveled through the United States. In Philadelphia he received a telegram from Mack Sennett suggesting that he join Keystone. He was hired. In the films the young Charles Spencer Chaplin's spasmodic numbers were to be superimposed—an exaggerated but captivating symmetry—on those little entertainments the titles of which can be found in La Grange's *Registre,* and which Molière and his companions trotted around the provinces and then performed in Paris in those covered tennis courts which, for better or for worse, they transformed into theaters. Nothing remains of those shorts but their titles: *Plan-plan, Les Indes, La Casaque, La Fin Lourdaud. . . .* A whole series is devoted to the maneuvers of Gros-René, a puny humbug masked with scabby flour, along with Gorgibus, father of Madelon, a pot-bellied, loud-mouthed, soot-covered giant, the very one Charlie Chaplin had constantly to confront in the forty reels of such films as *Mabel's Busy Day* or *The Masquerader,* and then

"Poquelin and Chaplin." From *Molière, Dramaturge* by Jacques Audiberti. Copyright 1954 by L'Arche, Paris. Translated and reprinted by permission of the publisher and the author. The pages printed here, and translated by June Guicharnaud, are from Chapter Two, "Lignes Générales et Analogies."

in shorts at Essanay Films, and in the longer movies at Mutual, and throughout *The Gold Rush,* which was his declaration of independence.

Two of those entertainments, *Le Médecin volant* and *La Jalousie du barbouillé,* derive from the anonymous swarms of the Italian masked farces which sustained the wandering companies. Similarly, of all the early mechanical little comedies, *Shoulder Arms* and *The Sunny Side* stand clearly out.

From then on, there was the progression *The Pilgrim, Le Misanthrope, The Kid, Tartuffe, Les Femmes savantes,* and *City Lights,* ending in *Limelight* and *L'École des femmes,* both of which retraced, in parallel terms, the same scratch cutting into the soul of man, a theater animal par excellence, forever behind, forever beyond.

Once the rush was over, the doors broken open, the gold acquired, every word and every caper calling forth rivers of ecstatic commentaries, Molière and Charlie Chaplin each still—in the unity of an operative and homogeneous life in which proceeding meant returning—came together, at all points, with his distant and original silhouette, which each inflated to the most fabulous radiance possible. In the cast-off clothing of the comedian in *Limelight,* who dies in a big packing-case, as in the white-haired millionaire for whom the earthly globe hasn't enough downy dwelling-places, one tracks down, adores, applauds—affectionate X-ray! prophecy in the rear-view mirror!—the tramp and dandy who turned sharp corners on the wings of his old shoes. Not a milligram of preconceived philosophy existed in the derby of the young acrobatic and curly-haired renegade of the Karno Pantomime Company, under the friendly whip of Mack Sennett. But the moments of dreamy melancholy on that almost stenciled white and black face were fondled with an ever-growing insistence, sustained by a camera that sensed the future. On the screen we have, literally and visibly, followed the epic of a seed managing, through shorter and shorter periods of trial and error, finally to become fixed in its perfect state, that deified specimen of man—exiled, solitary, lost, saved.

Similarly, in the successful, opulent, and proclaimed Molière, the height of comedy, one of the kings of a literature which he brought to heel and mastered, the clown wriggles, laughs, cries—intact, not repudiated—the clown smeared with flour and jealousy who, on days when fairs were held, declared to the spectators that of all men he was the most unhappy, because of his wife: she drives him wild, she doesn't stay at home, she associates with all sorts of people, "que tu es misérable, pauvre barbouillé!"

The works of Chaplin and those of Molière grow, from one to the other, under the weight of almost continual good fortune. Farce becomes an ethic, the cream pie a philosophy. The puppets are greeted as monumental champions of a humanity which is no longer obsolete or theoretical but which everyone can touch, there and then. Their scope is all the wider in that it does not require the fit of fury, as in tragedy. While the tragic hero, Trojan or Castilian, struggles, as a totality, in the raging urgency of choosing between love and honor, the comic type harbors unceasingly, within himself, antagonistic tendencies which are as difficult to conciliate as to confess. Besides, they almost always stop short of the crime, of the official offense. To the delight of the audience, the man one laughs at gives blatant proof, in his bearing and in his manners, of his personal and permanent hybridity, postulated most of the time by the title of the work. In one there are nothing but ignorant pedants, ingenuous little foxes, worldly neurasthenics, beribboned and fraudulent gentlemen, raving bourgeois, fornicating clericals, despondent libertines, doctors in spite of themselves, ridiculous *précieuses,* and learned women. In the other *The Great Dictator* and *Monsieur Verdoux* finally and unexpectedly underline in red the permanent duality of the visionary vagabond.

In both cases Jean-Baptiste or Charles Spencer appear, in person, as the supreme common denominator of the martyrs in their insolubly comical repertory. Twin glory! A crown for two heads!

Lecturers at cinema clubs ask questions of this kind:

> If Charlie Chaplin, after having heard an edifying sermon, spontaneously and joyously returns the contents he had stolen from some poor people's trunk (*The Immigrant*), should he not also, in the same spirit of abnegation, have drunk the swimming-pool water, despite his disgust, in order to please the girl friend who asked him to (*The Cure*)?

And professors giving the *baccalauréat* examination propose such subjects as: "Is it true, on the grounds of Agnès' temperament, that for Molière woman is, as Gustave Lanson would have it, the little instinctive, illogical, and disconcerting animal that our contemporaries are fond of depicting?" (*Bar-le-Duc.*)

Chronology of Important Dates

1622   Jean-Baptiste Poquelin born in Paris.

1632-37(?)   Studies at the Collège de Clermont. According to legend, often taken by his grandfather to watch Italian comedians and French tragedians at the Hôtel de Bourgogne. Begins law studies.

1638   Birth of Louis XIV.

1640   Poquelin meets Italian actor Tiberio Fiorelli (Scaramouche) and Madeleine Béjart.

1642   Death of Richelieu.

1643   Death of Louis XIII. Birth of Armande, daughter or sister of Madeleine Béjart and future wife of Molière. Poquelin founds "L'Illustre Théâtre" with the Béjart family and other actors.

1644   Poquelin adopts the name "Molière." Bankruptcy of "L'Illustre Théâtre." Molière imprisoned for debt in the Châtelet. Molière's father pays his debts.

1645   Molière and the Béjarts join the Dufresne company, of which the comedian Gros-René is a member. They tour the provinces until 1658 (Lyon: 1655-57; Rouen: 1658).

1650   Molière becomes director of the company. Protected by the Prince de Conti.

1653-55   Molière writes farces and his first comedy, *L'Étourdi* (1655). Conti withdraws his protection and joins the devout "Confrérie du Saint-Sacrement."

1656   *Le Dépit amoureux.*

1658   At the Louvre in Paris, Molière and his company perform Corneille's *Nicomède* for the young King, as well as Molière's own farce *Le Docteur amoureux*: "The King deigned to laugh." Molière shares the theater of the Petit Bourbon with the Italians (who leave France in 1659).

1659   Success of *Les Précieuses ridicules*. The young Lagrange (or La Grange) joins the company.

1660   Destruction of the Petit Bourbon. After a few months, the King gives Molière the theater of the Palais Royal. *Sganarelle ou le Cocu imaginaire.*

1661   Italian comedians return to Paris, with Domenico Biancolelli (Arlequin), who becomes a friend of Molière's. *Dom Garcie de Navarre* ("comédie héroïque"). *L'École des Maris. Les Fâcheux,* in a "Fête offerte au Roi par Fouquet." Louis XIV personally assumes power.

1662   Molière marries Armande. *L'École des femmes.*

1663   Controversy around *L'École des femmes.* Molière accused of impiety, then of incest. *La Critique de "l'École des femmes." L'Impromptu de Versailles.*

1664   *Le Mariage forcé.* Louis XIV godfather of Molière's son (who dies shortly after). For the feast given at Versailles by the King for his mistress Mlle de La Vallière, "Les Plaisirs de l'île enchantée," Molière and his company participate in the great pageants and perform Molière's *La Princesse d'Élide,* as well as the first version of *Tartuffe,* in three acts. *Tartuffe* banned in Paris. Molière will fight until 1669 to obtain the authorization to produce it. Colbert becomes the King's most important minister.

1665   *Dom Juan, ou le Festin de Pierre,* withdrawn after initial success. Louis XIV names Molière's company "Troupe du Roy." *L'Amour médecin.*

1666   Molière's health failing. Marital difficulties with Armande. *Le Misanthrope* (a modest success). *Le Médecin malgré lui.*

1667   Louis XIV at war in Flandres. Molière produces second version of *Tartuffe,* which is immediately banned. *Mélicerte* and *Le Sicilien* given as part of the "Ballet des Muses" at Saint-Germain-en-Laye.

1668   *Amphitryon. George Dandin. L'Avare* (a flop). Molière and Armande separated, but they continue to act together.

1669   Third version of *Tartuffe* authorized. *Monsieur de Pourceaugnac* at Chambord.

1670   *Les Amants magnifiques* at Saint-Germain-en-Laye. *Le Bourgeois gentilhomme* at Chambord.

1671   *Psyché* (in collaboration with Corneille and Quinault) in the "salle des machines" at the Tuileries. *Les Fourberies de Scapin. La Comtesse d'Escarbagnas* at Saint-Germain-en-Laye.

1672   *Les Femmes savantes.* Death of Madeleine Béjart.

1673   *Le Malade imaginaire.* February 17: during the fourth performance, Molière falls ill, and dies the same night around ten o'clock. Until

Louis XIV intervenes to prevent scandal, parish priest refuses burial. Lully takes over the Palais Royal and makes it into the Opéra. Armande, Lagrange, and others join the Compagnie du Marais, rue Guénégaud.

1680   The King merges the Rue Guénégaud company with the Hôtel de Bourgogne, so founding the Comédie Française.

Notes on the Editor and Authors

JACQUES GUICHARNAUD, editor of this volume, is the author of *Modern French Theatre from Giraudoux to Beckett* (in collaboration with June Beckelman), *Molière, une aventure théâtrale*, and a few works of fiction. He is also the translator of several plays by Tennessee Williams and the short stories of Ring Lardner. He is Professor of French at Yale University.

JACQUES AUDIBERTI is a French poet, novelist, and eminent contemporary playwright. Of his numerous plays, *La Fourmi dans le corps* was performed in 1961 at the Comédie Française.

PAUL BÉNICHOU is Professor of Romance Languages at Harvard University. In addition to his *Morales du Grand Siècle*, he has written articles on Jean-Jacques Rousseau, Benjamin Constant, and Mallarmé. He is a student of popular Spanish poetry as well, and the translator of José Luis Borges.

RENÉ BRAY (1896-1954), one of the best known French scholars of classical literature, wrote what is still one of the most authoritative works on the subject, his doctoral dissertation (1927) *La Formation de la doctrine classique en France*. His *Molière, homme de théâtre* was somewhat revolutionary when it was published in 1954. After having edited the works of Molière for the collection "Les Belles Lettres," he began another monumental edition for the "Club du meilleur livre," but died before completing it.

JACQUES COPEAU (1878-1949) is celebrated for his lasting influence on the arts of acting and producing. Cofounder of *La Nouvelle Revue Française*, he created in 1913 the Théâtre du Vieux Colombier. His staging of *Les Fourberies de Scapin* in 1917 was one of the great events in the history of Molière performances.

JAMES DOOLITTLE, head of the Department of Romance Languages and Literatures at the University of Cincinnati, divides his interests between Diderot and the seventeenth century. Author of *Rameau's Nephew: A Study of Diderot's Second Satire*, he has published articles on related subjects as well as on Corneille and Molière.

CHARLES DULLIN (1885-1949), one of the great actor-directors of the Thirties, recreated Molière's *L'Avare*, in which he played the part of Harpagon. This production has been almost unanimously considered the best of the twentieth century thus far.

RAMON FERNANDEZ (1894-1944), son of a Mexican diplomat, was a French novelist and critic, author of studies on Gide, Proust, and Balzac, as well as of *La Vie de Molière* (1929).

LIONEL GOSSMAN, author of *Men and Masks, a Study of Molière,* is a member of the Department of Romance Languages at The Johns Hopkins University.

H. GASTON HALL, lecturer in French at the University of Glasgow, is the author of an exegesis of Molière's *Tartuffe,* as well as of the critical edition of Desmarets de Saint Sorlin's *Les Visionnaires.*

J. D. HUBERT, Professor of French at the University of California, has written, in addition to his *Molière and the Comedy of Intellect,* a study of *Les Fleurs du Mal* and an *Essai d'exégèse racinienne,* which has had great influence in the field.

GUSTAVE LANSON (1857-1934), the author of a world-famous *Histoire de la littérature française,* is the most eminent representative of the historical method in the study of literature. Although the trend today is away from that genre of criticism, some of his works—such as the article "Molière et la farce"—prefigure more modern interpretations.

WILL G. MOORE, Fellow and Tutor at St. John's College, Oxford, is the author of the revolutionary *Molière, a New Criticism; French Classical Literature, an Essay*; and several articles.

ROBERT J. NELSON, Professor of Romance Languages at the University of Pennsylvania, is a student of the French drama. He is the author of *The Play within the Play; Corneille, His Heroes and Their Worlds*; and is currently working on a study of Rotrou.

ALFRED SIMON is Professor of Literature and Philosophy in France, drama critic for the review *Esprit,* author of *Molière par lui-même,* and coeditor of the *Oeuvres complètes de Molière* (Club des Libraires) .

ANDRÉ VILLIERS is an eminent student of the theater. In addition to his study of *Dom Juan,* he is the author of *La Psychologie du comédien* and *Le Théâtre en rond.*

Memorable Twentieth Century Performances of Molière's Plays in France

AMPHITRYON

1. Directed by Jean-Louis Barrault. Paris, Théâtre Marigny, 1947.

Prologue, with moving clouds, machines, and the usual Barrault horses. Setting, in perspective, in the Italian style of the eighteenth century. Madeleine Renaud (Alcmène), Jean-Pierre Granval (Sosie), and Jean-Louis Barrault (Mercure), along with the rest of the company, in possibly the most "musical" performance ever given of the play: elegant, amusing, a perfect reconstitution of a *divertissement* for the Roi-Soleil. A biting emphasis on certain lines in which satire is shown to be more important than aristocratic poetry. A perfect example of how frivolous beauty may be an expression of ambiguous indictment.

2. Paris, La Comédie Française, 1959.

An opportunity for the actor Robert Hirsch (Sosie) to star. Setting inspired by a seventeenth century engraving: ships on the right, the ramparts of a city on the left. The action takes place on the quay. Exasperating production inasmuch as Hirsch uses the same very personal tricks that he does in a Feydeau *vaudeville* or as Scapin. But his role as the star has a meaning here: we know that in the original performance, Molière played the part of Sosie. Interpretation: the weak, cowardly, but lovable common-man is victimized, but on the *theatrical* level he is the *victor* of the rather silly adulterous adventure between problematical gods and precious aristocrats.

L'AVARE

1. Directed by Charles Dullin. Paris, Théâtre de Paris, 1941.

Small and almost hunchbacked, Dullin well suited to the title role. His voice precise—but its precision a result of enormous effort to control natural difficulties in elocution, as was the case with Molière. Star of the show, but integrated in the whole, Dullin—sensitive to the general structure of the play—made *L'Avare* a perfect comedy, midway between farce and drama. Considered by several generations of the twentieth century to be the ideal Harpagon.

2. Directed by Jean Vilar. Paris, Théâtre National Populaire, 1952.

Stage too vast for the comedy and Vilar too thin for Harpagon (whereas in the case of Dom Juan, his thinness brought out the character's ambiguity). Here, emphasis put on Daniel Sorano, in the role of La Flèche. However, as Dullin had died in 1949, the avid public at least found in Vilar's interpretation the same principles of purity that it had in Dullin's.

LE BOURGEOIS GENTILHOMME

1. Paris, La Comédie Française, 1944.
Jourdain played by the great movie actor Raimu, with ballets directed by Serge Lifar. Much publicity, but the year 1944 was a difficult one, and the spectacle overpowered the movie actor, who was perplexed in his role of a classical protagonist. Nevertheless, a new interpretation of Jourdain.

2. Paris, La Comédie Française, 1951.
Jourdain played by Louis Seigner. Setting by Suzanne Lalique: a gigantic spiral stairway transformed the bourgeois salon into a fanciful ballroom in which poetry could soar to the heights. The old (Seigner, Beatrice Bretty) and the young (Jean Meyer, Jacques Charron) of the respectable Théâtre Français had a real fling. The production brought out the play's biting satire, as well as its sumptuously spectacular aspect, without stifling the comedy itself.

DOM JUAN

1. Directed by Louis Jouvet. Paris, Théâtre de l'Athénée, 1947.
Dom Juan played by Jouvet; the role of Sganarelle sacrificed. Sumptuous and pseudoclassical setting by Christian Bérard. Very Spanish costumes. A chilling, aging, voluntarily damned Dom Juan. Sganarelle's last speech the occasion for an impressive tableau (a gaping tomb, with skeleton), subduing the farcical aspect. Yet a production responsible for *Dom Juan's* reacceptance as a performable and fascinating play.

2. Directed by Jean Vilar. Paris, Théâtre National Populaire, 1953.
Dom Juan played by Vilar, a bit thin (exhausted?), in a handsome costume, this time in the French style. A Sganarelle who carried weight, played by the extraordinary actor Daniel Sorano. Thus the real dialogue of the play re-established. Still more intellectual, less "baroque," and more ambiguous than Jouvet's, Vilar's *Dom Juan* was much better balanced.

L'ÉCOLE DES FEMMES

Directed by Louis Jouvet. Paris, Théâtre de l'Athénée, 1936.
Arnolphe played by Jouvet; Agnès, by Madeleine Ozeray. Elegant and celebrated setting by Christian Bérard: chandeliers; a tall house, with triangular walled-in garden; walls could open, allowing the characters to go from street to garden at will. Arnolphe obsessed, but given a grotesque laugh, making him funny even in the so-called tragic scenes (Act V, Scene 4, for example). Yet Jouvet avoided making it a complete farce. However questionable and questioned, this production contributed more than any other to reintroducing Molière to the general theater public.

LES FOURBERIES DE SCAPIN

1. Directed by Jacques Copeau. Paris, Théâtre du Vieux Colombier, 1920 (first performed in New York, 1917).

2. Directed by Louis Jouvet. Paris, Théâtre Marigny, 1949.

Two great Scapins in the twentieth century: Jacques Copeau and Jean-Louis Barrault. The two productions cannot be dissociated, for they are related to one another by Louis Jouvet, Copeau's collaborator and Barrault's director. Copeau rejected the French Scapin in favor of a really Italian one: the virtuoso. But audiences of the Twenties were struck more by scenic innovations than by the role of the hero. Jouvet imposed about the same setting and staging on Barrault (architectural background in the shape of a port; Naples suggested by a few painted backdrops—this time by Bérard; Géronte's umbrella gag; etc.) but let him add his own gymnastics as a mime and an acrobat. With Barrault, all the space and every object on stage became functional, the pretext for gags. Both performances were an embodiment, on the French stage, of the nearest thing to "pure theater." They have been questioned, but they are landmarks. (Robert Hirsch's more recent interpretation of Scapin, at the Comédie Française, had him dressed as a modern Neopolitan sailor and added a human and shady side to him.)

GEORGE DANDIN

Directed by Roger Planchon. Cité de Villeurbanne (Lyon), 1958.

New trend among some of the younger French directors: how to make a short play last for over two hours. In this case, by adding to the unrealistic farce numerous tableaux of realistic peasant life in the seventeenth century, some inspired by paintings by the Le Nain brothers. Speeches interrupted by scenic changes, then go on. Very moving Dandin. A beautiful *Brechtian* show, but little relation to Molière.

LE MALADE IMAGINAIRE

Directed by Daniel Sorano. Paris, Théâtre National Populaire, 1957.

Daniel Sorano restored to the title role its basic contradiction: real physical health, shown by his activity and movement and general bearing, in opposition to his complaints and obsessions. A remarkable illustration of the simple *conflict* that rends the souls of almost all Molière's heroes.

LE MÉDECIN MALGRÉ LUI

Directed by Jacques Copeau. Paris, Théâtre du Vieux Colombier, 1920 (first performed in New York, 1918).

To judge from what little we know about Copeau's "bare stage" revival of this farce—from a few photographs, a few texts—it was, thanks to the genius of Copeau and his group, the revelation of what comedy is all about.

LE MISANTHROPE

1. Directed by Jacques Copeau. Paris, Théâtre du Vieux Colombier, 1920 (first performed in New York, 1919).

Alceste played by Copeau; Célimène, by Valentine Tessier. Setting: a few Louis XIV armchairs, in front of a Gobelins tapestry—and nothing else. An "inner" Alceste, but one rich in violent gestures. A sober staging, but no fixed tableaux: an abundance of movement intended to reveal the characters' souls.

2. Directed by Jean-Louis Barrault. Paris, Théâtre Marigny, 1954.

Alceste played by Barrault; Célimène, by Madeleine Renaud. Setting: black and white, an almost abstract stylization of an ideal seventeenth century engraving. A young Alceste, as he was meant to be. Choleric and *prancing*. His very real suffering not that of an old sage: it attracted sympathy but did not preclude a smile. Impression that he was making a "youthful mistake"—but a mistake that would mark him for life. One serious flaw: the marquis, too puppet-like, too effeminate. Célimène, marvelously exasperating through being absolutely herself, as she was meant to be.

3. Paris, La Comédie Française, 1958.

Jacques Dumesnil: an apoplectic Alceste. An interpretation that leaves no room for the question: Should he be mocked or admired?

TARTUFFE

1. Directed by Louis Jouvet. Paris, Théâtre de l'Athénée, 1950.

Tartuffe played by Jouvet. The handsome but not very Molièresque setting by Braque. Jouvet would seem to have believed in a partially sincere Tartuffe, whose fall was caused by the temptation of the flesh. Hence a spectacle oriented toward the complications of a modern drama à la Mauriac. In short: too serious —a kind of seriousness that has nothing to do with Molière. A regal Dorine; an Orgon out of a bourgeois drama. The whole undertaking a mistake perhaps— but a superb mistake.

2. Directed by Fernand Ledoux. Paris, La Comédie Française, 1951.

Finally, a basically sensual and obviously hypocritical Tartuffe. And funny in his ignominy. Jean Marchat was to take over the part somewhat later, with the same transparent unctuosity.

Note: As this volume was going to press, we learned that Roger Planchon, director of the Centre Dramatique de la Cité de Villeurbanne (Lyon), has just produced a *Tartuffe* in Brechtian style.

Also, Jean-Louis Barrault, in his *Salut à Molière,* produced for the first time at the New York City Center in March 1964, gave Act III, Scene 3, of *Tartuffe,* with Pierre Bertin playing the title role: despite the actor's age, the tension between the hypocritical mask and the real sensuality was played to perfection.

Selected Bibliography

BIBLIOGRAPHIES AND DOCUMENTS

Edelman, Nathan, ed. *The Seventeenth Century* ("Molière," pp. 226-43). Vol. III of *A Critical Bibliography of French Literature*, ed. David Cabeen and Jules Brody (Syracuse: Syracuse University Press, 1961).

Jurgens, Madeleine, and Elizabeth Maxfield-Miller. *Cent Ans de recherches sur Molière* (Paris: Archives Nationales, 1963).

Saintonge, Paul, and Robert W. Christ. *Fifty Years of Molière Studies, a Bibliography, 1892-1941* (Baltimore: The Johns Hopkins Press, 1942).

————. "Omissions and Additions to *Fifty Years of Molière Studies*," *Modern Language Notes*, LIX (1944), 282, 85.

Young, Bert Edward, and Grace Philputt Young, eds. *Le Registre de La Grange (1659-1685)* (2 vols. Geneva: Droz, 1947). Facsimile reproduction, with note on La Grange.

PRINCIPAL EDITIONS OF THE COMPLETE WORKS OF MOLIÈRE

Bray, René, ed. (8 vols. Paris: Les Belles Lettres, 1935-52).

————, and Jacques Scherer, eds. (3 vols. Paris: Club du Meilleur Livre, 1954-56).

Copeau, Jacques, ed. (10 vols. Paris: Cité des Livres, 1926-29).

Despois, Eugène, and Paul Mesnard, eds. (13 vols. Paris: Hachette [Collection des grands écrivains de la France], 1873-1900).

Jouanny, Robert, ed. (2 vols. Paris: Classiques Garnier, 1960).

Rat, Maurice, ed. (2 vols. Paris: Gallimard [Collection Pléiade], 1933).

EDITIONS OF CERTAIN INDIVIDUAL PLAYS, WITH COMMENTARIES

Amphitryon, ed. Pierre Mélèse (Geneva: Droz, 1950). Scholarly edition.

L'Avare, ed. Charles Dullin (Paris: Editions du Seuil, 1946). Stage directions by the famous actor-director.

L'Avare, ed. Jacques Arnavon. In *Notes sur l'interprétation de Molière* (Paris: Plon, Nourrit et cie., 1923). Stage directions; tendency toward naturalism.

Dom Juan, ed. Jacques Arnavon (Copenhagen: Glydendal, 1947). Stage directions; tendency toward naturalism. Dom Juan killed at the end in an ambush.

L'École des femmes (L'Interprétation de la comédie classique; comment jouer un chef d'oeuvre de Molière), ed. Jacques Arnavon (Paris: Plon, 1936).

L'Étourdi ou les Contre–temps, ed. Pierre Mélèse (Geneva: Droz, 1951). Shcolarly edition.

Les Femmes savantes (Mise en scène), ed. Jacques Arnavon (Paris: Desfossis, 1912).

Les Fourberies de Scapin, staged by Jacques Copeau, presented by Louis Jouvet (Paris: Éditions du Seuil, 1951).

Le Malade imaginaire, ed. Pierre Valde (Paris: Éditions du Seuil, 1946). Stage directions.

Le Misanthrope (L'Interprétation de la comédie classique), ed. Jacques Arnavon (Paris: Plon, 1930). Stage directions; naturalism.

Le Misanthrope, ed. Gustave Rudler (Oxford: Blackwell, 1947). Scholarly edition and detailed critical analysis of the play. Outstanding.

Tartuffe, ed. Fernand Ledoux (Paris: Éditions du Seuil, 1953). Stage directions.

Le Tartuffe and *Le Médecin malgré lui,* ed. Jacques Guicharnaud (New York: Dell, 1962). Introduction is a critical analysis of the plays. In English.

OUTSTANDING ENGLISH TRANSLATIONS

The Misanthrope, trans. Richard Wilbur (New York: Harcourt, Brace & World, 1955).

Tartuffe, trans. Richard Wilbur (New York: Harcourt, Brace & World, 1963).

BIOGRAPHICAL AND CRITICAL STUDIES

Adam, Antoine. *Histoire de la littérature française au XVIIᵉ siècle* (Paris: Domat, 1953), III, 207-408. Analysis of the plays as theatrical works, in the light of the philosophy of the times.

Arnavon, Jacques. *Notes sur l'interprétation de Molière* (Paris: Plon, Nourrit et Cie., 1923). An interpretation that attempts to break away from the academic and scenic conventions of the nineteenth century.

————. *La Morale de Molière* (Paris: Éditions universelles, 1945). An ethic of "feeling."

Audiberti, Jacques. *Molière, Dramaturge* (Paris: L'Arche, 1954). A short, rather muddled work, which says more about Audiberti than about Molière. Nevertheless, its unexpected parallels and unorthodox assertions open new doors on the subject. See the excerpt included in this volume.

Bénichou, Paul. *Morales du Grand Siècle* (Paris: Gallimard, 1948). "Molière," pp. 156-218. Basing his study on the analysis of a few plays (including *Amphitryon* and *Dom Juan*), the author situates Molière in the evolution of the ethics and manners of the seventeenth century. A brilliant synthesis of sociology and literature, although literature is not considered a mere "product." See the excerpt included in this collection.

Bray, René. *Molière, homme de théâtre* (Paris: Mercure de France, 1954). The works explained in terms of Molière's profession as actor and director, of the traditions and exigencies of the stage, as well as of Molière's poetic imagination.

Cairncross, John. *Molière bourgeois et libertin* (Paris: Nizet, 1964).

Descotes, Maurice. *Les Grands rôles du théâtre de Molière* (Paris: Presses universitaires de France, 1960). An account of how Molière's plays and characters have been interpreted by great actors, and how the drama critics reacted. Unfortunately, no precise chronology of premières and revivals.

Doolittle, James. "The Humanity of Molière's *Dom Juan*," *PMLA*, LXVIII, 3 (June 1953), 509-34. An interpretation of the play through a study of its inner mechanism. See the excerpt included in this collection.

Dussane, Beatrix. *Un Comédien nommé Molière* (Paris: Plon, 1936). A sentimental and fictionalized biography by a famous actress.

Ehrmann, Jacques. "Notes sur *L'École des femmes*," *Revue des sciences humaines*, CIX (Janvier-Mars 1963), 5-10. A new interpretation of the play in terms of the dialectic of the "secret."

Fernandez, Ramon. *La Vie de Molière* (Paris: Gallimard, 1929). Trans. Wilson Follet. *Molière, the Man Seen through the Plays* (New York: Hill and Wang, 1958). Molière's personality and temperament as revealed through a critical analysis of his works. A bit Freudian and Pirandellian. The most convincing of the works of this genre.

————. "Molière," in *Tableau de la littérature française de Corneille à Chénier*, ed. André Gide (Paris: Gallimard, 1939). A study of the underlying forces in Molière's works. Close interaction of psychology and criticism. See the excerpt included in this collection.

Gossman, Lionel. *Men and Masks, a Study of Molière* (Baltimore: The Johns Hopkins Press, 1963). Half the book is devoted to an analysis of *Amphitryon, Dom Juan, Le Misanthrope, Le Tartuffe,* and *George Dandin;* the other half, a combination of new criticism and "structuralist" criticism, situates Molière's vision of the world and his art in the times in which he lived. See the excerpt included in this collection.

Guicharnaud, Jacques. *Molière, une aventure théâtrale* (Paris: Gallimard, 1963). An analysis of *Tartuffe, Dom Juan,* and *Le Misanthrope,* showing how Molière's use of the comic mask, in greater and greater depth, leads to an awareness of the irreducibility of human nature and a dramaturgical impasse.

Hall, Gaston. "A Comic *Dom Juan,*" *Yale French Studies,* No. 23 (Summer 1959), 77-84. Reprinted in this collection.

———. *Molière: Tartuffe* (London: Edward Arnold, 1960). W. G. Moore's method applied to one play. In English.

Hubert, Judd D. *Molière and the Comedy of Intellect* (Berkeley and Los Angeles: University of California Press, 1962). An internal analysis of the plays. The unity of each is explained in terms of a theme, an idea, a dramatic or satirical presupposition. See the excerpt included in this collection.

Jasinski, René. *Molière et Le Misanthrope* (Paris: Armand Colin, 1951; second edition, Paris: Nizet, 1964). An extraordinary wealth of information on the circumstances and philosophy of the times. An analysis of the temperament of Alceste and of Célimène's coquetry. The author follows rigorously the tradition of literary history, sees the play as "one of the masterpieces of personal literature," and considers Philinte the embodiment of a higher wisdom, dear to Molière.

Jouvet, Louis. "Molière," *Conferencia,* XXXI (1937), 281-99.

———. "Molière," *Conferencia,* XXXII (1938), 655-75. On *L'École des femmes.*

———. "Pourquoi j'ai monté *Dom Juan,*" *Conferencia,* XXXVII (1948), 451-68.

———. "Pourquoi j'ai monté *Tartuffe,*" *Conferencia,* LVII (1950), 27-38. The famous revivals of Molière by this celebrated actor-director, explained by himself. Theatricalism is emphasized. These articles had considerable influence on the general public, which up until then had considered Molière's comedies as reserved for the Sorbonne and for the education of children.

Lancaster, Henry Carlington. "The Period of Molière," in *A History of French Dramatic Literature in the Seventeenth Century,* Part III (2nd ed. Baltimore: The Johns Hopkins Press, 1952). Useful mainly for its source material.

Lanson, Gustave. "Molière and Farce" (trans. Ruby Cohen), *Tulane Drama Review,* VIII, 2 (Winter 1963), 133-54. Contrary to the traditional thinking which refused to consider Molière as anything but a philosopher and serious portrayer of human nature, the author, using all his sound erudition, shows for the first time and definitely that the art of Molière has its roots in farce. See the excerpt included in this collection.

Lewis, Wyndham D. B. *Molière: The Comic Mask* (New York: Coward-McCann, 1959). A biography, with short summaries of the plays. Somewhat elementary, a few factual errors, but very informed and highly readable in its nonchalance.

Meyer, Jean. *Molière* (Paris: Librairie académique Perrin, 1963). The last biography to date, by an actor.

Mongrédien, Georges. *La Vie privée de Molière* (Paris: Hachette, 1950). Molière's life as an actor, by a scholar.

Michaut, Gustave. *La Jeunesse de Molière, les débuts de Molière à Paris, les luttes de Molière* (3 vols. Paris: Hachette, 1921-25). Notes for the fourth volume are to be found in Michaut's edition of Molière's *Oeuvres complètes* (Paris: Imprimerie nationale, 1949). A basic work, scholarly and historical; somewhat outdated in its interpretations. Unfortunately, never completed.

——. "La Biographie de Molière," "Molière dans son oeuvre," and "La Légende d'Alceste," in *Pascal, Molière, Musset* (Paris: Éditions Alsatia, 1942). The great literary historian replies with vigor to the younger biographers and critics, particularly Ramon Fernandez. Although there are more modern critical methods than his, the author keeps the battle going in a most lively fashion. His image of Molière may perhaps be out-of-date, but it was never that of a corpse.

Moore, Will G. *Molière, a New Criticism* (Oxford: The Clarendon Press, 1949). Reprinted by Doubleday in 1962, with an additional "Post-Script." Making a clean sweep of the overwhelming amount of material that was stifling Molière's works, the author revolutionized the study of Molière with his method of internal analysis. The unity of the plays and the very essence of comedy are thus disclosed. See the excerpt included in this collection.

Palmer, John L. *Molière* (New York: Brewer and Warren, 1930). A straightforward biography, in English.

Romano, Danilo. *Essai sur le comique de Molière* (Berne: A. Francke, 1950). Somewhat confused, but an attempt to discover the essence of the comic element by side-stepping the rather limiting explanation of Bergson.

Sauvage, Micheline. *Le Cas Don Juan* (Paris: Éditions du Seuil, 1953). Dom Juan among the other Dons. Primarily an analysis of the role of Elvire and the retribution she demands.

Simon, Alfred. *Molière par lui-même* (Paris: Éditions du Seuil, 1957). Illustrated. A new interpretation of Molière's career; the man, his works, and the exigencies of the theater are grasped as a whole and in the context of the period. Often allusive. See the excerpt included in this collection.

——. "Les Rites élémentaires de la comédie molièresque," *Cahiers de la Compagnie Madeleine Renaud—Jean-Louis Barrault*, No. 15 (Paris: Juilliard, Jan. 1956). The article is included in this collection.

Vedel, Valdemar. "Molière," in *Deux Classiques français vus par un critique étranger*, trans. from the Danish by E. Cornet (Paris: Champion, 1935). The man and his works seen in the context of the French seventeenth century. Molière's originality. The extent of his "realism."

Villiers, André. *Le Dom Juan de Molière, un problème de mise en scène* (Paris: "Masques," 1947). The first serious attempt to rehabilitate the play, on the dramatic level as well as on the ideological level. An analysis of the play, of Dom Juan's psychology, and also of his possible relation to the heroes of today's theater. See the chapter included in this collection.